P9-CLO-714

AN OUNCE OF PREVENTION

Don
Cahalan

AN OUNCE OF PREVENTION

Strategies for Solving Tobacco, Alcohol, and Drug Problems

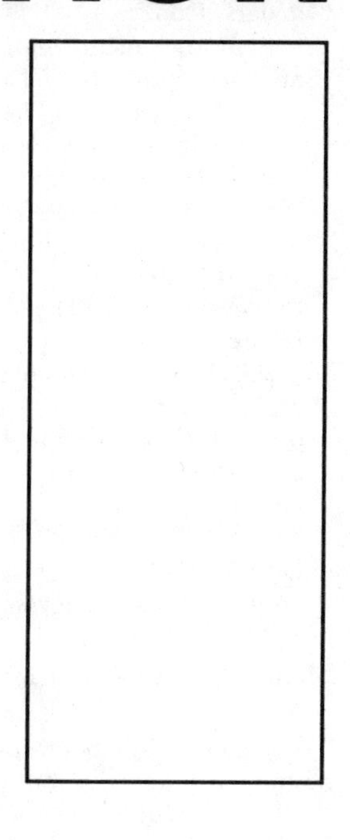

Jossey-Bass Publishers
San Francisco • Oxford • 1991

AN OUNCE OF PREVENTION
Strategies for Solving Tobacco, Alcohol, and Drug Problems
by Don Cahalan

350 Sansome Street
San Francisco, California 94104
&
Jossey-Bass Limited
Headington Hill Hall
Oxford OX3 0BW

Library of Congress Cataloging-in-Publication Data

Cahalan, Don.
An ounce of prevention : strategies for solving tobacco, alcohol, and drug problems / Don Cahalan.
p. cm. — (The Jossey-Bass health series)
(The Jossey-Bass social and behavioral science series)
includes bibliographical references and index.
ISBN 1-55542-348-5
1. Alcoholism—United States—Prevention. 2. Tobacco habit—United States—Prevention. 3. Drug abuse—United States—Prevention. 4. Health promotion—United States. I. Title. II. Series.
[DNLM: 1. Alcoholism—prevention & control—United States. 2. Health Promotion—methods—United States. 3. Substance Abuse—prevention & control—United States. 4. Tobacco Use Disorder—prevention & control—United States. WM 270 C132o]
RC565.C27 1991
362.29'17'0973—dc20
DNLM/DLC
for Library of Congress 90-15642
CIP

Manufactured in the United States of America

The paper in this book meets the guidelines for permanence and durability of the Committee on Production Guidelines for Book Longevity of the Council on Library Resources.

JACKET DESIGN BY WILLI BAUM

FIRST EDITION

Code 9152

A joint
publication
in
The Jossey-Bass
Health Series
and
The Jossey-Bass
Social and Behavioral Science Series

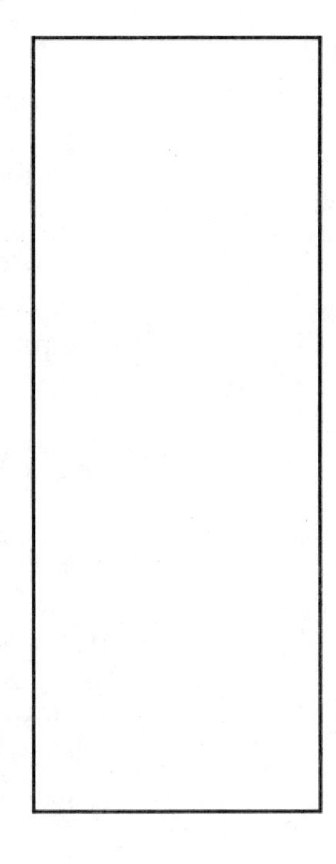

Contents

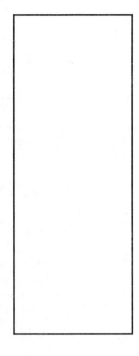

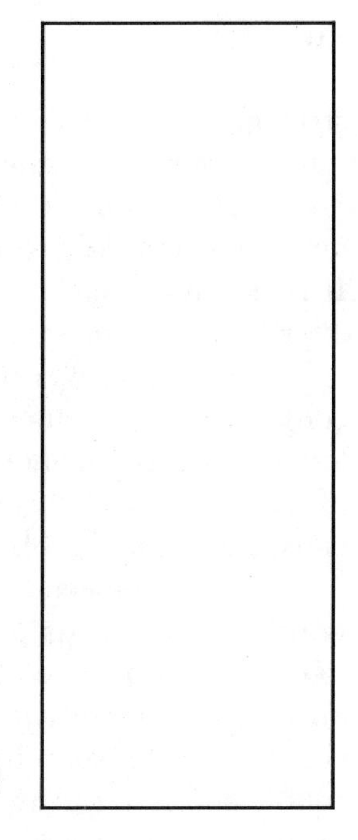

Preface

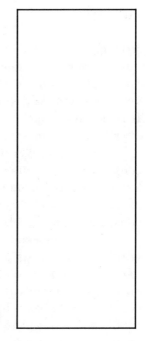

The title of this book, *An Ounce of Prevention,* should bring to mind the rest of that old adage, " . . . is worth a pound of cure." Yet when we become fully aware of the damage being inflicted on our society by tobacco, alcohol, and other drugs, it will become all too clear that unless we make more effective use of that ounce of prevention, we are never going to get that pound of cure.

Since the Prohibition era, our country has been spending ever-expanding sums yearly on the medical treatment of tobacco-caused illnesses and on treatment or incarceration of alcoholics and drug addicts. But while there has been considerable success in reducing the ravages of American health caused by tobacco, the prevalence of serious alcohol- or illicit drug-related problems has hardly been shrinking at all. Obviously, trying to cope with such problems *after* they have reached the stage of deep-seated addiction is ineffective. What is needed are ways to *prevent* such problems *before* they become chronic. Accordingly, this book is directed primarily to the discussion of some of the newer strategies to inoculate and shield the general public from damage caused by tobacco, alcohol, and illicit drugs—

strategies that are winning public approval without creating undue barriers to personal freedoms.

This book provides information on recent national developments in the prevention of harm from addictive substances. It is the first book to describe in detail the recently developed coordinated strategies and programs on which the federal government and prevention-oriented nonprofit organizations are cooperating to reduce the level of health and economic problems caused by alcohol, illicit drugs, and tobacco. An abundance of recent research has made it clear that all three substances are causing serious problems for certain particularly vulnerable populations, especially adolescents and those of lower socioeconomic status. Thus prevention programs need to be designed to cope with misuse of all three substances through integrated and consistent education and control strategies. This book discusses recent research on the common elements in tobacco, alcohol, and illicit drug misuse in the United States and on how prevention programs are being designed to cope with them in combination. While space limitations in dealing with such a broad topic obviously preclude meeting the full informational needs of researchers, the book's emphasis on the *common factors* to be considered in most addiction research will be helpful both to research specialists and to those concerned with general issues of public policy regarding addictive substances.

An Ounce of Prevention is based on the premise that only a *realistic public health approach,* rather than a moralistic or punitive policy, can make real progress in reducing the heavy toll taken each day by addictive substances. The emphasis is on *realistic,* because the old-fashioned public health approach to dealing with noxious substances by forbidding their use altogether has not worked in the past; and we are still very much aware of how Prohibition failed because it was not supported by the real consent of the governed.

This book summarizes the growth of American markets for alcohol and other addictive drugs and the impact these substances have had on American well-being. While there are signs of slight downturns in aggregate use of some addictives, there is still tremendous demand for these products in our country.

We will not get very far in limiting the damage caused by these drugs until we bring down this domestic demand. In identifying the chief villain in our use of addictive drugs, we will have to admit that Pogo was right when he said, "We have met the enemy and he is us." It has been expedient to spend billions of dollars on medical care for alcoholics and the victims of tobacco-caused illnesses and on the revolving-door jailing of drug addicts while only a pittance (estimated at 77 cents per capita per year) is being spent to combat early addiction to tobacco, alcohol, and illicit drugs.

Audience

The information in this book should be of interest to professionals and administrators in health care administration, public health, social welfare, public policy, and political science and law. It is hoped that this information will encourage them to continue to exert needed leadership in promoting more effective prevention and remedial programs in their communities and in the nation as a whole.

Overview of the Contents

Chapter One provides a brief summary of some of the major federal agencies and national organizations playing a role in the prevention or treatment of substance addiction and discusses some of the more significant changes in such organizations during the last few years.

Chapter Two summarizes the major favorable and unfavorable factors that have affected the prevention of tobacco, alcohol, and other drug problems within the last generation. *Unfavorable* factors include cultural shortcomings such as the American public's preoccupation with "go-for-the-gusto" immediate gratifications reinforced by the media, the alienation of the rootless and poverty-stricken (especially among the young), the formidable amounts spent on marketing and lobbying by the alcohol and tobacco industries, and the lack of incentive on the part of many in the medical and social welfare professions to play a more active role in prevention. *Favorable* factors include an increasingly receptive attitude toward primary prevention attributable to the health movement and mounting public concern over the high level of alcohol and other drug abuse. This favorable climate in turn has reinforced the development of better-funded, more realistic prevention strategies on the part of federal agencies and cooperating organizations for linking together programs to deal with all three types of addictive substances in a much more comprehensive set of national and local community programs than ever attempted before in the United States.

Chapter Three summarizes the impact of prevention programs that have reduced cigarette consumption markedly during the last generation, leading to expectations that from the antismoking campaigns valuable pointers will also arise on ways of minimizing the damage from misuse of alcohol and other drugs. Also discussed is the irony involved in some federal agencies' working to reduce deaths due to smoking while other federal agencies work to maintain the tobacco industry's tax breaks and agricultural subsidies.

Chapter Four explains that smoking is one of the most stubborn addictions because of the insidious qualities of nicotine and the fact that the average smoker experiences many more reinforcing sessions than does the average drinker or user of illicit drugs. The relative effectiveness of various smoking addiction treatment methods is discussed, as well as the possible reasons why women smokers generally find it much harder to quit than men do.

Chapter Five begins by making some distinctions between clinical alcoholism and the myriad other types of alcohol-related problems in America, and then discusses recent trends in drinking behavior. Recent evolutionary changes in the roles of government and private agencies are discussed, with emphasis on some encouraging new developments.

Chapter Six updates the chapters "How Well Do Alcohol Treatment Programs Work?" and "Economics and Management of Treatment" in my book *Understanding America's Drinking Problem: How to Combat the Hazards of Alcohol* (1987). As in that book, this section draws on the opinions of nationally recognized leaders in the field of alcoholism treatment as well as the findings of several new federally sponsored or privately conducted studies. All of them agree that while the treatment of alcoholism in the United States is slowly improving, it is still lacking in real long-term effectiveness despite the billions of dollars that are being spent on it.

Chapter Seven discusses why we are still far from winning the war on illicit drugs, which constitute a multibillion dollar market. The discussion opens with a summary of national statistics on trends in the use of the major illegal mood-modifying drugs by subgroups within the population. The chapter then deals with the implications of cocaine, the substance of primary current emphasis in the federal "War on Drugs." Evidence and expert opinion are presented on how the present emphasis on cutting off the *supply* will continue to be a futile and dangerous enterprise so long as we do not find more effective means of reducing the *demand* for these drugs within our own populace.

Chapter Eight discusses the woeful inadequacies in the drug treatment resources now available in the United States. It cites the conviction among many experts that present methods are too punitive and will continue to be ineffectual until addicts are provided with humane and positive close personal supervision and help in building new lives, liberated from the poisonous environments that drew them into addiction.

Chapter Nine emphasizes that public health–oriented prevention programs are likely to be more effective in general than moralistic or law-and-order drives. Effective efforts to minimize the damage done by such mood-modifying drugs as tobacco, alcohol, heroin, and cocaine must require the cooperation of all four of Sir Edmund Burke's "estates" in our society: the executive and legislative branches, organized religion, and the media, as well as the general public. This chapter summarizes some of the practical steps that can be taken to reduce the consumption of tobacco, alcohol, and other addictive drugs, including exerting continued pressure on the media to stop glamorizing smoking, drinking, and macho hectic and violent lifestyles and thus providing poor role models for our society.

The central perspective of Chapter Ten is that the prevention of problems arising from use of addictive substances can be improved materially, but only if we adopt long-range programs to deal with the *root causes* of persistent misuse of psychoactive substances: hopelessness on the part of many city youth because they lack employable skills, inadequate social supports from the family and the community, and our society's prevalent emphasis on short-term gratification. The experiences of other industrialized countries in dealing with misuse of addictives is drawn on in suggesting better solutions to some of our problems.

In addition to the reference section, there is a resource at the end of the book that provides selected sources of information on the use of alcohol, tobacco, and illicit drugs and on preventive and treatment programs.

Acknowledgments

I wish to express my appreciation for the helpful data and insights on prevention issues provided through interviews or correspondence. In the Rockville, Maryland, area, within the Alcohol, Drug Abuse, and Mental Health Administration, the following individuals were particularly helpful: Loran Archer, deputy director of the National Institute on Alcohol Abuse and Alcoholism (NIAAA), Brenda Hewitt, special assistant to the director, NIAAA, and Jan Howard, chief of the Prevention Research Branch, NIAAA; Zili Amsel, chief of the Prevention Research Branch, and William Bukowski, program director for Intervention Research, National Institute on Drug Abuse (NIDA); Robert W. Denniston, director, Division of Communication Programs, Office for Substance Abuse Prevention (OSAP); Sandra Diaz, National Clearinghouse for Alcohol and Drug Information; and Tanner Wray, Office on Smoking and Health, Centers for Disease Control, U.S. Public Health Service.

From Washington, D.C., I received helpful information from: Jay Lewis, editor of *The Alcoholism Report* newsletter; Christine Lubinski, director of public policy, National Council on Alcoholism and Drug Dependence; Patricia Taylor, alcohol policies project director, and Michael Jacobson, executive director, Center for Science in the Public Interest; and Alexander C. Wagenaar, chair, National Coalition to Prevent Impaired Driving, and associate professor, School of Public Health, University of Minnesota.

From the Marin Institute for the Prevention of Alcohol and Other Drug Problems, Thomas Greenfield, associate director/research, David Jernigan, associate director/Media and Policy Center, and James Mosher, program director, were especially helpful.

From the School of Public Health, University of California at Berkeley, Christine Campbell, reference librarian, and associate professor Lawrence Wallack gave valuable assistance. Librarian Christina Miller from the Prevention Research Center in Berkeley was also very helpful.

From the Alcohol Research Group (ARG) in Berkeley, I very much appreciate the technical assistance provided by Judith Lubina, information specialist, and David Smith, project coordinator. And as with several of my prior writings, a special note of appreciation is due Andrea Mitchell, director of the library at ARG, for general editorial assistance and for tracking down a lot of hard-to-find information about prevention programs bearing on problems caused by tobacco, alcohol, and illicit drugs.

Berkeley, California
March 1991

Don Cahalan

The Author

Don Cahalan is professor of public health (emeritus) at the University of California at Berkeley. He received both his B.A. degree (1937) in psychology and journalism and his M.A. degree (1938) in psychology from the University of Iowa and his Ph.D. degree (1968) from George Washington University in social psychology. Cahalan's direction and analysis of social surveys have spanned a half-century. During much of the latter half of his career he has directed national and regional studies of drinking behavior and problems, sponsored primarily by the National Institute on Alcohol Abuse and Alcoholism and its predecessors. Out of these studies he has published nearly fifty articles and four books: *American Drinking Practices* (1969, with I. H. Cisin and H. M. Crossley), *Problem Drinkers: a National Survey* (1970), *Problem Drinking Among American Men* (1974, with R. Room), and *Understanding America's Drinking Problem: How to Combat the Hazards of Alcohol* (1987).

Earlier, after service as a naval officer in World War II, Cahalan served as associate professor of psychology and social science at the University of Denver, as director of attitude research for the U.S. Army and Air Force in Europe, and as senior research analyst in the National Opinion Research Center at the University of Chicago. After spending several years in the New York area conducting market research, he moved in 1962 to George Washington University to work with Ira Cisin in his Social Research Group in directing the first national probability sampling survey on American drinking practices. In 1968 he moved to Berkeley, where he merged the research resources set up a decade earlier in the State of California Department of Public Health with the national survey resources of Ira Cisin's Social Research Group under the aegis of the University of California at Berkeley's School of Public Health. He founded and directed the Alcohol Research Group and its federally funded alcohol research and training programs, now headed by Robin Room, until his formal retirement in 1979.

Cahalan is a life member of the American Psychological Association and the American Association for Public Opinion Research. He is also a member of the Society for the Psychological Study of Social Issues and the American Public Health Association, and he serves on the advisory boards of the Prevention Research Center of Berkeley and the journal *Drugs and Society*.

An Ounce of Prevention

PART ONE

Challenges and Opportunities

CHAPTER ONE

Putting Prevention on the National Agenda

This chapter will summarize the development and evolution of the principal federal agencies and nationally known private organizations in which prevention of tobacco, alcohol, or other drug problems is a primary objective. Space considerations preclude covering in detail the many other federal agencies that play a collateral or subordinate part in prevention, or the myriad of state and local organizations, public and private, that have sprung up over the last generation. Readers who are interested in more detail on prevention-oriented organizations should lobby the new Office for Substance Abuse Prevention (OSAP) within the Department of Health and Human Services to prepare such an inventory.

A generation ago, the number of governmental and private agencies with any real influence in promoting the prevention of tobacco, alcohol, and other drug problems could be counted on the fingers of two hands. The entirely legal tobacco and alcohol companies even then had billions of dollars in profits to invest in advertising and lobbying to maintain their markets with a minimum of interference, and were enjoying many millions of dollars in tax benefits and other subsidies for tobacco and alcohol from our own federal government. Thanks largely to the powerful lobbying efforts of the tobacco and alcohol industries as well as the bad taste Prohibition left in the American public's mouth, it was not until the 1980s that the federal government spent more than a handful of money on activities that could be identified as preventive.

As for private support of prevention research and action programs: Out of $2.6 billion contributed by major foundations in 1987 to social and humanitarian causes, research, prevention, and treatment of alcohol and other drug problems received $26 million—only about 1 percent, but nearly twice as much as in 1982. A survey by the Foundation Center of New York found that the number of foundations making grants in the alcohol and drug field rose from one in four in 1980 to two in five in 1987. For 1983 to 1987, alcohol and drug treatment facilities and social service providers received 48.3 percent and prevention programs 36.2 percent of the foundations' total funding. However, in 1987 alone, prevention's share had risen to 52 percent, and treatment and services had fallen to 37 percent. Among recent significant financial contributors to alcohol and drug programs are the Kaiser Family Foundation, the Cowell Foundation funding of the Policy Initiatives Project of the Trauma Foundation of San Francisco, the Commonwealth Fund, the Conrad Hilton Foundation, the Metropolitan Life Foundation, Pew Charitable Trusts, New York Community Trust, and the J. M. Foundation (University of California at San Diego, 1990c, pp. 13–14). Other foundations active in funding prevention are the Kroc Foundation, the Robert Wood Johnson Foundation, and the Buck Trust (the latter supports the Marin Institute for the Prevention of Alcohol and Other Drug Problems, discussed later).

As the scope of activities of governmental and private agencies in coping with problems caused by tobacco, alcohol, and other drugs continues to grow, it is becoming harder and harder to estimate just how much money and effort are being expended on prevention. Further, often it is difficult to assess the scope of primary prevention as against secondary and tertiary prevention because they tend to become intertwined in practice if not in theory, and often very basic research (such as on polio) has wound up having powerful preventive effects. But in any case, it is certain that far more effort and attention are being expended today on primary prevention than even a few years ago.

Prior to the creation of the National Institute on Alcoholism and Alcohol Abuse (NIAAA) in 1971, the only federal agencies specifically designated with any authority over tobacco and alcohol were the Food and Drug Administration (which played a very minor part in purity standards) and the Bureau of Alcohol, Tobacco, and Firearms of the Treasury Department (which saw its primary role as maintaining orderly markets for the cigarettes and alcoholic beverages to yield substantial taxes for the Treasury's coffers). The first report of the Surgeon General on smoking and health did not appear until 1964. Moreover, the first national probability sample survey of drinking practices, which Ira Cisin of George Washington University and I launched that same year, was funded on a shoestring budget provided through a handful of interested scientists in the National Institute of Mental Health, because there was no federal alcohol agency in those years.

The National Institute on Alcohol Abuse and Alcoholism (NIAAA)

A considerable impetus to dealing with some of the problems surrounding misuse of alcohol was provided by the formal founding of the NIAAA in 1971, which was stimulated especially by the leadership of Senator Harold Hughes of Iowa with the enthusiastic backing of the National Council on Alcoholism (NCA). However, the NCA's emphasis at first was devoted almost exclusively to getting those who could be defined clinically as alcoholics into better treatment. Also, the alcohol industry for years heavily subsidized the NCA so as to be able through its influence (its money and its three members on the NCA eight-member board) to steer the NCA away as much as possible from any efforts to limit alcohol consumption. Thus it was not until after

Ernest Noble (executive vice president of NCA in 1982 and former director of the NIAAA) dropped the alcohol industry members—and the industry's funding—from the NCA and got his national board to approve a manifesto calling for a substantial redirection of the organization toward primary prevention programs (Lewis, 1982) that the influential NCA organization began to emphasize lobbying for prevention.

Chapter Three of my book *Understanding America's Drinking Problem: How to Combat the Hazards of Alcohol* (1987) presents a summary of some of the changes that have taken place within NIAAA over its first twenty years. The agency first grew out of the National Center for the Prevention and Control of Alcoholism in 1969 (retitled in 1970 the Division of Alcohol Abuse and Alcoholism) within the National Institute of Mental Health (NIMH). Its first budget was a tiny $6.4 million for its initial year, which funded sixty-eight research and twelve training grants and fellowships. Effective lobbying by the NCA and other constituency groups, and notably the leadership of Senator Hughes of Iowa, led to the formal establishment of NIAAA (separate from NIMH) in 1971 and authorized alcoholism treatment project and formula grant programs with a budget that soon jumped to $87.5 million per year. In 1974 Congress established an umbrella agency, the Alcohol, Drug, and Mental Health Administration (ADAMHA), which now superintends the operations of the NIAAA, the National Institute on Drug Abuse (NIDA), and NIMH, as well as the newer groups described later.

A NIAAA summary sheet in August 1975 reviewed increases in its budget from $17 million in 1971 to $218 million in 1974, listing its principal accomplishments for its first five years as being the passing of a Uniform Alcoholism and Intoxication Treatment Act (since adopted in most states): the acceptance of public drunkenness as a medical and not a criminal issue; increase in third-party payments from insurance companies covering alcoholism; the implementation of special programs focusing on African-Americans, Hispanics, and Native Americans; cooperation with the Department of Transportation on programs for rehabilitation of drinking drivers; and the setting of standards for certification of alcoholism treatment counselors. During that same period, substantial resources were also devoted to grants and contracts to support basic and applied alcohol research in the biomedical and behavioral sciences.

In 1979, NIAAA published its first comprehensive account of its collaboration with other federal agencies in solving alcohol problems. Many projects had been (and are continuing to be) conducted in conjunction with such agencies as the Veterans Administration; the Department of Justice; the Department of Education; National Institutes for Arthritis, Metabolism, and Digestive Diseases; the Heart, Lung, and Blood Institute; the National Institute on Drug Abuse; the National Cancer Institute; the National Institute of Child Health and Human Development; the National Institute on Aging; the National Institute on Neurological and Communicable Disease and Stroke; the National Institute of General Medical Science; the Health Services Administration; and the Department of Labor.

In 1977, a NIAAA Alcohol Research Centers (ARC) program was created to provide continuity for a number of research programs considered important to NIAAA's long-range goals. A dozen such centers (one financed by the Department of Veterans Affairs) are now operating, most of them affiliated with universities with strong research facilities. Most of these centers have a biomedical research emphasis. Exceptions include the Alcohol Research Group of Berkeley (now directed by Robin Room), which I founded within the University of California School of Public Health with the mission of studying the social epidemiology of alcohol problems through national and community surveys, and the Prevention Research Center of the Pacific Institute for Research and Evaluation.

The PRC, the one ARC exclusively devoted to prevention issues, was commissioned only after Congress mandated that at least one ARC should be dedicated primarily to the prevention area. Utilizing a public health systems model throughout all its research, it was founded in 1983 by an interdisciplinary team headed by Lawrence Wallack, James Mosher, and Friedner Wittman from the Alcohol Research Group. Under its director, Harold Holder, whose primary background has been in public health research, the PRC's major research projects include studies of individual and environmental factors associated with alcohol problems within the worksite, peer influences on adolescent values and attitudes about drinking, risk factors associated with alcohol-impaired driving, and the effectiveness of beverage server training to reduce intoxication among customers. Other key studies have focused on the structure and function of alcohol beverage control agencies, legal issues and legislation related to alcohol use, family and community studies of Mexican-American drinking and alcohol problems, and computer simulations of community factors influencing alcohol use and abuse as an aid to local prevention planners. The PRC also has begun community prevention trials (modeled after the heart disease and cancer prevention trials mentioned in later chapters) to seek effective strategies to reduce alcohol-involved trauma.

The emphasis in the Reagan years on whittling down the role of federal agencies and delegating more activities to the states forced the NIAAA to begin shifting its community-based treatment projects to state control under block grants, with supervision not by NIAAA but by its umbrella agency, ADAMHA. As a result, NIAAA budgets are now allocated almost exclusively to research into alcoholism and other alcohol-related medical problems, alcolhol-related deaths and injuries, epidemiology, public information activities and training grants, and some prevention activities. Although NIAAA has a Prevention Division, much of its prevention advocacy work is being carried out through the separate Office for Substance Abuse Prevention (see below) under vastly expanded funding.

In keeping with its present primary emphasis on research rather than treatment, the NIAAA now has four primary research divisions: Basic Research, including neurosciences and behavioral research and biomedical research; Intramural Clinical and Biological Research; Clinical and Prevention Research; and Biometry and Epidemiology (Gordis, 1988).

As pointed out by Jan Howard (1990, p. 244), chief of the Prevention Research Branch in NIAAA, NIAAA's prevention research responsibilities lie primarily in the areas of conducting systematic searches for effective strategies to reduce the incidence and prevalence of alcohol abuse and alcoholism, and for mechanisms to ensure the diffusion and adoption of effective prevention strategies. Unlike OSAP (Office for Substance Abuse Prevention, the new agency described later), NIAAA does not support prevention services or demonstration projects unless these activities are a direct part of a NIAAA research endeavor.

The types of prevention research programs under which NIAAA is currently inviting grant proposals include: economic and socioeconomic issues in alcohol abuse and alcoholism prevention, treatment, and epidemiology; prevention of alcohol abuse among the young and in the aging population; causative processes and primary and secondary prevention of worksite-related alcohol problems; recognition, management, and prevention in primary health care settings; and measuring the impact of alcohol warning labels.

The effectiveness of the NIAAA in a role other than largely basic research was seriously threatened under Reagan's proposed budget for the fiscal year 1987. However, the new drug initiative ("War on Drugs") that was hastily passed by Congress in the fall of 1986 and substantially augmented by the 1988 enabling legislation did mean some augmentation for NIAAA's total budget. This budget was $124,064,000 for 1989 and is being raised to an estimated $162,722,000 for 1991 (plus the allocation of an estimated $8,335,000 for the special Treatment Outcome Research project, discussed in some detail in Chapter Six).

As shown in Table 1, which summarizes estimated allocations for the five institutes under ADAMHA, NIAAA is getting a smaller allocation than any of the other four (Lewis, 1990b).

Table 1. Alcohol, Drug Abuse, and Mental Health Administration Estimated Budget Authority for FY 1991.

Agency	*Budget (dollars in thousands)*
Office of Treatment Improvement	$1,448,187
NIMH	527,786
NIDA	407,074
OSAP	251,892
NIAAA	162,722
(plus Treatment Outcome Research)	8,335

Source: Adapted from Lewis, 1990b, pp. 1–2.

NIAAA Director Enoch Gordis told Congress he had every reason to credit newly installed Health and Human Services (HHS) Secretary Louis Sullivan with being just as strong a supporter of progress in the alcoholism field as his predecessor, Otis Bowen, the last secretary of HHS. Bowen had launched a number of initiatives and two major national prevention-oriented conferences as well as the creation of the National Citizens Commission on Alcoholism (Lewis, 1989c).

Strategies for survival as well as the personal professional interests of the current leaders of NIAAA have worked toward increasing emphasis on scientific research and the avoidance of controversy (for example, over constraints on alcohol consumption). Some alcohol-control or alcohol-taxing activists are disappointed that NIAAA does not take a more militant stance concerning controls. However, the current NIAAA management remains cautious about coming out strongly for controls, contending that it would weaken its reputation for soundness of research by getting involved in such advocacy. As NIAAA Director Enoch Gordis (1990, p. 186) explains NIAAA's position: "In most cases, U.S. alcohol-related policy implementation has resulted from a convergence of many factors, including scientific evidence, public perception of the extent and impact of a problem, and public advocacy for specific policies to address specific problems. By itself, science is rarely the sole basis for policy development and implementation, and should not be in a society as complex as that in the U.S. A mix of economic, religious, and political pressures also affects U.S. policy development, and in many cases these factors may be more persuasive than the best scientific evidence. However, science can contribute valuable information to the policy formulation and decision-making process. Therefore, the NIAAA has developed an ongoing role in supporting research on alcohol-related public policies to provide additional information to policymakers to aid them in deciding among policy options."

Actually, as indicated in Chapter Four, the NIAAA is conducting a wide variety of research into the effects of changes in laws and regulations affecting alcohol availability, price, minimum legal drinking age, hours and other conditions of sale, and drinking-driving. It is also studying issues concerning health warning labels on alcohol containers, as well as possible constraints on alcohol advertising. However, the NIAAA strategy is to steer a conservative course to avoid being labeled "neoprohibitionist." Somewhat ironically, while the setting up of the Office for Substance Abuse Prevention (under hasty congressional insistence) as a parallel entity within ADAMHA brought its complications for NIAAA, OSAP's taking on of activist community-centered programs also is helping to shield NIAAA from much controversy.

The Office of Treatment Improvement (OTI)

The OTI "holding corporation" for the ADAMHA umbrella organization was established primarily for the purpose of dispensing formula and other grants to states and municipalities. Such grants for treatment and rehabilitation at one time were administered by NIAAA and NIDA, but were decentralized during the Reagan era.

The National Institute of Mental Health

Since the founding of NIAAA, the NIMH is no longer so intimately involved in research on the prevention of tobacco, alcohol, or other drug problems. However, it still collaborated extensively with NIAAA and the other branches of ADAMHA in studies of the interaction of the use of addictive substances with mental health problems.

Other Federal Agencies with Alcohol Control Authority

Many federal agencies have some control over the dispensing or management of alcohol. These were described in detail in Chapter Three of *Understanding America's Drinking Problem; How to Combat the Hazards of Alcohol* (Cahalan, 1987). Summarizing briefly: Mosher and Mottl (1981) have enumerated the agencies under four types of jurisdiction: *land-based* (such as the Department of Defense for military installations, National Forest Service and National Park Service, Bureau of Land Management, and Bureau of Indian Affairs); *safety-based* (Occupational Safety and Health, Consumer Product Safety Commission, Food and Drug Administration, and so on); *transportation-based* (National Transportation Safety Board, Department of Transportation, Federal Aviation Administration, and so forth); and *economic-based* (Internal Revenue Service as regards deductions for alcohol advertising expenses and purchase of alcohol for "business purposes," and the Bureau of Alcohol, Tobacco, and Firearms [BATF] in the Treasury Department, whose primary duty is to see that excise and import duties are collected).

Concerning the BATF: While it is supposed to have control over the advertising and labeling of alcoholic beverages, it has had a history of determined resistance to exercising such responsibilities. Chapter Two of my 1987 book relates the continued criticism over many years of the BATF by consumer advocacy agencies such as the Center for Science in the Public Interest and the National Council on Alcoholism for its slowness to respond to pressures to exercise more control over advertising and labeling.

One recent instance of BATF foot-dragging was its refusal to testify before the Senate Governmental Affairs Committee on recommendations made by then-Surgeon General Koop's Workshop on Drunk Driving—reportedly on grounds that "health and safety" are not within the agency's purview. At the same time, BATF, in what was regarded as an unusual stance, took the position that the Governmental Affairs Panel does not have express authorizing jurisdiction over BATF. BATF representatives reportedly cited the fact that one of the workshop's recommendations was to shift authority over advertising to Housing and Human Service's Public Health Service (Lewis, 1989h). The BATF reluctantly later assented to cooperating in prescribing standards for container labeling; but as discussed in Chapter Five of this book, it has taken continuing vigilance on the part of consumer groups to get it to prescribe labels that are large enough and pointed enough to serve any real preventive purpose.

National Institute on Drug Abuse

Much of the following summary history of NIDA has been drawn from the 1989 article by Charles R. Schuster, NIDA director. In response to the substantial increase in the American use of illicit drugs (particularly marijuana and heroin) in the late 1960s and early 1970s, a Special Action Office for Drug Abuse Prevention was established within the executive office of the president. In addition, NIDA was established within ADAMHA in 1974, just a couple of years after NIAAA, with the mission of conducting research on the cause and treatment of drug abuse and the ultimate objective of eliminating the demand for illicit substances. Another function was to manage national programs of drug abuse treatment, prevention, training, and data collection. NIDA's mission stayed virtually the same until 1981, when the new Reagan administration transferred responsibility for treatment and prevention services to the states through block grants—much as happened with NIAAA's treatment outreach programs.

The next major change in NIDA's responsibilities came in 1986 under the Anti-Drug Abuse Act, when funding for AIDS research was increased from $7.1 million to $31.3 million in an attempt to find ways to prevent the spread of the disease among intravenous drug users and their sexual partners and to their children. At the same time, NIDA's research funds were increased by $27 million. The act also created within ADAMHA a separate Office for Substance Abuse Prevention, which took over many of NIDA's prevention activities and was charged with coordinating a national prevention program involving states, communities, the media, and organizations of concerned citizens. (Research on drug prevention strategies, however, remained a NIDA responsibility.) Also in 1986, a presidential executive order directed the federal government, the country's largest employer, to become a model for eliminating drug abuse from American workplaces; the Office of Workplace Initiatives was established within NIDA to carry out this directive.

The many units within NIDA include the Division of Epidemiology and Prevention Research, which now annually monitors trends in substance abuse to aid in setting institute priorities, and the Drug Abuse Warning Network, which collects information on drug-related hospital emergency room episodes and medical examiner cases. Other units are the National Household Survey on Drug Abuse, which has collected data on individual respondents' use of illicit drugs at frequent intervals beginning in 1972, and the High School Senior Survey, instituted in 1975 and conducted annually among many thousand seniors and also among former seniors during follow-up interviews. Research units within NIDA include a Division of Preclinical Research, dealing with new knowledge on a molecular or cellular level about drug use; a Division of Clinical Research, which supports basic and applied studies in drug abuse treatment and prevention; and the intramural NIDA Addiction Research Center in Baltimore, with five branches conducting studies on the causes, hazards, treatment, and prevention of drug abuse and addiction and the nature of the addictive process. Others are the Division of Applied Research, which includes the Office of Workplace Initiatives, focusing on drug testing and the establishment of testing standards; Health Services Research; and Community Research, which is primarily concerned with financing AIDS-related outreach demonstration projects. NIDA also collaborates with international organizations interested in controlling drug problems, including the United Nations, the World Health Organization, the Council of Europe's Co-operation Group to Combat Drug Abuse and Illicit Trafficking in Drugs, the Pan American Health Organization, and the Organization of American States.

NIDA also funds many training grants and Research Scientist Development Awards for those agreeing to devote their skills full-time to substance abuse research for five years, and Visiting Associates/Scientists funding to foster scientific interchange. In addition, NIDA maintains a substantial research dissemination and public education activity through encouraging publication in scientific journals by grantees and staff members, and also publishes information for the general public concerning illicit drug problems in such channels as its quarterly newsletter *NIDA Notes*.

Much of the research supported by NIDA is conducted through grants to scientists who either initiate applications directly to NIDA or who respond to a NIDA request for proposals. As with NIAAA and NIMH, grants are subject to peer review. NIDA also makes contracts with investigators, and (as mentioned earlier), it supports its own Addiction Research Center in Baltimore, which has its own Scientific Advisory Board.

Office for Substance Abuse Prevention (OSAP)

OSAP was created under the authority of the Anti–Drug Abuse Act of 1986 (Lewis, 1986b) to consolidate drug and alcohol prevention activities under ADAMHA, the umbrella organization. At first there were four major divisions: Information Resources (including the Clearinghouse, Publications, Media and Public Affairs), Community Assistance (Schools, Parents, Practitioners, Community Organizations, and Special Populations), Demonstration Programs (high-risk youth), and Evaluation and Research Coordination. During its first few years OSAP has focused on providing national leadership in identifying effective prevention programs, distributing information, and supporting community-based prevention initiatives, particularly for youth and families in high-risk environments.

OSAP's primary objectives are summarized as follows in a recent fact sheet:

> OSAP's goal is to promote the concepts of no use of *any* illegal drugs and no illegal or high-risk use of alcohol or other legal drugs. (High-risk alcohol use includes drinking and driving, and drinking while pregnant, drinking while recovering, drinking when using certain medications, drinking if a child of an alcoholic, drinking to intoxication.) The guiding principles behind OSAP's prevention work are based on the premises that 1) the earlier prevention is started in a person's life cycle, the more likely is its success; 2) prevention programs should be

> knowledge-based and incorporate state-of-the-art findings and practices drawn from scientific research and expertise from the field; 3) prevention programs should be *comprehensive,* e.g., include components of education, health care, social service, religion, and law enforcement, as well as family involvement; 4) programs should include process as well as outcome evaluations to ensure that knowledge derived from prevention programs is synthesized usefully and disseminated to the field; 5) the most successful programs are likely to be those that are initiated and conducted by the community members themselves [Office for Substance Abuse Prevention, 1990a, pp. 1–2].

OSAP's activities include: carrying out demonstration projects targeted to specific high-risk groups; assisting communities in developing long-term, comprehensive prevention programs that involve all sectors of the community; operating a national clearinghouse of publications and other materials and services; developing and carrying out media campaigns and other knowledge-transfer programs; providing training in prevention of addictive disorders for health care and allied professionals, parents, youth, and multicultural groups; and providing technical assistance to help communities, organizations, and others develop and implement prevention efforts.

OSAP planned to award about 377 grant awards in fiscal year 1990 in the areas of prevention demonstrations targeting youth at high-risk, model prevention projects for pregnant and postpartum women and their infants, grants for conferences to exchange information on prevention objectives and methods, and grants to states to provide assistance for community alcohol and other drug abuse prevention activities.

The experiences gained through the 130 OSAP demonstration grants funded in 1987 for prevention efforts directed at high-risk youth are described in OSAP Technical Report 1 (Office for Substance Abuse Prevention, 1990b), available on request (see the resource at the back of the book). Details are provided, for each grant, on the objectives and current status of the project and the identity and addresses of the project directors. The technical report also provides a summary of prevention strategies that is designed to be helpful for those planning similar projects.

A major information resource is OSAP's National Clearinghouse for Alcohol and Drug Information (NCADI). See the resource for a brief summary of the many free information services available through NCADI.

OSAP has the central objective of concentrating on youth to persuade them not even to start using any nonmedical drugs, including tobacco as well as alcohol and such illicit drugs as crack, heroin, PCP, and so on (DuPont, 1989). OSAP links tobacco with alcohol and illicit drugs in its prevention recommendations because there are abundant research findings to show that cigarettes are a key "gateway" substance to adopting more mood-altering substances such as alcohol and other drugs.

Again, OSAP was created in 1986 through the new Drug Act, which also gave expanded funds to NIDA. As noted in the preface to OSAP's Monograph 1 (DuPont, 1989), it became clear that prevention could not deal with alcohol separately from other drugs, nor tobacco (which was outside the mandate of NIDA and NIAAA, although tobacco is clearly linked to the use of the others). OSAP was created in recognition of this, and knowledge that there exist high-risk environments that contribute to a whole range of problems—including teen pregnancy, increased homicides, and low literacy—which should be dealt with in a concerted fashion. Further, there were almost inevitable jurisdictional and budgetary turf conflicts that contributed to the administration's deciding on setting up the separate OSAP institute to deal with prevention activities for tobacco, alcohol, and other drugs, particularly among youth. However, as discussed earlier, both NIAAA and NIDA maintain active prevention research branches.

Chapter Two of this book summarizes some of OSAP's current primary activities. Chapter Nine will speculate how its funding of many community-based prevention programs linking emphasis on prevention of use of tobacco as well as alcohol and other drugs on a grass roots basis is likely to have a profound long-term effect on the future of local as well as national public health–oriented activities.

The general strategy of OSAP focuses on youth through high school and on special high-risk populations, especially those in inner cities. Its activities are summarized in Chapter Two.

Office of National Drug Control Policy

In the fall of 1986, Congress passed the Omnibus Drug Enforcement, Education, and Control Act of 1986 (H.R. 5484) providing additional funds for enforcement, treatment, education and prevention of illicit drugs. President Reagan added funding through a series of budget amends to fund activities under the Drug-Free Workplace Act, the Drug-Free Schools Act, the Substance Abuse Services Amendments, the Drug Interdiction and International Cooperation Act, the Anti-Drug Enforcement Act, and the Public Awareness and Private Sector Initiatives Act. Reagan also issued an executive order establishing a policy against the use of illegal drugs by the federal government's civilian employees, in hopes of setting an example to the nation's private employees (Lewis, 1986a).

Public Law 100-690 of the 100th Congress, entitled the Anti–Drug Abuse Act of 1988, established the Office of National Drug Control Policy (ONDCP) within the executive office of the president. In September 1989, President Bush unveiled a new National Drug Control Strategy, with the objective of explaining the nature of the illicit drug problem in America and presenting a policy that included roles for the federal government, state and local governments, and the private sector, to "restore order and security to American neighborhoods, to dismantle drug trafficking organizations, to help people break the habit of drug use, and to prevent those who have never used illegal drugs from starting" (Office of National Drug Control Policy, 1990, p. 1). William J. Bennett, former Secretary of Education under the Reagan administration, was named director of the new White House drug office, serving until he resigned in November 1990.

As of mid 1990, Congress has passed legislation to implement some of the policies proposed by the strategy and has appropriated $9.5 billion in funds to carry them out—with additional funds being debated by both Congress and the administration. For fiscal 1991, the administration has proposed that the funding be increased to more that $10.6 billion—an amount that dwarfs most federal budgets outside of the Department of Defense (Office of National Drug Control Policy, 1990, p. 7).

Not much of this vast sum is to be spent directly by the ONDCP, but its expenditure is to be monitored by ONDCP in the wide variety of initiatives to be described in Chapters Seven and Eight. Funds are to be spent through a wide array of federal and state agencies, with an estimated 70 percent being spent in law enforcement. However, a little-noticed provision in the 1988 Anti–Drug Abuse Act explicitly states that the jurisdiction of the ONDCP (then headed by Bennett) "does not extend to alcohol abuse programs," but says the intent is that alcohol and drug programs should be "fully coordinated," particularly in the areas of education, prevention and treatment. Senate Judiciary Chairman Joseph Biden (D-Del.), the lead author of the section establishing the ONDCP, has said that the term *drug* means the same as *controlled substance* as defined in the Controlled Substance Act. "As a result, the (ONDCP) director's jurisdiction does not extend to alcohol abuse programs" (Lewis, 1989f). Lewis seems to be saying that the ONDCP's apparent lack of direct jurisdiction over federal alcohol programs is seen as keeping NIAAA's funding out of the budget authority conferred on ONDCP by the 1988 act. Senator Biden has stated that the intent of Congress was not to give the ONDCP Director dictatorial authority over the budgets of other agencies.

Office on Smoking and Health

The primary role of the Office on Smoking and Health, established in 1978 within the Centers for Disease Control of the U.S. Public Health Service, is to coordinate the distribution of information about the effects of smoking directed toward either the general public or research interests. It cooperates with a broad range of other governmental agencies such as the Department of Agriculture, the Federal Trade Commission, and the National Cancer Institute. It aids in publicizing the almost-yearly Surgeon General's reports on the epidemiology and health consequences of nicotine use (see Chapter Three), as well as a host of popular public information pamphlets and selected technical monographs (see the resource).

Nongovernmental Organizations Active in Prevention

Chapter Four of my book *Understanding America's Drinking Problem: How to Combat the Hazards of Alcohol* (1987) presents a summary of some of the activities of a few of the myriad organizations that have sprung up since the early 1970s in the alcohol and drug field. A *Resource Directory* published by the National Association of State Alcohol and Drug Abuse Directors (NASADAD) (Butynski, 1985) provides an overview of ninety-three such organizations, and others have been founded since. OSAP also has published a new *Citizen's Alcohol and Other Drug Prevention Directory* (1990c), developed by NASADAD, which provides a very detailed inventory of the prevention programs of many nonprofit associations and governmental agencies.

Most of the organizations listed in the 1985 NASADAD Resource Directory are still in existence and many of them have prevention programs. The most active nationally known ones include the National Council on Alcoholism and Drug Dependence (NCADD), Mothers Against Drunk Driving (MADD), and the Center for Science in the Public Interest (CSPI). The scope of these three organizations is described below, along with the Students Against Drunk Driving (SADD), the National Commission Against Drunk Driving, the National Coalition to Prevent Impaired Driving, the Advocacy Institute, and the prevention campaigns of the American Public Health Association relevant to tobacco, alcohol, and illicit drugs.

NCADD (which recently changed its name from NCA) is the oldest nonprofit agency dealing with alcohol problems, having been founded in 1944. From its beginnings, as discussed in Chapter Four of my 1987 book, its primary mission was to get better treatment and decriminalization for alcoholism. In recent years it has been putting more emphasis on lobbying intensively for more constraints on alcohol sales such as increased taxes, limitations on alcohol advertising, and efforts to provide more emphasis on container labels about the hazards in alcohol consumption. Hamiltom Beazley, president of NCADD, said in recommendations made to President Bush on the day of a White House briefing on drunk driving that the "pricing, marketing and advertising [he mentioned alcohol advertising expenditures of $2 billion a year] of alcoholic beverages contribute to the massive problem of drinking and driving." His recommendations: BATF should apply rules to require warning notices on drinking-driving and health risks, should prohibit the depiction of risky activities (including all references to speed on autos, motorcycles, and boats), and should prohibit "current or traditional heroes of the young or active or retired, amateur or professional athletes or athletic events" in alcohol advertising or promotions. It should also require broadcasters to give equal time for health and safety messages to promote accurate information about drinking, especially directed toward those under twenty-one; should eliminate alcohol advertising and promotion and sponsorships of events on college campuses and eliminate billboards on alcohol advertising from mass transit systems and sports stadiums; and should require that billboard alcohol advertising should be allowed no closer than 500 feet from residences, schools, parks, churches, community centers, or other places youth might gather. Finally, it should require that deductibility of alcohol advertising expenditures be eliminated (Lewis, 1989k, p. 2).

On the occasion of the announcement of the expansion of the NCA title to include drugs, Beazley said that while their mission remains essentially the same, "We enter the new decade with the opportunity to explicitly link alcohol with other drugs in the public mind. Drug dependence inevitably begins with alcohol and often coexists with alcoholism in today's world." The change affects NCADD's nearly 200 independently administered affiliates in thirty-eight states (Lewis, 1990a, p. 9).

The NCADD consistently has pushed for a much stronger federal role in the control of alcohol problems and in treatment. The convictions of its national management are set forth vigorously in statements before congressional committees, such as the one by Christine Lubinski, NCADD Director for Public Policy, before the Senate Committee on Governmental Affairs on May 25, 1988. She took a strong stand for granting increased authority over alcohol regulation to the Department of Health and Human Services, either through the Food and Drug Administration or through the NIAAA. Her statement reads in part:

> The history of federal involvement in alcohol is a history of fragmentation, non-communication and agencies working at cross-purposes. Although NIAAA represents the heart of the federal alcohol effort, NIAAA lacks any authority over regulations or federal policy of any kind governing beverage alcohol. Despite NIAAA's placement within the Public Health Service, there has been complete resistance within both the executive and legislative branches of government to utilizing the public health model to address alcoholism and alcohol-related problems. Within the public health model, disease prevention must address the agent, the host, and the environment. It has taken us decades as a nation to resist blaming the host—the individual with alcoholism—for his or her condition. But our obsession with the host continues as we focus our attention almost exclusively on treating the illness, with little willingness to take necessary steps to reduce the size of the problem. And what is the legacy of this limited view? During debate of the Hughes Act in 1969, estimates of the cost of alcoholism and related problems to the nation were pegged at $12 billion. Today, the cost of these problems is slated to be $120 billion a year.

> And how have federal institutions responded? While NIAAA funded treatment programs in the past and today funds research to identify a genetic predisposition to alcoholism, the Bureau of Alcohol, Tobacco and Firearms (BATF) continues to promulgate regulations in the economic interests of the alcohol beverage industry with little regard for the impact of any policy on the public health. The Food and Drug Administration (FDA) diligently monitors the dissemination of legal drugs to physicians and consumers while the nation's favorite legal drug, alcohol, continues to be exempt from any consumer information or protection initiatives implemented over the last two decades. The Federal Trade Commission (FTC) has repeatedly refused to investigate or further regulate alcohol advertising. This is while increasing numbers of ads promote alcohol as a beverage positively associated with health, sex, athletics, risky activities, economic and social success. These ads and other marketing strategies are the single greatest source of alcohol education for American children, but how frequently have we looked at them in the context of prevention and education programming? [Lubinski, 1988.]

MADD, another private agency concerned with alcohol, has been quite effective in its lobbying with legislatures and administrations concerning one limited but important objective: raising the penalties for driving under the influence of alcohol. For some time MADD was criticized because in its early days when it was enjoying substantial subsidies from the alcohol industry, it was refusing to join in with other agencies in advocating higher taxes for alcohol and for container labeling. Those subsidies now apparently have ceased.

However, MADD does continue to have problems with internal dissension (Snyder, 1990). A former local California

MADD chapter president has complained that the MADD administration is abandoning its grass roots base to focus on big-time fund raising and political power building, at the expense of the original purpose: personal involvement in lobbying for tougher drinking-driving laws and enforcement. She said that some years ago MADD had up to thirty chapters in the state, but has lost nearly a third. She claimed that MADD siphons off too large a share of local money to headquarters: that the bulk of the money goes for salaries at the top while unpaid volunteers struggle to keep going at the local level.

She also said that "The 'national' is reluctant to support tough legislative insurance reforms against drunk drivers or initiatives to raise the sales tax on alcohol, and the reason is that they are afraid to step on the toes of some of their biggest contributors" (Snyder, 1990, p. A7).

A spokesperson at MADD's headquarters in Hurst, Texas, conceded that the organization has not made all members happy: Now that they have a $40 million budget and 1.5 million members, they are "a group trying to achieve legislative progress by filing briefs instead of standing in the streets. We have had a positive effect on more than 1,000 pieces of anti–drunk driving legislation on the State and Federal level" (Snyder, 1990, p. A7). She went on to say that as the result of pressures from groups like MADD, the number killed in drunk driving accidents has decreased from about 28,000 in 1988 to an estimated 23,251 in 1989. But friction between the locals and the nationals has gone on for some time.

SADD also is setting up a separate coalition consisting of agencies dealing with youth and underage drinking and driving. Both MADD and SADD have received substantial subsidies in the past from the alcohol industry, but MADD is said to be no longer accepting industry donations.

There is still another drunk-driving organization, the *National Commission Against Drunk-Driving,* which was set up to carry out the recommendations of Reagan's Commission on Drunk Driving, whose initial board was dominated by old-line politicians and representatives of the alcohol industry. This group boycotted the Surgeon General's 1988 workshop, contending that some of the panels were biased in favor of restrictive measures against the advertising, broadcasting, and alcoholic beverage industries. This commission is heavily subsidized by the alcohol industry.

The National Coalition to Prevent Impaired Driving was officially launched in Washington in early 1990, with the mission of promoting ten key recommendations from the Drunk Driving Workshop conducted by then Surgeon General Koop (1989). The coalition chair is Alexander C. Wagenaar, associate professor of public health at the University of Minnesota, who said that membership in the coalition will be "screened to prevent the influence of the alcoholic beverage industry." The ten initial key recommendations of the coalition, as reported by Lewis (1990b, p. 2), are:

1. Reduce blood alcohol content (BAC) from the usual .10 percent to .04 percent by the year 2000 and establish zero level for drivers under 21.
2. Increase excise taxes on alcohol beverages and tax them equally.
3. Have each state fund comprehensive alcohol-impaired driving programs.
4. Reduce availability of alcoholic beverages.
5. Pass legislation in each state to confiscate driver's licenses on the spot for those above legal BAC ("administrative license revocation").
6. Match alcohol advertising with an equal number of pro-health and pro-safety messages.
7. Restrict certain alcohol advertising and marketing practices, especially those reaching underage youth.
8. Conduct public information efforts based on social marketing and communications strategies and on sound learning principles.
9. Conduct drinking-driving education within worksites, communities, health care agencies, and schools.
10. Increase enforcement of drinking-driving laws and expand the use of sobriety checkpoints.

In passing, one development encouraging to the coalition has been the gradual tightening of the state-by-state regulations on blood alcohol levels that are deemed prima facie evidence of impaired driving. California and Vermont recently lowered the BAC limits to .08 percent, joining Oregon, Utah, and Maine in adopting that standard. Seven additional states are considering that rule, although most states still have a .10 percent law. (University of California at San Diego, 1990b, pp. 9–10).

Members of the National Coalition's board include representatives from the following organizations: the American Medical Association, American Public Health Association, Center for Science in the Public Interest, Christian Life Commission of the Southern Baptist Convention, Cork Institute on Black Alcohol and Other Drug Abuse of Morehouse School of Medicine, and National Drug Information Center of Families in Action. Other groups represented include the Marin Institute for the Prevention of Alcohol and Other Drug Problems, National Council on Alcoholism and Drug Dependence (formerly NCA), National Governors' Highway Safety Representatives, Remove Intoxicated Drivers, Robert Wood Johnson Medical School, Texans' War on Drugs, University of Michigan Transportation Research Institute, and University of Minnesota School of Public Health.

MADD declined membership in the coalition and said it would form an "advertising review council" composed of other anti–drunk driving activists and public health advocates. It explained that it planned to cooperate with the National Coalition on matters of common interest, but preferred to work toward voluntary (rather than compulsory) improvement in alcohol advertising. Thus far, MADD does not appear to be doing very much in this direction.

The Washington-based *Center for Science in the Public Interest* (CSPI), a nonprofit consumer advocacy organization founded in 1971, has continued to mount intensive lobbying campaigns for the same types of controls advocated by NCADD to reduce alcohol problems, as well as for cigarette constraints. One of its most successful campaigns has been providing the leadership for Project SMART, a continuing lobbying activity by a coalition of advocacy groups directed toward legislators and administrators to reduce or eliminate alcohol advertising. (See the resource for a list of some of its recent publications.)

CSPI's *Marketing Disease to Hispanics: The Selling of Alcohol, Tobacco, and Junk Foods* (1989), an illustrated paperback by Maxwell and Jacobson, tells how the tobacco and beer companies are pushing their product to the high-risk Hispanic population, especially vulnerable youth. They contribute liberally to Hispanic fiestas and other meetings, blanket Spanish communities with billboards, and advertise heavily in print and broadcast media. "Open up a Spanish-language magazaine and you'll likely see attractive ads for cigarettes and liquor. Attend a convention of one of the major national Hispanic organizations, and you'll be handed free samples of cigarettes and be able to belly up to a free bar sponsored by a beer company that's open during the entire event" (Maxwell and Jacobson, 1989, p. ix). In 1988, CSPI ran a successful drive to persuade a large Spanish-language television network to halt showing ads for hard liquor. CSPI currently is working with Hispanic groups on other campaigns to bring about better control of alcohol and drug marketing.

Another activity of the CSPI is publicizing the financial linkage between the alcohol and tobacco industries and politicians and others who might be unduly influenced by industry contributions. One such instance is the recent publication of a newsletter issue entitled "Legislating Under the Influence: the Booze Merchants, Money, and Congress" (Taylor, 1989). It revealed that more than $4 million was paid out to members of Congress during two recent election cycles (1985–86 and 1987–88). This CSPI newsletter listed twenty senators as each having received from $13,500 to $33,100 from the alcohol industry during those two election periods, and 20 U.S. representatives who got $14,500 to $34,000. The members of the House Ways and Means and Senate Finance Committees especially have been favored with alcohol industry contributions, and since 1951, understandably there have been no *recorded* votes by the tax-writing Ways and Means and Senate Finance Committees on proposals to increase taxes on alcoholic beverages. This kind of information should be of interest to those who are advocating reducing (if not eliminating) this now perfectly legal form of vote buying.

Michael Jacobson, executive director of the CSPI since its beginnings twenty years ago, was the 1988 recipient of the Leadership Award of the Alcohol and Drug Section of the American Public Health Association. On that occasion, he summarized some of the growing number of successful campaigns waged by CSPI and other nonprofit advocacy groups (such as NCADD and MADD). These include the 19 percent increase in federal hard liquor taxes in 1984 (the first such increase since 1951); requirements to label dangerous sulfite preservatives in alcoholic beverages; the warning labels now required on all alcoholic beverages; promotion of Surgeon General Koop's 1988 workshop on drunk driving, and some progress on the advertising front through CSPI-led Project SMART (Stop Marketing Alcohol on Radio and Television). Jacobson (1990, p. 11) hopes that the perceptual climate for alcohol is changing: "The legislative victories have been modest and infrequent, but all the activity around the alcohol issue in the last decade contributed to a new way of thinking about booze. Booze for the first time is losing some of its glamour—the image which the industry has spent billions of dollars to build. More and more people are realizing that booze is not the key to happiness and success. De-alcoholized wine and non-alcoholic beer are becoming increasingly trendy, and what had been seen as a moral problem or a medical problem is being seen increasingly as a public health problem that this nation needs to tackle."

In closing that address, Jacobson summarized the unfinished business of CSPI and cooperating groups as including: eliminating alcohol advertisements on radio and television or the balancing of each ad with a health or safety message, further increases in alcohol taxes and devoting a portion of that revenue to support alcohol education and treatment programs, adding rotating messages on the dangers of drinking to the labels on alcoholic beverages, banning all alcohol marketing to those under twenty-one, and prohibiting inner-city billboards advertising alcohol and tobacco. Jacobson (1990, p. 12) closed by saying, "Finally, the number of outlets selling alcoholic beverages should be restricted in many places. Does it make sense to sell liquor in supermarkets, as is done in California and some other states? Does it make sense to sell booze in every corner store in the inner city?"

The Advocacy Institute of Washington, directed by Michael Pertschuk and David Cohen, has prevention-oriented goals that are similar and complementary to those of the CSPI. It concentrates on the study and teaching of advocacy strategies and skills for nonprofit organizations to apply in effecting policy changes. The Institute launched the Smoking Control Advocacy Resource Center in 1987; and both Michael and Mark Pertschuk have been active in developing and publicizing antismoking strategies, as discussed in a Stanford University conference of July 1990 proceedings published by the University of California at San Diego (Winter 1991). More recently, the Institute has been concentrating also on alcohol problems, such as issues concerning alcohol taxes, alcohol ads on billboards, revocation of licenses of drunken drivers, and curbing the spread of heavy drinking promoting on holiday occasions such as Halloween. (See the resource at the end of the book for a summary of the Advocacy Institute's prevention strategies and for sources of more information on the Institute's activities and publications.)

The American Public Health Association (APHA) in recent years has passed many resolutions calling for further constraints on cigarettes, alcohol, and other drugs, and it appears to have provided considerable reinforcement within prevention circles toward greater emphasis on a public health (as opposed to a moralistic) approach to prevention. One instance is the policy statement adopted by the governing council of the APHA at its 1986 annual meeting, which was prepared by James Mosher, who has been active in the Alcohol and Drugs section of the APHA from its inception and was chairperson-elect for 1990. The resolutions include four on alcohol tax policy that were later recommended by Surgeon General Koop for congressional consideration (as discussed in Chapter Five). These APHA policy statements are excellent sources for well-documented public health and economic arguments (directed at Congress and federal and state agencies) for such measures as increases in alcohol and tobacco taxes and constraints on alcohol and tobacco marketing (Mosher, 1987).

A more recent APHA set of policy statements (American Public Health Association, 1989b, p. 361) takes note that APHA has adopted numerous resolutions and position papers on alcohol advertising, alcohol tax policy, minimum drinking age, alcohol education, alcoholism treatment and prevention, and alcohol-related birth defects—all of which focus at least to some degree on special issues with youth. On tobacco, APHA has as a major priority to make the United States tobacco-smoke-free by 2000, as well as banning cigarette sales in health facilities, prohibiting the advertising of tobacco products, and increasing tobacco taxation. On illicit drugs, the APHA position paper cites the Drug Abuse Warning Network (DAWN) finding from a survey of deaths in the thirty largest metropolitan areas in the United States (excluding New York) that cocaine accounted for 604 fatalities and heroin/morphine, 1,072 fatalities in 1984. It also points to NIDA estimates that drugs other than alcohol are involved in 20 percent of all car crashes, or about 8,000 deaths per year. As with alcohol-related casualties, a large share of these deaths were among young people.

The article says that "drug problems can only be understood by reference to their social, physical, cultural and economic environments. Alcohol and tobacco are legal, culturally accepted, relatively inexpensive, easily accessible, and highly profitable for a legal industry. Illicit drugs, on the other hand, are closely linked to criminal behavior, are highly profitable for an illegal industry, and are not socially accepted. . . . These and other environmental factors have a profound impact on drug usage and drug problems. . . . Drug problems should be viewed collectively as 'a public health problem, instead of merely a problem of criminal deviancy.' Strict punitive measures should not take priority over drug treatment and prevention goals" (American Public Health Association, 1989b, p. 362).

APHA contends that in focusing on illicit drugs, the government has virtually ignored tobacco and prescription drugs as drug issues, and has treated alcohol problems only tangentially. The heavy expenditures in the War on Drugs are on paramilitary hardware and law enforcement activities. The 1988 War on Drugs legislation called for spending about one-half of the over $2 billion in authorized funding on "supply reduction" activities (AHPA, 1989b, p. 362). The APHA article asserts that the War legislation encourages incursions on basic civil rights as regards unreasonable searches and seizures, and ignores the economic, social, and political underpinnings of drug problems. "Program cuts in basic health care, economic policies that lead to homelessness and unemployment and continued lack of attention to the problems of underdevelopment may result in increased drug problems despite the commendable goals of the War on Drugs" (AHPA, 1989b, p. 362). Also, the APHA is concerned about what it considers to be insufficient funding for research and evaluation.

One example of the increased activism toward better control over alcohol and other drugs among public health professionals in recent years is the acceptance of the chair of the National Coalition to Prevent Impaired Driving by Alex Wagenaar of the University of Minnesota's School of Public Health. The generation of public health educators and practitioners that witnessed the shortcomings of Prohibition has largely died off (Room, 1984), and there now seems to be less fear within the newer generation within APHA of being labeled "neoprohibitionists" by the alcohol industry.

Public health professionals continue to have misgivings about the manner in which the federal government is conducting its War on Drugs. As Robert Denniston, chairperson of the Alcohol and Drugs Section of the APHA, commented concerning the suggestions made by APHA and some other 500 organizations and individuals to the Public Health Service in the development of the Year 2000 Objectives for the Nation,

> In reviewing many of the comments from our Section, including my own, most of us were examining the bark on the trees instead of the shape of the forest. While highly valuable in the process, technical comments neglected some of the underlying causes of the problems we work to solve, including structural problems in this society. Perhaps that's in part why we've got a "war on drugs" with users being declared the sole enemy. We all know that everyone loses in a war.

> This last point brings to mind a quotation that seems relevant to the Year 2000 Objectives and, especially, our effort to reduce problems with alcohol, tobacco and other drugs. "Every gun that's made, every warship launched, every rocket fired signifies a theft from those who hunger and are not fed, those who are not clothed," said Dwight David Eisenhower. "This world in arms is not spending money alone. It is spending the sweat of its laborers, the genius of its scientists, the hope of its children" [1990, pp. 2-3].

The APHA's prevention activities are closely associated with those of a number of more regionally based nonprofit prevention research and advocacy groups. One of the most recent of these is the Marin Institute for the Prevention of Alcohol and Other Drug Problems of San Rafael, California, founded in 1987 with substantial long-term funding from the Beryl Buck Foundation. This nonprofit institute compiles data on current and proposed laws and regulations regarding alcohol control. James Mosher, the program director, whose combined legal and behavioral research training has been helpful in drafting model control legislation, has been appearing frequently before state and federal legislative bodies to testify in support of more control over the sale and dispensing of alcohol. The Marin Institute is unique in its combination of nationally oriented prevention research programs, its program of assisting community advocacy groups in organizing and running prevention campaigns, and in serving as an alcohol and drug information resource for community organizations or state or federal agencies.

To sum up the current outlook for improvement in primary prevention in excessive use of alcohol, tobacco, and other drugs: All the current activity should have a synergistic effect in making community and governmental agencies more prevention-conscious and interested in working together toward mutual goals. Mosher and Jernigan (1989, p. 246) hoped this is about to happen: "Changing policy requires learning to organize new constituencies, becoming effective in the political and economic arena, developing new funding sources, and offsetting the barriers to effective public health reform. It demands a coordinated, concerted effort from diverse professionals—researchers and evaluators, program personnel, citizen activists, government administrators, educators, health care providers, health planners, and others. The potential benefits are enormous. Not only do we have a chance to reduce dramatically the tragic toll of alcohol-related problems on society. The approach envisioned here also holds the potential of broadening citizen support and activism on behalf of public health goals and agendas across the board."

CHAPTER TWO

What Makes and Breaks Prevention Programs

No doubt the considerable increase in official support for prevention programs directed toward reducing the damage being done in our society by tobacco, alcohol, and illicit drugs stems in large part from the growing realization that it is enormously expensive to try to cope with such problems *after* they occur, because once people become strongly habituated to using one or more of these substances, it is extremely difficult to rehabilitate them. But even under the best of auspices, effective prevention measures are bound to continue to be expensive and controversial because addictive substances are already so heavily entrenched within our society.

Throughout this book, "effective prevention measures" to minimize the damage done by tobacco, alcohol, and other drugs are defined as those that operate to limit casualties or other losses significantly without being so disruptive as to fail to maintain a workable level of popular support. (By this criterion, the prohibition of the sale of alcoholic beverages in the 1920s could not be termed "effective" even though it reduced the rate of liver cirrhosis by one-third.) This book will attempt to cover most of the major types and degrees of prevention measures that may be applied to limit problems related to tobacco, alcohol, and other drugs.

The most sweeping measure is to prohibit the use of the substance altogether—which is the law now applicable to such drugs as marijuana, cocaine, and the opiates. Other measures include increasing taxes, which has been applied on tobacco and alcohol at intervals throughout our history. Increases currently are being advocated as a means not only of reducing consumption but also of raising additional funds to help pay for the damage caused by these substances. Other measures that have been adopted or proposed include warning labels attached to tobacco and alcohol containers, warnings required in conjunction with advertising of alcohol or tobacco, and other constraints on advertising such as rules against using sports celebrities. Other alternatives include prohibition or limitation in certain situations (such as smoking in enclosed public buildings or on airplanes, and drinking in public parks or at sporting events), zoning regulations limiting the number and localities of licensed establishments for service or off-premises sale of alcoholic beverages, enforcement of server liability laws intended to curb excessive drinking, and prohibition of sale of alcohol or tobacco to minors.

"Prevention" here is taken to mean not necessarily the complete elimination of a problem, but at least a significant reduction or minimization (Room, 1974b). In any effective prevention program, there needs to be a careful assessment, before the inception of the program and at frequent intervals during its progress, of the costs and benefits that are likely to ensue. Often this is a very frustrating experience because it entails the apples-and-oranges comparison of the value of saving a guesstimated minimum number of lives through a prevention program, against the cost of a guesstimated number of dollars and public inconvenience and disruption.

The old axiom that the effectiveness of laws depends in the long run on the consent of the governed especially rings true in the case of constraints on the use of tobacco, alcohol, and other drugs used to relieve tension or to feel better. Depriving a substantial minority of the people of ready access to their favorite drugs in the interest of promoting their own benefit in the long run (as well as substantial benefits to the majority) can be successful only if a large majority stand firm in support of the prevention measures. There also needs to be the full backing of the media as well as fair administration of the laws by government authorities with the hardihood to stand up against attacks against the constraints on the part of powerful commercial interests.

The fact that certain groups are more vulnerable to all three addictions makes the task of preventing the problems caused by these drugs easier in some ways and harder in others. As noted in Chapter Five, those who have high levels of problems with alcohol are most likely to be young, male, of lower socioeconomic status, and from large cities. The same can be said generally for addiction to tobacco (see Chapter Three) and illicit drugs (Chapter Seven). The task is made easier to the extent that the common vulnerabilities of young, lower-status, urbanized males suggests that to be effective, prevention programs directed toward this group should make a concerted effort to deal with all three addictions at the same time. And the task is made harder by the interaction of a variety of influences toward use of addictive substances within this group—such as the macho or risk-taking values in the youth culture, the fact that young males tend to be subject to fewer responsibilities and constraints than others, that lower-status youth often resort to drugs to feel more adequate, and because drinking and illicit drug use is usually associated with dropping out of school or the closing off of other avenues toward success in life—all of which makes addictions more deep-seated. Young lower-status male addicts also are commonly regarded as threatening to people and property, thus heightening their alienation from others and making prevention and treatment of their addictions even more difficult.

Forces Hindering Prevention Programs

Public health authorities take pardonable pride in the fact that most of the infectious diseases that were the foremost causes of death at the beginning of the twentieth century—such as tuberculosis, smallpox, and malaria—have been substantially reduced by persistent long-term prevention campaigns. But the rough sledding for most addiction prevention programs in modern America is self-evident in the fact that after many generations of effort and many billions of dollars have been expended by federal, state, and local government and private agencies in attempts to control the spread of addictions, use of addictive substances in the United States still is causing more than 600,000 deaths per year (Ravenholt, 1984).

Several important elements within the American culture have made it difficult to develop effective addiction prevention programs:

The most obvious one is that throughout our history a very large proportion of our population has derived satisfaction from smoking to reduce tension and from drinking alcoholic beverages for temporary relief of stress and as a generally accepted medium for enhancing sociability. In addition, opiates and cocaine have long been resorted to by a fairly substantial minority for temporary escape from physical or emotional pains or stress. Thus the prevention of problems from use of tobacco, alcohol, and illegal drugs is not at all in the same league as the prevention of infectious diseases like tuberculosis or smallpox—since tobacco, alcohol, and other drugs not only have brought their users a great deal of pleasure, but also have fostered continued use because of their addictive qualities.

Another handicap for tobacco, alcohol, and drug prevention programs is that the average American is a very individualistic being who bristles at having anyone tell him or her what not to do, an attitude strongly reinforced by the country's unfortunate experience with Prohibition a half-century ago.

Another element in American individuality is the apparent growth in recent generations of a tendency to put a high value on immediate short-term gratification. Our government itself has fostered pursuit of such feel-good gratifications by its own long delays in applying belt-tightening measures to reduce the crushing burden of public debt that otherwise will fall on our children and grandchildren, by its failure to invest sufficient funds in research and development to improve long-term living conditions, and by its failure to provide real incentives to encourage personal savings for future needs. It has also been guilty of a laissez-faire attitude of near indifference about doing anything substantial to remedy the fact that the rich are getting richer and the poor are getting much poorer—with consequent damage to our living standards and productivity. Our communications media (especially television) have catered to the "me" generation, too, by an increasing emphasis on frenetic hurry-hurry-hurry advertising and a bias toward favoring superficial sensationalism rather than reasoned depth in presenting the news. As discussed in the next chapter, the print and broadcast media are fighting any controls over cigarette or alcohol advertising (a large share of their revenues come from those sources), ostensibly on the grounds of "commercial freedom of speech"—even though the constitutional supports for such alleged freedoms are virtually nonexistent.

How Special Interests Hinder Prevention

Obviously, one of the most formidable barriers against reduction of tobacco and alcohol problems is the billions of dollars spent yearly in advertising tobacco and alcohol, and the many millions spent by the interrelated alcohol and tobacco industries to defend their products against any further controls or taxes through heavy contributions to members of Congress and militant public campaigns. As discussed at many points in this book, in these defensive efforts they are usually joined by the advertising industry. Many publications and broadcasting stations are also reluctant to cooperate in voicing approval of any moves toward further constraints on tobacco and alcohol because they would consider it bad for business.

Another barrier to addiction prevention programs is that entrenched commercial and political interests tend to commend and reward those who provide alcoholics and other addicts with expensive treatment programs, but are apathetic or hostile to movements that might keep those addictions from developing in the first place. These interests include not only the manufacturers of cigarettes and alcoholic beverages, but also some professionals engaged in the treatment of alcoholics who fear that expenditures on prevention of addictions will result in less funds being available for treatment of those already addicted. One may guess also that many physicians and counselors are reluctant to get involved publicly in addiction prevention campaigns for fear of becoming regarded as bluenoses by their clients, or are reluctant to question or advise their individual clients about smoking, drinking, or use of other drugs for fear of offending them.

Proving Prevention Effectiveness Is Not Easy

Another difficulty in achieving successful prevention programs is the complexity and difficulty of proving their effectiveness in a culture that is skeptical about any campaign that is not an immediate success, and in which it is difficult or impossible to test program effectiveness through a controlled experiment. One instance is a real-life experiment my colleagues and I conducted in the 1970s in three California counties through television commercials designed to extol the merits of moderation in improving one's physical fitness and attractiveness and social life. We conducted before-and-after probability sample surveys on drinking behavior attitudes, comparing results for one county where three television commercials were shown repeatedly and where there also was print media reinforcement of the same moderation messages, another county where only television was used, and a third control county where neither television or print media were used. The whole experiment took several years to conduct and report, at a cost to the state of California of more than a half million dollars. But, as we had predicted, the outcome was that while the so-called "Winners" campaign did manage to make modest changes in information levels and attitudes about drinking, it did not result in any real change in drinking behavior (Wallack and Barrows, 1982–83). In fact, many of the people we questioned after they had seen the commercials assumed that they were actually commercials extolling the merits of drinking beer or wine—because these television viewers had been inundated for so long by real beer and wine commercials!

A useful critique of difficulties in conducting research on prevention campaigns (Kumpfer, 1989) summarizes a number of risk factor issues in research on alcohol and other drug abuse:

1. The lack of empirically tested causal models and other methodological problems (such as lack of control groups, too-small sample sizes, unrepresentative samples, nonstandard data collection techniques, and lack of triangulation of data sources).
2. Lack of adequate statistical analysis procedures. Often researchers will rely too heavily on high simple correlations between a certain factor (such as use of marijuana) and drug use when a multivariate analysis would show that other factors (such as closeness to parents) were actually better predictors.
3. Specificity of risk factors. For example, risks of drug abuse are different for different drugs, different levels of use, different age groups or age cohorts, and different races.
4. Failure to remember that the etiology of drug *use* is different from that for drug *abuse*. For example, the majority of youths who experiment with cigarettes, alcohol, or drugs will not become regular users.
5. Lack of specificity of risk factors. For example, considerable study has been conducted to determine whether drug use causes crime or crime causes drug use, when it is most likely that they are covariates for most of the youth who are manifesting a psychiatric syndrome that includes antisocial personality and chemical dependency.
6. More longitudinal studies are needed to measure the etiology of risk factors related to alcohol and other drug abuse, in order to establish more conclusively whether the causal relationships found in past studies are true or whether they might be limited to special sets of circumstances or processes of measurement.

Wallack (1981) has provided a congruent list of seven barriers to effective prevention programs: (1) improper or inadequate application of behavioral science models, (2) administration and coordination problems in implementation, (3) evaluation designs based on assumptions irrelevant to program needs, (4) a narrow conceptualization of the problem and of what is to be prevented, (5) unrealistic expectations (which can hinder continuation of future prevention efforts), (6) a sole focus on the individual rather than the system as the point of intervention, and (7) a lack of attention to relevant elements in the environment that can negatively impact the success of the program.

Kumpfer (1989, pp. 310–311) draws attention to the fact that although there has been a significant drop in the use of tobacco and other addictive drugs by youth since 1981, a substantial percentage of adults still use them, and thus there is still a great need for more prevention efforts among adults. She notes that the governmental commitments for prevention are mostly verbal instead of financial: that although alcohol and other drug abuse in 1986 cost each person in the country about $850, only 77 cents per person was spent on alcohol and drug abuse prevention. Public concern about drugs appeared to have changed dramatically by the fall of 1988, and Congress authorized several billion for prevention. "Unfortunately most of this money will be spent on supply reduction techniques that have demonstrated little effect on actual use patterns" (Kumpfer, 1989, p. 347). Kumpfer points out that the Rand report on *Strategies for Controlling Adolescent Drug Use* (Polich, Ellickson, Reuter, and Kahan, 1984) details reasons why supply-reduction interventions are ineffective and probably have pushed youth into using more harmful drugs.

The trouble with many proposed addiction prevention campaigns that can have a significant impact on the convenience and habits of the general public — such as increases in tobacco or alcohol taxes, or constraints on the hours of service — is that it is very hard to set up a realistic controlled experiment to test out the effectiveness of such campaigns by applying such tax increases or other constraints within limited areas and comparing behavior results after a test period against results in exactly comparable areas where there were no added constraints. One difficulty with such experiments is that the ethics and political feasibility of applying constraints to a test locality will be questioned — the issue will be raised as to why those people should be forced to put up with the inconveniences caused by the experiment. Another hazard is that the tobacco or alcohol manufacturers (and advertising interests that might be affected) readily can sabotage or suspend such experiments by raising a hue and cry and letter-writing campaigns within the test areas about "commercial civil rights."

In any case, the application of addiction control campaigns are seldom preceded by any scientific pilot testing, both because of their sponsors' concern over such resistances from manufacturers or marketers, and because such campaigns normally are launched by politicians or administrators who feel strongly enough about the issues and have the hardihood to take the risks in launching a control campaign when they sense that the time is ripe. One recent instance of this is the strong denunciation leveled by Dr. Louis Sullivan, Secretary of Health and Human Services, against the racism he saw in the proposed test marketing in heavily black Philadelphia of the new "Uptown" brand of cigarettes with a campaign directed primarily at African-Americans. Because the secretary himself is African-American, he was able to speak with enough moral outrage and political clout to induce the manufacturer hastily to cancel the launching of the new brand.

It appears that most control programs are launched only when the iron is sufficiently hot, but the sponsors are reluctant to hold up their campaigns for the many months to years it might take to run a conclusive test experiment. This practical reality may induce evaluators to reconcile themselves to lacking sufficient time and resources to pretest prevention programs adequately before they are put into effect, although they should guard against being pressured into taking sides by endorsing proposed programs unless there is a reasonable weight of evidence to warrant such recommendations.

Jan Howard, head of the NIAAA Prevention Branch, views the difficulty of deciding upon preventive action in a somewhat similar perspective:

> Ideally, Prevention programs should reflect and build upon the state of the art. They should be

> guided by existing research findings and, if possible, carry the inquiry further. Unfortunately, there is a dearth of proven strategies for the primary prevention of alcohol abuse and alcoholism. And, thus, administrators who are committed to prevention activity must frequently choose between less-than-preferred options. They can delay intervention until the evidence for one or another strategy becomes more convincing; they can undertake expeditious or long-term research in preparation for intervention; they can select an intervention on the basis of promise rather than proof; or they can conduct a natural experiment, intervening and testing at the same time. Obviously, any of these options constitutes action, but the time period for the implementation of prevention strategies (as opposed to research) will vary with the choice. In the first two cases, intervention might be postponed indefinitely [1990, p. 248].

Forces Favorable to Current Prevention Campaigns

Despite the many forces operating to thwart additional measures to control smoking and drinking problems, the era of the 1990s has seen the evolution of a number of influences that are having a significant effect on the potential success of proposed additional controls. These influences have tended to reinforce each other in a snowball fashion: For example, the general public's acceptance with at least lip service of the "good health" movement (Cahalan, 1987) has encouraged national and community leaders to lend further support to public health–oriented prevention measures. The encouragement provided by these leaders has made it easier in turn for governmental and private agencies concerned with prevention to get the budgets and moral support needed to be able to mount successful control programs. And the evolution and strengthening of the skills of public and private agencies in turn have made it easier for them to attract well-qualified people and the other resources needed to sustain the adoption of effective prevention programs.

Another factor encouraging greater emphasis on primary prevention is the great increases of recent years in medical costs generally, which in turn have multiplied the costs of treatment of people afflicted with alcoholism or other drug addiction. With the growing body of research indicating that primary prevention is more cost-effective than resorting to treatment only after addiction has become chronic, there should continue to be more demand for primary prevention to reduce overall medical costs as well as to avoid distress not only among those who might become addicted but also among those around them.

There is as yet no single federal agency of any size formally charged with reducing the toll of lives lost because of addiction to tobacco. However, the Office of the Surgeon General and several of the National Institutes of Health (notably the National Cancer Institute) have been devoting much time and attention to this issue for the last twenty-five years, with considerable success. In addition (as discussed in Chapter One), an Office on Smoking and Health has been established within the Centers for Disease Control to assist in coordinating information and research on the effects of tobacco. Senator Edward Kennedy (D-Mass.) in November 1989 introduced a bill (S. 1883; short title "Tobacco Product Education and Health Protection Act of 1990") to amend the Public Health Service Act to establish a center for tobacco products, inform the public about the hazards of tobacco use, disclose and restrict additives to tobacco products, and require labeling of tobacco products concerning their hazards.

As related by an article in the APHA's *The Nation's Health* (American Public Health Association, 1990), Senator Kennedy's bill, backed by Senator Orrin Hatch (R-Utah) from the Senate Labor and Human Resources Committee, would create the first large-scale federal tobacco education program. It would provide a Center for Tobacco Products at the Center for Disease Control, as well as $50 million per year for counteradvertising to discourage tobacco use, $50 million to states for enactment and better enforcement of prohibition of sales to minors, and

$25 million to encourage schools to be smoke-free. APHA has joined thirty-eight other organizations in support of the bill. In addition, the proposed bill would establish new regulatory authority for disclosure of additives and requirements for labeling, analogous to the types of requirements normally imposed by the Food and Drug Administration. Kennedy noted that the $50 million for counteradvertising is equal to only 2 percent of the tobacco industry's $2.5 billion advertising budget: "It's still a David-and-Goliath battle, but at least we are providing enough to pay for David's slingshot" (American Public Health Association, 1990, p. 1). He plans to continue pushing a high priority for the bill.

As discussed in Chapter One, the new Office for Substance Abuse Prevention (OSAP), which now is the principal federal agency dealing with prevention of tobacco, alcohol, and other drug problems, is off and running with a budget of more than $250 million. The National Institute on Alcohol Abuse and Alcoholism (NIAAA) has grown (although rather slowly) over the years since its formal founding in 1971, until its budget now runs approximately $160 million per year, with about 6 percent of the total being allocated to prevention-oriented research or demonstration activities. The National Institute on Drug Abuse (NIDA), although founded three years later than NIAAA as part of the umbrella agency of the Alcohol, Drug, and Mental Health Administration (ADAMHA), has zoomed past NIAAA in recent budgets to approximately $400 million per year because of public demand and the demand of politicians to intensify the War on Drugs; of this total, about 3 percent is allocated for activities directly under the Prevention Research Branch.

At its inception, NIAAA was not very concerned with programs to prevent alcohol problems because its primary constituency was treatment-oriented groups like the National Council on Alcoholism (Cahalan, 1987, chap. 3). Not long after the founding of NIDA, it became clear that there was need for a more concerted effort to prevent both alcohol and other drug use from increasing, since abundant research findings had established that there is a high relationship between the adoption of and addiction to cigarettes and alcohol and other drugs. The vastly increased funding under the War on Drugs provided the opportunity for the founding of the new Office for Substance Abuse Prevention in 1986, and from its inception OSAP has had the primary federal responsibility for facilitating programs to minimize the misuse of all three types of addictive substances. Accordingly, the remainder of this chapter will focus on OSAP's current objectives and activities.

OSAP has concentrated on the compilation, assessment, and distribution of information deemed potentially useful in advancing prevention programs. Its Division of Communication Programs turned out in 1989 a series of three highly readable paperback monographs that can be very helpful to community, city, or state governmental or private organizations concerned with prevention; other program guides are in preparation. OSAP Monograph 1, edited by Robert L. DuPont (1989), former director of NIDA, summarizes a prevention strategy that focuses on youth of the most vulnerable age (twelve to twenty) for adopting the use of tobacco, alcohol, and other drugs. The monograph provides basic information on recent trends in the use of various addictive substances, discusses what strategies seem to work and which do not, and gives a summary of action and research programs vital to continued progress in prevention.

A central rationale for OSAP's urging a prevention strategy that concentrates its attention on the young well before most of them ever try to use tobacco, alcohol, or illicit drugs stems from survey findings that show that the period of greatest risk for initiating use of cigarettes is in the sixth and seventh grades. The ninth grade is the time of greatest risk for beginning alcohol use and for experiencing the first loss of control over drinking, and for beginning the use of marijuana. Thus the OSAP (1989, p. 12) conclusion is that the most crucial period for prevention is during the fifth through ninth grades.

While the University of Michigan national surveys of tobacco, alcohol, and other drug use by high school seniors show that consumption has fallen slightly in recent years (Johnston, O'Malley, and Bachman, 1989), Figure 1 indicates that for almost all of the substances surveyed (all of which are illegal for youth), usage among seniors is still large enough to occasion concern, and is still especially large for alcohol, cigarettes, and marijuana.

Figure 1. Prevalence and Recency: Percent of 1987 U.S. High School Seniors Who Had Used a Drug in Their Lifetimes, in the Past Year, or in the Past Month, by Drug Type.

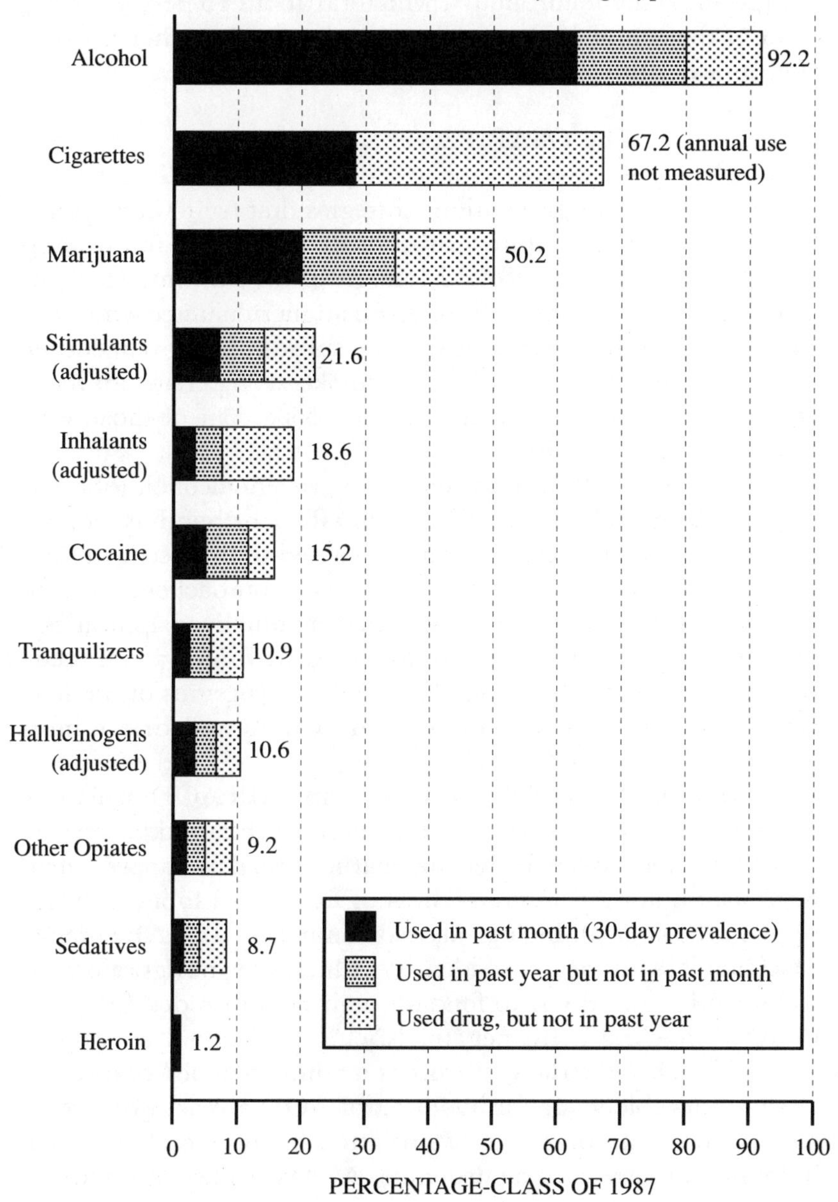

Source: Adapted from L. Johnston, P. O'Malley, and J. Bachman, 1989, p. 67.

As noted in Chapter Six, these usage figures among those still in school do not take into account the obviously higher consumption by school dropouts, who total about 15 percent of the total of the senior high age group and a much higher proportion among inner-city youth.

The OSAP Prevention Strategy

The importance of prevention strategies that try to keep youth from *even trying* prohibited substances is seen in the finding reported in the same OSAP Monograph 1 (DuPont, 1989, p. 69) that the percentage of those *ever* using a substance who were *still* using it in their senior year ran a substantial 70 percent for users of alcohol, 44 percent for ever-smokers, 38 percent for those who have ever tried marijuana, and 25 percent of those who have ever tried cocaine.

In the OSAP strategy, efforts to prevent alcohol, tobacco, or illicit drugs (labeled "AOD" in OSAP's shorthand usage) fall under three categories: programs targeted to the needs of particular groups of young people, large-scale approaches to youths in a given school or community, and individualized approaches by parents and others directly involved with individual teenagers. OSAP's efforts are now focused on programs of the first type, with much attention directed to cigarette smoking as both a health risk and a "gateway" drug.

In OSAP's Monograph 1, prevention of AOD problems among youths in high-risk environments is featured because it should be more cost-effective than earlier broadside approaches. Risk factors for AOD are seen as of five broad types: family, peer, psychological, biological, and community. OSAP emphasizes that it is important to identify vulnerable youngsters early in life and to intervene to fend off their adoption of AOD, but to avoid labeling them negatively.

The OSAP strategy focuses on young people because the most vulnerable years for adoption of AOD are ages twelve to twenty, with the peak age of initiation being age fifteen. But in inner cities and among dropouts, AOD use may begin much earlier: There prevention must start in the elementary and preteen years. The younger the first use of a drug, the more likely the person is to have AOD problems. Peak incidence (or use) is between twelve and twenty years, and peak prevalence (or the aggregate number of users at a specified time) falls between eighteen and twenty-five. This OSAP Monograph 1 notes that the rates of use among those over forty for marijuana and cocaine are lower than among younger people because the over-forty group was less exposed to these drugs when in their vulnerable teenage years.

The report (DuPont, 1989, p. 4) says concerning diminution of parental influence in the teens, "If adolescence is seen as a free ride, as a time only for having fun without responsibility, or as a time when adult functioning is demanded in the absence of meaningful support, serious problems may result, including AOD use." DuPont (1988), Kandel (1985), and others have found that AOD use is particularly at risk when young persons use it with support from peers, when it is perceived as an acceptable norm, and when it continues over time. The more frequent and longer the use, the more likely it is to be accompanied by a wide range of negative experiences, from truancy and school failure to criminal behavior and suicide.

In this OSAP report, all use of illegal drugs and all use of legal drugs at an illegal age is defined as "abuse." The OSAP focus here is on the use of four drugs by teenagers: tobacco, alcohol, marijuana, and cocaine. The first three are described as "gateway" drugs because they are traditional entry substances, with crack cocaine also being a gateway drug in poor urban communities.

Consistent with NIAAA doctrine since the 1970s, this OSAP report says that it is highly questionable to teach adolescents to drink "moderately," because the most recent High School Senior Survey (Johnston, O'Malley, and Bachman, 1989) found that 35 percent of high school seniors drank at least five drinks on a single occasion at least once in the two weeks before the survey. Even "moderate" drinking among youth (which is at least illegal) is seen as providing a cover to legitimize more dangerous drinking.

OSAP stresses the importance for favorable bonding between child and parents or teachers as a source of support. "Adults, particularly parents, must mix controls with support and encourage the growth that must lead inevitably to separation. The adolescent must struggle with sudden new urges, with physical changes, with a need to fit into the peer group without losing a sense of self. The potential for conflict between parent and child and the possibility of disruption to adolescent growth and development are considerable" (DuPont, 1989, p. 9).

The importance of close attention by parents or their surrogates to the after-school behavior of their children is underscored by the study of Richardson and colleagues (1989). This investigation focused on substance use among children who regularly care for themselves after school (latchkey children). The data, collected from 4,932 eighth-grade students, indicated that self-care is an important risk factor for alcohol, tobacco, and marijuana use; and data from 2,185 parents validated these findings. Eighth-grade students who took care of themselves for eleven or more hours a week were twice as likely to use illegal substances as those who were supervised. This relationship held at all levels of sociodemographic status, extracurricular activities, sources of social influence, and stress. Path analyses suggest that risk taking, having friends who smoke, and being offered cigarettes may partially explain the relationship between self-care and substance use. The authors infer that the eighth-grade students who select friends who smoke and place themselves in situations in which they are offered cigarettes may be manifesting a desire to display their sense of maturity and independence, and that it is also possible that more time in self-care results in more unnoticed solitary trials of substances, as well as trials motivated by peer pressure.

OSAP emphasizes the need not to confuse "addiction" (actual withdrawal symptoms) with habituation that develops because of becoming psychologically dependent on the effects of the drug. OSAP warns that confusion of true neurophysiological addiction with psychological dependence has led in the past to lower societal resistance to marijuana and cocaine use (which do not necessarily lead to true withdrawal symptoms); in turn this has contributed to higher use of these two substances within the last two decades.

Youth has become a much more risky time of life over the last twenty to thirty years: The death rate for those age fifteen to twenty-four (the peak ages for AOD use) has risen even when it has been falling among older groups. The suicide rate among youth has doubled from 1960 to 1985, especially in association with AOD use (Murphy, 1988). Homicides in this group have tripled between 1950 and 1980 and have become the leading cause of death for nonwhite males fifteen to twenty-four; one-third of the accidental deaths in the same age group are drinking-driving deaths. During the 1960s, academic SAT scores began a long slide, hitting lows in 1980 and now rising, but still much lower than two decades ago. "Although generalizations are hazardous, it can be said that during the past 20 years there has been a deterioration in the health and behavior of teenagers, which has resulted in increased crime, out-of-wedlock pregnancies, sexually transmitted diseases, suicides, and lowered academic performance. And, in tragic association with all of these increased problems, there has been a large increase in drug use and no diminution in alcohol use. All of these problems reflect impulsiveness on the part of teenagers, the loss of positive bonding to adults and to social institutions such as religious settings and schools, and other factors that appear to be contributing to problems for teenagers in America" (DuPont, 1989, p. 18).

"Health information" stressing the harmful effects of AOD was the leading prevention approach when an AOD epidemic among youth became apparent twenty years ago. Many schools still stress this approach, even though by itself it usually is found to be ineffectual (Flay and Sobel, 1983). In fact, youth are somewhat more *likely* to use drugs after exposure to health information about drugs unless other antidrug influences are present (Swisher, Crawford, Goldstein, and Yura, 1971). Two variants of health information, fear arousal and moral suasion, do not appear to be very successful either. Neither of two additional types of health education ("affective education," based on the observation that many people who use drugs have difficulty expressing anger and love, and "values clarification," another humanistic approach) has been found to be very effective (Moskowitz, 1989).

These findings are consistent with those in the meta-analysis by Rundall and Bruvold (1988) of forty-seven smoking and twenty-seven alcohol school-based intervention programs published since 1970. Results indicated that smoking and alcohol interventions have very modest effects on immediate behavior. Smoking interventions, however, have been more successful than alcohol interventions in altering students' long-term behavior. All of the alcohol programs and all but one of the smoking programs successfully increased knowledge concerning the risks in use of these substances, but attitude changes were much more difficult to achieve. The authors concluded that for immediate smoking outcomes and long-term alcohol outcomes, innovative interventions that provide social reinforcements and developmental behavioral models are more effective than traditional "awareness" programs designed to inform adolescents about the health risks involved in smoking and drinking.

One innovative means of applying peer pressures to discourage the use of addictive substances is the drug-free pledge campaign in San Francisco's racially mixed century-old Mission High School. The graduating class has been divided into clusters of five students, with an adult mentor from the school or business community assigned to each cluster for a ten-week period. The fifty mentors sign the same drug-free pledge as the students, and they attend a two-hour training seminar focusing on substance abuse and counseling techniques. Mentors make encouraging phone calls to students, accompanying them on visits to business offices or other future potential job sites and on field trips for cultural and recreational activities and to find part-time or summer jobs. At the same time, seniors play big brother and big sister with juniors, juniors will adopt sophomores, and sophomores will carry the drug-free message to the freshmen. The principal of Mission High says, "We're a different school than we were 20 years ago. The cultural climate is different. So many kids have part-time jobs or do volunteer work that they don't have time to develop drug problems" (Zane, 1990, p. A26).

The OSAP Monograph 1 touches on some of the larger-scale recommended prevention campaigns (discussed in further detail in its later monographs) that are designed to raise the resistance of young people to the peer pressures and marketing appeals that push the consumption of cigarettes, alcohol, or other drugs. Some generic approaches being applied to larger populations, sometimes identified only as to age and locale (such as national media campaigns, or all the youth in a selected community) or all populations covered by a given agency (such as in the development of school policies about AOD use), are covered in this monograph. Such large-scale efforts typically attempt to change attitudes and beliefs about use and acceptability of AOD, and to decrease community tolerance, such as by stiffening school policies and getting communities to get rid of their "head shops."

This OSAP report concludes that the changes in public awareness, attitudes, and behaviors within the past decade is without precedent. Examples: successful efforts to cut down on smoking in public places, heightened feelings of concern over the effects of alcohol on one's guests or customers, and increase in the disapproval of use of marijuana. The report emphasizes the importance of communitywide campaigns that combine the efforts of citizens' groups and public officials, in which public display of the main messages in the campaign is reinforced through such devices as slogans on T-shirts or billboards.

This report concedes that there is need for greater effort to tailor prevention initiatives to help deal with the special problems of ethnic minorities, and need for more individualized prevention efforts and research within such groups. Especially at risk are youths with a family history of alcoholism or of antisocial behavior, inadequate parental direction and discipline, and approving or apathetic parental attitudes and behavior concerning alcohol and other drug use. One of the most powerful predictors of AOD use by adolescents is the using behavior of their best friends. Another high-risk group is those who have a stronger bond to their peers than to their parents (Jessor and Jessor, 1978). Factors correlated with alcohol and drug use include school failure, low interest in school and achievement, rebelliousness and alienation, early antisocial behavior, and heavy early AOD use. Character traits strongly associated with alcohol and drug problems include lack of empathy for others' feelings, lying, pursuit of immediate gratification, and insensitivity to punishment. Thus it is seen why health education alone is unlikely to produce major further reductions in AOD use unless these other influences are considered.

Kumpfer (1989), in her chapter in the OSAP monograph edited by Schaffer and others, mentions nine categories of youth presumed to be at especially high risk of becoming chronic users of tobacco, alcohol, and illicit drugs: children of AOD abusers; victims of physical, sexual, or psychological abuse; school dropouts; pregnant teenagers; economically disadvantaged youth; delinquent youth; youth with mental health problems; suicidal youth; and disabled youth. High-risk youth are the major targets of the $24 million in newly awarded community demonstration/evaluation projects, many of which involve communities with many minority youth.

While traditional public health practice separates health programs into primary, secondary, and tertiary prevention, the OSAP advisory committee recommended throwing together all primary and secondary prevention (to be called "intervention") under three groupings: programs targeted at particular youth populations; working with an entire community or large population groups, such as in media campaigns; and prevention efforts targeted to particular individual youths, teachers, or parents who work with their own children to reduce AOD use. The OSAP committee considered the latter to be the most important and most complex.

The OSAP committee identified six age groups for recommended prevention activities: from conception through fourth grade, fifth through seventh grades, eighth through tenth grades, eleventh and twelfth grades, college, and the years after schooling. The OSAP committee considered it important to divide AOD prevention efforts according to these six groups (as is common in education but not in public health) because the prevention needs of a fifth-grader are different from those of a ninth-grader. As regards the very youngest group, research has shown that the mother's use of AOD has an impact on the child's cognitive functioning. The fifth through seventh grades are most important in terms of preventing initial AOD use (smoking and drinking, and crack in high-risk areas). The eighth through tenth grades is the time when most young people who are ever going to use drugs will begin. While college-bound high school students generally use AODs less than noncollege ones, once they go to college they tend to catch up. There are very high rates of alcohol and other drug use in college, often the cause of quitting college or of being thrown out. Finally, the entry into the world of work is often associated with increased AOD use, probably because the individuals are now largely outside of the influence of parents.

The committee of experts advising OSAP on this 1989 monograph were rather ambivalent about the efficacy of *punishments* in controlling adolescent alcohol and drug use, although they conceded that some negative reinforcements or sanctions can help if coupled with positive reinforcements for appropriate behavior. This perspective is in keeping with Kurt Lewin's dictum (1936) that negative reinforcements almost always challenge the offender to find detours to avoid punishment, doing nothing to change the disapproved habits.

The committee was very divided on the issue of urine testing as a deterrent for drug use by the young. The controversial character of such testing, which entails public embarrassment of sensitive and often-rebellious adolescents, is borne out by a continuing rash of civil liberties protests and court cases concerning such tests as required for eligibility to participate in sports or enrollment in special school programs.

Among the substantial number of recent studies measuring the relative effectiveness of various approaches to adolescent drug prevention is a meta-analysis comparison of results for experimental and control groups for 143 programs within the United States (Tobler, 1986). Five major modalities were compared for effectiveness: knowledge, attitudes, use, skills, and behavior. The programs that emphasized influences relevant to the adolescents' peers (rehearsal in developing skills in refusing alcohol or other drug use and in communicating and decision making) were the most effective among various modalities in limiting use of alcohol, soft and hard drugs, and cigarettes. Programs with primary emphasis on imparting knowledge, or affective or emotional appeals, were ineffectual. The peer-relevant programs were not only the most effective, but also were the most cost-effective for the general school-based programs. The author speculates that the relative success of communication and decision-making skills in such peer-relevant programs may be because they can be acquired quickly, while basic attitudes are not as readily changed within this age group.

Research also has shown the effectiveness of multimodal prevention campaigns that combine school-based programs for youth, mass media cooperation in advancing prevention messages, parent organization and education, community organization, and publicity for health-enhancing programs in yielding synergistic reductions in alcohol and other drug use. One notable example of this approach is the Midwestern Prevention Project, which has been operating in an eight-county area in Kansas and Missouri since 1984. The results of the first two years of the project were reported by Pentz and others (1989). During this period, 22,500 sixth- and seventh-grade adolescents received intensive mass media exposure and participated in school-based prevention programs combined with parental involvement in prevention-related homework. Included were ten-session youth educational programs on skills training for resistance of drug use, ten homework sessions involving active interviews, and role-playing with parents and family members. Mass media elements included in-school exposure to newspaper articles and television news clips of project staffs about the progress of the program. The project also incorporated a televised press conference reporting baseline rates of drug use in the Kansas City area, with a total of sixteen television, ten radio, and thirty print media events broadcast and made available through the schools during the two-year period. Findings: During the second year of the campaign, drug use prevalence rates for the 1984 cohort of sixth- and seventh-grade students in the intervention schools showed a substantial slowing down relative to control schools, in general and when adjusted for grade, race socioeconomic status, and urbanicity.

Another multicommunity research project to test the effectiveness of programs to inhibit the use of the "gateway drugs" of alcohol, tobacco, and marijuana was conducted recently by the Rand Corporation in its "Project ALERT" in a wide range of socioeconomic and ethnic environments in thirty California and Oregon schools in urban, suburban, and rural areas; nine of the thirty schools had minority populations of 50 percent or more (Bell, Gareleck, and Ellickson, 1990). Utilizing a social influence model, the curriculum sought to develop students' motivations and skills to reduce drug pressures. The curriculum consisted of eight weekly sessions for seventh-graders and three booster sessions presented during eighth grade. The program emphasized active student participation in learning new drug resistance skills. The thirty schools were divided into three groups of ten each: Students in one group received Project ALERT sessions conducted by students only; another group of schools received the Project ALERT sessions conducted by teachers but assisted by older teen leaders; and the third group of schools did not participate in the sessions, thus serving as a control group. Findings: The rate of marijuana initiation in the Project ALERT schools after the program was one-third lower than in the control group of schools. Regular and daily smoking by those who already had experimented with cigarettes before the training program was reduced by as much as 50 to 60 percent, with the program being equally effective both in schools with substantial minority populations and in predominantly white schools. However, while the program initially was successful against alcohol, the reduction in drinking had eroded by the time the students reached the eighth grade. One conclusion was that "the program was most successful against the socially disapproved substances; it was less effective in counteracting the forces that promote alcohol use. As long as the media and most adults directly contradict the message, social influence programs are not likely to realize their potential against alcohol" (Bell, Gareleck, and Ellickson, 1990, p. viii). Another conclusion was that "adolescents who are confirmed smokers need a more aggressive program than one based solely on the social influence model. They have already developed pro-smoking attitudes and a network of friends who smoke, drink, and/or use marijuana. Most of them also have a record of problem behaviors, such as stealing and truancy; they tend to receive poor grades; and many come from disrupted or impaired family environments. If the program promoted associations with nonusing peers and showed confirmed users how to quit, it might make more headway with the early smokers, but it would not address their deeper problems, of which smoking is only one symptom" (pp. viii–ix).

The first OSAP monograph on prevention ends with recommendations for more research on the risk factors described earlier, more research on differences in the effects and attractions of various drugs, and more longitudinal studies of AOD use, but only those with experimental manipulation of key variables. Meanwhile, OSAP sees much value even in retrospective studies, and in case-control epidemiologic studies, which often at least show which causal relationships are in need of further examination. The report especially stresses the need for more developmental studies, especially in poverty populations.

OSAP Monograph 2 (Schaffer and others, 1989), jointly sponsored by the American Academy of Child and Adolescent Psychiatry, contains twelve chapters describing recent research findings highly relevant to understanding the etiology of tobacco, alcohol, and other drug dependency. The monograph entitled *Prevention Plus II: Tools for Creating and Sustaining Drug-Free Communities* (Office for Substance Abuse Prevention, 1989) contains more than 500 pages of highly detailed strategies and descriptions of promising specific community or state prevention programs around the nation, along with program planning guides. It even provides the names, addresses, and telephone numbers of those to contact within various community, state, or federal prevention activities for needed help or advice. (See the resource on how to procure such information.) Many other details on the rationales and resources for the prevention strategies advanced by OSAP are presented in Chapters Three, Five, and Seven of this book.

OSAP also has launched an ambitious program of demonstration grants to stimulate neighborhoods throughout America to organize for the purpose of supporting locally initiated prevention programs on such issues as improving zoning on liquor stores and driving out drug dealers. This program is discussed in Chapter Nine.

The OSAP prevention strategies are being closely coordinated with the general objectives of the Public Health Service in its latest decennial plans (U.S. Department of Health and Human Services, 1990). These Year 2000 Objectives, in addition to covering a very broad range of improvements in health protection and preventive services, call for a reduction in cigarette smoking to no greater than 15 percent among people age twenty and older, reduction of the initiation of smoking by youth to no more than 15 percent of the prevalence among persons ages twenty through twenty-four, and increase to at least 50 percent the proportion of current smokers age twenty and older who will make a serious attempt to quit smoking during a year. Other objectives involve getting at least 60 percent of pregnant women smokers to quit and reducing to no more than 25 percent the proportion of children age six and younger who are exposed to cigarette smoke at home. The Year 2000 Objectives also call for very substantial reductions during the next ten years in alcohol-related motor vehicle crash deaths, cirrhosis deaths, poisoning deaths, and emergency room visits attributable to alcohol and other drugs; substantial reductions in use of tobacco, alcohol, and other drugs; and substantial increases in awareness on the part of the general public and of health professionals of the dangers in alcohol and other drugs. The Year 2000 Objectives also would demand substantial increases in primary and secondary school education programs on alcohol and other drugs, extension of the adoption of alcohol- and drug-free work environment policies, and extension to all states of driver's license suspension/revocation laws and programs for those found to have been driving under the influence of intoxicants. In addition, they call for substantial increases in the availability of drug treatment, particularly for intravenous users.

So much new stimulus toward improving prevention programs is coming out of federal agencies such as OSAP, NIAAA, and NIDA these days that it will take a few years of assessment and evaluation to find out what types of approaches work best. The common policy behind most of the federal prevention efforts appears to be to stimulate and encourage prevention initiatives on a community level. Certainly a number of federal agencies are providing, free for the asking, many new guidelines for future prevention initiatives and their evaluation. Some of these types of information, and how they may be obtained, are presented in the resource.

PART TWO

The Legal Drugs: Tobacco and Alcohol

CHAPTER THREE

Reducing Tobacco-Caused Deaths

The use of tobacco goes back many centuries, beginning among Indians in North and South America and introduced into Europe about 1560. In the 1570s, Sir Walter Raleigh popularized the weed in the English court, and its use spread rapidly among all classes of Elizabethan society. It was a source of solace for the poor and of relaxation for the rich. In 1604, King James (who hated Sir Walter) vehemently opposed smoking from motives of national pride, refuted its medicinal value, denounced it as "the lively image and pattern of hell," and increased tobacco taxes 4,000 percent (Austin, 1978, p. 2). While Ravenholt (1984) tells how several kings and potentates hundreds of years ago dictated harsh penalties for its use on moral or economic grounds, and notes that the harmful effects of tobacco were suspected centuries ago, he reports that the range and magnitude of damage was not firmly established until well into the twentieth century.

The invention of the cigarette rolling machine in 1881 was followed several decades later by increases in deaths from lung cancer and smoking-associated heart disease, which were detected through improvements in medical science and the rise of public health as a profession and epidemiology as a discipline. As Ravenholt (1984, p. 697) notes, although the classic report of Raymond Pearl in *Science* (1938) "clearly delineated the extraordinary impact of smoking on longevity, these disquieting findings were soon papered over by blatantly misleading advertising; and general recognition of the nature and magnitude of the morbidity and mortality hazard posed by tobacco did not occur until the second half of this century."

Although inhaling someone else's tobacco smoke is called "passive" because it is involuntary, it is anything but passive in its lethal effects. A new analysis (Glantz and Parmley, 1991) of eleven epidemiological studies throughout America shows that passive smoke (more appropriately called environmental tobacco smoke or ETS) increases the risk of death from heart disease by 30 percent among nonsmokers living with smokers. ETS damages blood platelet function and arterial endothelium and significantly reduces the capability of people to exercise, both those who are healthy and those with heart disease. ETS interferes with mitochondrial respiration and accelerates the development of atherosclerotic plaque in blood vessels. In short, environmental tobacco smoke is the third leading preventable cause of death, after active smoking and alcohol.

As to the specific damage caused by tobacco, Ravenholt (1984) estimates that the total number of excess deaths in the United States in 1980 attributable to smoking cigarettes was approximately 485,000. He estimates that additional deaths caused by pipe and cigar smoking, the passive inhalation of tobacco smoke, and the chewing and snuffing of tobacco probably raised the total U.S. tobacco death toll in 1980 to more than 500,000, or more than one-fourth of all deaths from all causes. These tobacco-related death tolls are identified as including many types of cancers, diseases of the circulatory, respiratory, and digestive systems, infant mortality because of low birth weight occasioned by mothers' smoking, and fires and other accidents. (Because smoking has decreased appreciably since 1980, the probable current death figures for tobacco would now be somewhat lower, although still high.)

Ravenholt points out that the United States is the second

largest producer of cigarettes (China being first). He criticizes our government for permitting heavy export of tobacco and the World Health Organization for spending less than one-thousandth of its resources on combating smoking despite the fact that tobacco now kills about two million persons worldwide annually. As the Berkeley *Wellness Letter* notes ("Fascinating Facts," 1989, p. 1), "Smoking kills more Americans each year than died in battle in World War II and Vietnam put together."

The federal government has set up a coordinating service to gather and circulate information on tobacco: the Office on Smoking and Health, within the Center for Chronic Disease Prevention and Health Promotion among the Centers for Disease Control in Rockville, Maryland. The Office on Smoking and Health provides, free or at nominal cost, such pamphlets or monographs as the periodic reports of the Surgeon General on smoking and health, a detailed monograph on smoking-cessation methods, one for management on reducing smoking at the worksite, a comprehensive inventory of major local smoking ordinances including data on workplaces, restaurants, and public places, and a periodically updated *Fact Book* on smoking, tobacco, and health (Office on Smoking and Health, 1989). (See the resource on the availability of these publications.) The latest government *Fact Book* on smoking (Office on Smoking and Health, 1989, p. 1) reports that "Cigarette smoking can legitimately be termed the most devastating preventable cause of disease and premature death this country has ever experienced. Each year it causes the death of nearly 400,000 Americans—115,000 from coronary heart disease, 27,000 from stroke, 136,000 from cancer, 60,000 from chronic obstructive pulmonary disease, and an estimated 50,000 deaths from other diseases and other causes."

The 1989 *Fact Book* also notes that the turning point in America's smoking epidemic came in 1964, when the Public Health Service issued its first report on smoking and health. The World Health Organization and health agencies in virtually all countries throughout the world now have antismoking programs in progress. Although smoking rates in the United States are still fairly high (31.7 percent of men and 26.8 percent of women age twenty and older in 1987), this represents a material drop since 1965 for men (then 50.2 percent smoked) and a small drop among women (then 31.9 percent). The decline has operated in every age group and income level, but has been greatest among college graduates, dropping by half, while hardly changing among those with less than a high school education.

The most harmful effect of teenage smoking is the likelihood of addiction, for the earlier people start, the more difficult it is to quit later in life. Most people who smoke would like to quit: At least two-thirds of all smokers have tried to quit and in any year, at least one-third try. But there are now more than forty million who have given it up. Quitting pays: Ten years later, the death rates of former smokers are about the same as for those who have never smoked.

This report notes that people who smoke cigarettes run greater risk of premature death than people who do not smoke, at every age and for men and women alike, with the risk being greater for men under sixty-five.

The costs of smoking include an estimated $22 billion in medical costs each year and another $43 billion in lost productivity. Medicare and Medicaid alone pay out at least $4.2 billion annually to care for those who are ill from cigarette-related illnesses. Smokers are at nearly twice the risk of dying of a heart attack than nonsmokers. The three major risk factors for heart disease are cigarette smoking, hypertension, and high blood pressure. Cancer is second to heart disease as a cause of death, and cigarette smoking is the largest preventable cause: 30 percent of all cancer deaths and nearly 90 percent of all lung cancer deaths are caused by smoking. Cigarettes are also a strong cause of cancers of the larynx, oral cavity, esophagus, bladder, pancreas, and kidney. Chronic obstructive lung disease is often caused by smoking, with crippling emphysema afflicting two million sufferers each year.

Smokeless Tobacco

The use of smokeless tobacco (usually in the form of snuff), a potent cause of mouth cancer and other oral diseases, increased during the 1980s, especially among youth. In 1986, Congress banned its advertising on radio and television and required health warnings in packages and advertisements.

However, this use of "smokeless tobcco" (as it is termed in the public health field) is reported by Boyd and Glover (1989) as not diminishing, and as incurring the risk of oral cancer, noncancerous oral pathology such as leukoplakias, and addiction. A California preliminary observational phase of a study aimed at curtailing smokeless tobacco use among youth (Braverman, D'Onofrio, and Moskowitz, 1989), interviewing school personnel and youth leaders and retail store managers, found that 81 percent of the stores in the sample carried smokeless tobacco, especially moist snuff. Most (78 percent) of their sample of school personnel and youth leaders were aware of advertisements for it, especially on television and in magazines.

When smokeless tobacco use and its correlates were assessed in a NIDA national household survey of residents twelve years of age and older, 11 percent had "ever tried" chewing tobacco, snuff, or other smokeless tobacco. Of these, 5 percent were former users and 3 percent used smokeless tobacco almost daily in the past year. Rates of use differed significantly by gender, age group, race, region, and metropolitan area size. Although females were far less likely to try it, those who did were as likely as males to be daily users. Smokeless tobacco users were also more likely to use alcohol, cigarettes, and marijuana. Those reporting almost-daily use were more likely to report poor health and hospitalization for illness or injury in the past year, even when other substance use was controlled, and also were more likely to report symptoms of depression. Some substituted smokeless tobacco for cigarettes, but youths age twelve to seventeen were more likely than older tobacco users to use both forms of tobacco regularly (Rouse, 1989).

The Adult Use of Tobacco Surveys for 1964–1986 for the prevalence of smokeless tobacco use among adults age twenty-one years and older, and data from the 1986 survey on prevalence, beliefs, ages of initiation, and demographic correlates of use by males age seventeen years and older, were also analyzed. The prevalence of smokeless tobacco use declined slightly among those twenty-one and older between 1966 and 1986. However, 5.2 percent of the males age seventeen and older still were using smokeless tobacco in 1986, and prevalence was highest among those seventeen to nineteen years old (8.2 percent). Smokeless tobacco use was most common among white men who were living in the southeastern United States, were unemployed, and were in blue-collar or service/labor employment. Most (77.4 percent) of users and 83.4 percent of nonusers said they believed that smokeless tobacco is a health hazard. Many current users (39.1 percent) had attempted to quit. Some current (6.4 percent) and former smokers (7.0 percent) had used smokeless tobacco as an aid to smoking cessation (Novotny, Pierce, Fiore, and Davis, 1989).

The 1985 Current Population Survey analyzed the use of chewing tobacco, snuff, and smokeless tobacco, finding that the prevalence of smokeless tobacco use varies considerably among and within regions of the country, being highest in the South and lowest in the Northeast. States with the highest smokeless tobacco use among males included West Virginia (23.1 percent), Mississippi (16.5 percent), Wyoming (15.8 percent), Arkansas (14.7 percent), and Kentucky (13.6 percent). Nationally, male use of such products was 5.5 percent, compared to less than 1 percent among women. White males are the primary consumers of snuff; fewer than 1 percent of African-American or Hispanic males use it. Higher percentages of blue-collar and service workers use it compared with white-collar workers. Snuff and chewing tobacco use among teenage boys in the United States increased dramatically between 1970 and 1985, at a time when their use of cigarettes was declining (Marcus, Crane, Shopland, and Lynn, 1989).

The *Fact Book* from the Office on Smoking and Health reports that the tobacco business is still eminently profitable, with six companies producing virtually all the cigarettes made in America. All are active in mergers, particularly with food companies. Total domestic sales of cigarettes in 1985 were $30.2 billion plus $1.2 billion in foreign sales, with net profits after taxes of $3.4 billion. Nearly $2.4 billion was spent in 1986 to promote cigarettes, including almost $1 billion for advertising.

Cigarette companies were the largest advertisers on television and radio until 1971, when Congress banned such advertising. They are now the leader in outdoor and transit advertising and among the leaders in magazine advertising.

In 1984, Congress required that cigarette ads and packages contain one of four health warnings, which are rotated every three months. But Congress—inconsistently—still continues to approve of a price-support subsidy for tobacco, which has cost the taxpayers well over half a billion dollars!

Role of the Surgeon General

One of the strongest advocates for trying to eliminate cigarette smoking altogether has been C. Everett Koop, militant Surgeon General of the 1980s. In 1982, he wrote a strong indictment of cigarette smoking and proposed a smoke-free America by the year 2000. He was vilified by tobacco companies, their lobbyists, some legislators who have received campaign contributions from the tobacco industry, and the governor of the tobacco-growing state of North Carolina because of his demands for stronger health warnings on cigarettes. Koop himself considers the anticigarette campaign one of the highest triumphs of public health: "We had 80 ordinances against smoking in 50 states at that time. It is now over 480 and that is [an example of] militant nonsmokers getting on the stick. Yesterday in Greensboro, N.C., they voted for restriction on smoking in the city. That is unbelievable. That is the home of the tobacco companies" (Dean, 1989, p. E8).

Some of the key points in a swan-song report issued just before Koop was replaced as Surgeon General by the new Bush administration were as follows (Koop, 1989):

Twenty-five years earlier, Surgeon General Luther Terry released the report of the Advisory Committee on Smoking and Health, America's first widely publicized official recognition that cigarette smoking is a cause of cancer and other serious diseases. That first report was based on more than 7,000 articles in the biomedical literature. It was issued on a Saturday morning to avoid a precipitous reaction on Wall Street. Press representatives were locked in the auditorium without access to telephones and were given ninety minutes to read it, and then Dr. Terry and committee members answered questions. This was one of the top stories of 1964.

Since then, the Federal Cigarette Labeling and Advertising Act of 1965 and the Public Health Cigarette Smoking Act of 1969 have been passed. These required health warning labels on cigarette packages, banned cigarette advertising on broadcast media, and called for an annual report on the health consequences of smoking. In 1964, the Public Health Service established the National Clearinghouse for Smoking and Health, which since has been responsible for twenty reports on health consequences. Some findings from Koop's 1989 report:

- Koop's foreword stated that the school and community programs and research that the PHS has supported on tobacco use and its damage "have changed the way in which our society views smoking. In the 1940s and 1950s, smoking was chic; now, increasingly, it is shunned. Movie stars, sports heroes, and other celebrities used to appear in cigarette advertisements. Today, actors, athletes, public figures, and political candidates are rarely seen smoking. The ashtray is following the spittoon into oblivion" (p. iv).
- "The most impressive decline noted in smoking has been among men, falling from 50 percent in 1965 to 32 percent in 1987" (p. iv). This report shows that without the campaign, there would have been 91 million American smokers fifteen to eighty-four years of age in 1985 instead of 56 million, and an estimated 789,000 smoking-related deaths were avoided or postponed between 1964 and 1985. Also, these decisions to quit smoking will result in avoidance or postponement of an estimated 2.1 million smoking-related deaths between 1986 and 2000. "This achievement has few parallels in the history of public health. It was accomplished despite the addictive nature of tobacco and the powerful economic forces promoting its use" (p. iv).
- Prevention programs are not yet reaching large numbers of young people. "The public health community should pay

at least as much attention to the prevention of smoking among teenagers as it now pays to smoking cessation among adults" (p. vi).

- If women's smoking continues to decline less than men's, by the mid 1990s women may smoke at a higher rate than men. Other heavy-smoking groups: African-Americans and Hispanics, and blue-collar workers (40 percent in 1985 compared to 28 percent among white-collar workers). The report notes that blue-collar workers are a major target of advertising and promotional campaigns, and that worksite smoking-cessation programs, employee incentive programs, and policies banning or restricting workplace smoking are effective strategies to reach this group (p.vii).

Antismoking Activity in the Workplace

Of increasing concern is the effect of "passive smoking" on nonsmokers, which is especially harmful among the young. As the Office on Smoking and Health *Fact Book* (1989) reports, forty-two states and more than three hundred municipalities restrict smoking in restaurants and other public places, and thirteen states have extended this protection to private work places. All federal agencies restrict or ban smoking in public areas and workplaces.

Among the myriad ways in which smoking in public places is discouraged, one of the most conspicuous recent developments has been the ban on smoking on all commercial flights, effective February 25, 1990, within the continental United States and to Puerto Rico and the Virgin Islands, and on all flights of less than six hours to Alaska and Hawaii. Foreign airlines flying within the United States are cooperating with the ban. Of the 755 airlines registered throughout the world, half operate out of three nations with antismoking legislation: the United States, Canada, and Australia. China banned smoking on all flights as long ago as 1968, and some other airlines, including British Air, Finnair, Malev (Hungarian), Scandinavian Airlines, and the Soviet Union's Aeroflot, have banned smoking on some domestic flights ("Where the Skies . . . ," 1990).

As to the railroads, Amtrak's policy effective April 1, 1990, permits passengers to smoke in sleeping compartments but bans smoking in first-class cars on all trains in the Northeast Corridor that do not require reservations. It permits smoking in smoking cars on reserved-seat Metroliners but bans smoking in most other situations and in stations smaller than 1,100 square feet. Amtrak's ultimate goal is to separate the 25 percent of their passengers who smoke from the 75 percent who do not, putting their smoking areas at the front or back of trains so that nonsmokers will not have to walk through the smoking areas to reach their seats ("Amtrak to Ban Most Smoking," 1990).

Business and industry are also joining in on constraints against smoking. Cranshaw (1990) tells of several companies that are offering incentives to their employees to quit smoking, both for reasons of health, health insurance costs, and employee morale in some cases. One company charges smokers $10 more per month for health insurance coverage. Another company charges smokers $180 per year for health insurance that is provided free for nonsmokers. Southern California Edison offers a voluntary five-point screening process, checking smoking, weight, blood sugar, blood pressure, and cholesterol, with $120 per year to those who pass the tests or obtain a doctor's certificate stating they are in a health remedial program—a sum sufficient to cover the employee's required contribution to the company's medical care program.

Jerome Schwartz's (1987, chap. 4) review of smoking cessation methods provides an extensive discussion of current worksite smoking policies and control programs in the United States and Canada.

There are ethical and civil rights limits to how far such health care cost containment can be pushed: One company ran into trouble when it tried to extend it to alcohol or drug-related ailments. One company representative voiced the principle that in order to adhere to appropriate insurance coverage for large groups, the sanctions should be applied only to those things that the worker *can* control: that an unwell person who is in a wellness program should not be penalized. But with the mounting costs of health care, in any case these kinds of healthy-behavior incentives are likely to increase.

Pressures Against Tobacco Marketing

Turning now to current trends in cigarette advertising and marketing: According to the Federal Trade Commission (Davis, 1987) total cigarette advertising and promotional expenditures reached $2.1 billion in 1984. From 1974 through 1984, total expenditures increased approximately sevenfold, or threefold after adjustment by the consumer price index. In 1985, cigarette advertising expenditures accounted for 22.3 percent, 7.1 percent, and 0.8 percent of total advertising expenditures in outdoor media, magazines, and newspapers, respectively. When *all* products and services were ranked according to national advertising expenditures, cigarettes were first in the outdoor media, second in magazines, and third in newspapers. The proportion of total cigarette advertising and promotional expenditures increased steadily, from 25.5 percent in 1975 to 47.6 percent in 1984.

Several advertising campaigns have targeted women, minorities, and blue-collar workers (Davis, 1987). Evidence that the cigarette industry is targeting the sale of menthol cigarettes to African-American consumers is suggested by a Buffalo study measuring the types of cigarettes smoked by whites and African-Americans. One group consisted of 70 white and 365 African-American adult smokers seen at a Family Medicine Center. The second population included 1,070 white and 92 African-American smokers who called a Stop Smoking Hotline in Buffalo. The results showed that, in both populations, African-Americans were twice as likely to smoke mentholated cigarettes as whites. In an attempt to evaluate the targeting of cigarette ads to African-American smokers as a possible explanation for black-white differences in brand preferences, cigarette ads appearing in magazines targeted to predominantly white or African-American readers were compared. Cigarette ads appearing in seven magazines were reviewed, four directed to predominantly white readers (*Newsweek, Time, People, Mademoiselle*) and three with wide circulation among African-American audiences (*Jet, Ebony, Essence*). The results showed that the magazines targeted to African-American readers contained significantly more cigarette ads, and more ads for menthol brand cigarettes, than magazines similar in content but targeted to white readers. However, the study did not attempt to determine whether cigarette advertising is the cause of the differences in preference of cigarette brands between white and African-American smokers (Cummings, Giovino, and Mendicino, 1987).

Smokeless tobacco was not affected by the ban on broadcast advertising of cigarettes that went into effect in 1971, and until 1986 both print and broadcast media were used to advertise it. The approaches used to advertise and promote smokeless tobacco products during the early to mid 1980s included traditional motifs that featured rugged-looking masculine models in sporting and outdoor settings as well as an expanded white-collar appeal. Promotional activities ranged from sponsorship of sporting events to offers for clothing bearing smokeless tobacco product logos. Despite the claims of manufacturers that advertising and promotional efforts were not targeted to youth, smokeless tobacco companies sponsored tobacco-spitting contests with teenage participants, a college marketing program, and college scholarships. Federal legislation was passed in 1986 that banned television and radio advertising of smokeless tobacco products and required manufacturers to include warning labels on their products on the potential health hazards of smokeless tobacco use (Ernster, 1989).

In January 1990, R. J. Reynolds dropped its Philadelphia test marketing of "Uptown," a new cigarette being marketed heavily to African-Americans, a day after Health and Human Services Sullivan (himself African-American) accused Reynolds of trying to create a "culture of cancer." About thirty organizations in Philadelphia had joined in the effort to fight Uptown. In response to a reminder that the U.S. Public Health Service has found that African-American men have a 58 percent higher incidence of lung cancer than white men and that African-Americans lose twice as many years of life as do whites because of smoking-related diseases, the R. J. Reynolds executive vice president of marketing said, "We regret that a small coalition of anti-smoking zealots apparently believes that black smokers are somehow different from others who choose to smoke and must not be allowed to exercise the same freedom of choice available to all other smokers. This represents a loss of choice for black smokers and a further erosion of the free-enterprise system" ("Cigarette Ads for Blacks Dropped," 1990, p. A2).

In an article immediately following the withdrawal of the Uptown cigarettes, which were challenged as being directed toward African-Americans, Cohen (1990) asserted that selling to women through ads in women's magazines is also reprehensible, for lung cancer has passed breast cancer as a cause of death at a time when smoking has diminished among men. The article noted that ads featuring Capri Super Slims and others brands emphasize the "slim" because cigarette makers know that many women are obsessed with their weight, and that those who smoke fear quitting because they will gain weight. Should either group have any qualms about smoking, the ads are there to put them at ease. The models are the epitome of healthfulness, and they are all slim. Cohen thought Dr. Sullivan should also blast cigarette companies for targeting women.

In the summer of 1989, the National Archives accepted $600,000 from Philip Morris, makers of Marlboro cigarettes, and allowed the company to use the Archives' name in ads celebrating the Bill of Rights. The Archives also agreed to sponsor a joint exhibit on the Bill of Rights and promised that it would use its "best effort" to locate such items as recordings of the voices of past presidents for use in the advertising.

Tobacco industry critics quickly attacked the deal. Sidney Wolfe, head of the Public Citizen Research Group, a Ralph Nader–founded consumer advocacy group, said the advertising "smears the Bill of Rights with the blood of all Americans killed as a result of smoking Marlboro and other Philip Morris cigarets." ("Lawmakers Want," 1990, p. 13.)

A Phillip Morris spokesman said the company is not advertising smoking or cigarettes with the ads, but just its corporate image. "We are celebrating the Bill of Rights," said Guy Smith, Philip Morris vice president for corporate affairs. "It is also a way for us to give the company an identity. We hope people will think better of the company ("Lawmakers Want," 1990, p. 13). One Philip Morris advertisement that appeared in *Harper's Magazine* (March 1990, p. 58) carried a photo of President Franklin D. Roosevelt when he designated December 15 as Bill of Rights Day. The advertisement ends saying, "Today, as we approach the bicentennial of the adoption of the Bill of Rights, let us all, as President Roosevelt asked of us then, 'rededicate its principles and its practice.'" Readers were invited to call a toll-free number or to write the Bill of Rights department of Philip Morris for a free copy of the Bill of Rights. Could it be possible that Philip Morris was not only using the prestige of the National Archives, President Roosevelt, and the Bill of Rights to promote its corporate image, but also slyly to remind the readers about the debatable commercial "freedom of speech" in cigarette advertising that it wishes to maintain?

National Council on Alcoholism (now National Council on Alcohol and Drug Dependence) President Hamilton Beazley promptly called the collaboration of Philip Morris and the Archives in the Bill of Rights promotion "appalling" in a letter to the National Archivist. As the letter said, "A Bill of Rights promotion sponsored by Phillip Morris, Inc., and Miller beer will be a tremendous disservice to the cause of personal freedom for the millions of Americans for whom the freedom from addiction is a prerequisite for enjoying the basic liberties guaranteed by the Founding Fathers in our remarkable and treasured Bill of Rights." Rep. Luken (D-Ohio) wrote to the Attorney General that "if Philip Morris can circumvent the law prohibiting it from advertising cigarettes [on television] by the transparent device used here, we may as well tear up the Federal Cigarette Labeling and Advertisement Act" (Lewis, 1989l, p. 6).

Another frequent anticigarette complaint by public health authorities was voiced by Health and Human Services Secretary Louis Sullivan: "An athlete or sports figure should not allow his or her good name, hard-earned image, or integrity to be exploited by the tobacco industry to push a product that, when used as intended, causes death. This blood money should not be used to foster a misleading impression that smoking is compatible with good health." He called on universities and other institutions to refuse to host events sponsored by tobacco companies, and he warned advertisers to "shun the temptation of this tainted money, stained by addiction, disease, and death" ("Athletes Urged to Spurn Tobacco 'Blood Money,'" 1990, p. A1).

Sullivan spoke at a meeting called by a coalition of health groups to protest sponsorship of women's tennis events by Virginia Slims cigarettes, which has been sponsoring such events for two decades. In rebuttal, a Philip Morris spokesperson said that it does not ask players to smoke or endorse smoking, but just to play tennis.

Sullivan also attacked tobacco advertising practices in general, calling on television stations to donate free air time to help educate viewers about the dangers of smoking. He asked hospitals to declare hospitals smoke-free zones and Department of Health and Human Services grantees to prohibit smoking where they work, and has written national convenience stores asking them to enforce laws prohibiting the sale of tobacco to minors.

The growing sentiment against smoking is evident in the results of a 1989 national survey by Peter B. Hart and the Roper Organization, which found that half the nation's adult consumers would support an outright ban on advertising of all alcoholic beverages and tobacco. And 57 percent said cigarette machines should be eliminated so that those below legal age could not get cigarettes so easily (Freedman, 1989, p. B1).

Even *Time* magazine, which has carried so much cigarette advertising, featured an article (Gallagher, 1990) on all the criticism the tobacco business has been getting: R. J. Reynolds's canceling of the Uptown brand directed at African-Americans, Secretary Sullivan's charge that smoking cost the country $52 billion a year ("Cigarettes are the only legal product that when used as intended cause death"), the smoking ban on all domestic flights, and announcements by state and local officials of additional antismoking initiatives.

R. J. Reynolds attempted to rebound with its new cigarette, Dakota, planned to be test marketed in its Project VF (for "virile female"), which describes the typical customer as an entry-level factory worker, eighteen to twenty, who enjoys watching drag races and aspires to "get married in her early 20s and have a family." Health experts and women's groups accused the company of targeting uninformed young women for death: Lung cancer among women has jumped more than fivefold in the past twenty years. The *Time* reporter (Gallagher, 1990, p. 41) noted that "target marketing has taken on an odious reputation as tobacco makers aim for the few groups that have been slow to kick the habit." A sociologist is quoted as saying, "You certainly don't see ads featuring 65-year-olds." A lobbyist for the Tobacco Institute disagreed: "Advertising doesn't get people to smoke. High school kids haven't seen ads for marijuana."

The article (Gallagher, 1990, p. 41) also noted that Congress was considering seventy-two bills to inhibit tobacco use, including Kennedy's proposed $185 billion Center for Tobacco products, which would have broad powers to regulate the industry.

California is conducting a new $28.6 million advertising war against smoking, designed to counter the marketing efforts of tobacco companies with equally sophisticated television, radio, and newspaper ads. "The goal is to persuade 5 million of the State's 7 million smokers to kick the habit by the end of the decade. Most ironic of all is that the campaign will be financed by smokers through the new 25c-a-pack cigarette tax. Says Thomas Lauria, a spokesman for the Tobacco Institute, 'Now smokers are paying for their own harassment'" (Castro, 1990, p. 61).

The tobacco companies spent $15 million to defeat this initiative, but failed. Governor Deukmajian tried to distance himself from the antismoking television campaign: His press secretary said, "We weren't aware of the ads. The approach was developed by the Department of Health Services and an advertising agency. Whether or not it is going to work remains to be seen" (Lucas, 1990, p. A1). The antismoking money came from a publicly generated statewide initiative, not through a legislative act. Many legislators receive substantial money from the tobacco and alcohol industry.

One of the thirty-second ads shows an actor portraying a tobacco company executive in a smoke-filled conference room with his employees, saying to them that 3,000 new smokers must be recruited every day to make up for the 2,000 who quit and the 1,000 who die of lung cancer, heart disease, and emphysema. ("We're not in this business for our health!" he concludes with a demonic laugh.) The tobacco interests are complaining that the ads are unfair, but the director of Health Services noted that preliminary statistics from the Federal Trade Commission showed that $3.2 billion was spent nationwide in 1988 to promote smoking, and that the antismoking ads are simply full disclosure, to let the people know that many of their decisions are actually a response to very clever tobacco industry advertising.

The *Time* article by Castro (1990) suggests how California's campaign opens another chapter in the fight against the marketing of alcohol as well as tobacco. New York, Chicago, and Dallas residents have been whitewashing inner-city billboards to obliterate ads for cigarettes and cognac. Secretary Sullivan attacked Virginia Slims for sponsoring tennis matches; the National Collegiate Athletic Association reduced alcohol advertising during postseason games. Congress is working on seventy-two bills to constrain tobacco products, and Senator Albert Gore of Tennessee and Representative Joseph Kennedy of Massachusetts have introduced bills (S. 2439 and H.R. 4493) that would require health warnings on all alcoholic beverage advertisements in television, radio, or print.

Castro's article says the new outcry has spread to Europe also: The French government plans to ban all tobacco advertising by 1993 and to restrict alcohol advertising to print media. "The recent outburst against vice marketing seems motivated by a larger social movement, suddenly abloom at the turn of the decade, in which citizens are demanding more socially responsible behavior from individuals and corporations alike. In a fashion, the war on drugs has carried over to legal but abusable substances" (Castro, 1990, p. 61). But this article in *Time,* which has been an exceptionally heavy carrier of cigarette advertising over the years, could not resist ending with a jab at the California campaign by saying, "To some extent, blaming advertisers for selling products that society has been unable to control by other means is like shooting the messenger" (p. 61).

More economic pressure on the tobacco industry was exerted by John Van de Kamp, then California state attorney general, who called for legislation to end California's tax write-off for tobacco advertising, saying that "this misguided tax subsidy of the tobacco industry will cost California about $15 million over the next 18 months. . . . What does California get for its money? We get to watch 30,000 of our friends and neighbors die painful, premature deaths every year. Plus we get the economic burden of $7 billion a year in lost productivity and extra health care and its costs for smokers." Such antideduction legislation is being written into an anticigarette bill by State Assemblyman Tom Bates (Barabak, 1990, p. A13).

Concerning the responsibilities of the tobacco companies for damage to the public's health, George Will (1990), a prominent conservative columnist, recently observed that democracy rests on three assumptions: personal responsibility, individual rationality, and the efficacy of information. Will said that smoking and attempts to hold cigarette companies liable for its costs show how all three assumptions, although valid as generalities, are problematic when it comes to specifics. Since 1954, 321 suits have been filed against cigarette companies, but none have been forced to pay any damages. One recent case was a New Jersey court's overturning of a $400,000 award to a widower whose wife died at fifty-eight after forty-two years of smoking. At issue was whether, when there were no health warnings prior to 1966, the manufacturer had misled the woman about the risks of smoking. The court found the woman was 80 percent to blame for her condition. Will contends that antismoking advocates want a risk-benefit liability rule, where a jury can find a manufacturer liable because the risk of its use far exceeds its benefits. Driving the tax up (it would cost at least $2.25 a pack to match the costs) would be politically impossible, but the price also can be driven up by a flood of liability suits. "Cigarette companies are winning in courts, but being routed in the culture. In the mid 1950s about half of all Americans older than 18 smoked. Today about 26 percent do. If liability law ever aligns with the flow of social feeling, the following scandalous numbers will change: America spends $35 billion annually on smoking-related illnesses and suffers $65 billion in lost productivity. Even pessimistic projections for AIDS deaths in the late 1990s amount to one-eighth the annual toll (390,000) from smoking" (Will, 1990, p. 28).

Concerning the influence of cigarette advertising revenues on the media: When the cigarette broadcast advertising ban took effect in 1971, cigarette manufacturers shifted advertising expenditures to the print media. In the last year of broadcast advertising and the first year of the ban, cigarette ad expenditures in a sample of major national magazines increased by 49 and then 131 percent in constant dollars. From an eleven-year period preceding the ban to an eleven-year period following it, these magazines decreased their coverage of smoking and health by 65 percent, an amount that is statistically significantly greater than decreases found in magazines that did *not* carry cigarette ads and in two major newspapers. This finding strongly suggests that media dependent on cigarette advertising have restricted their coverage of smoking and health. This may have significant implications for public health, as well as raising obvious concerns about the integrity of the profession of journalism (Warner and Goldenhar, 1989).

Evidently the mandated requirement of a readable health warning on cigarette advertising billboards is still being flouted. In a study of the readability of the Surgeon General's warning in cigarette advertisements in two outdoor media (billboards and taxicab advertisements) in metropolitan Atlanta under typical driving conditions, observers were able to read the entire health warning on eighteen (46 percent) of thirty-nine street billboards but on only two (5 percent) of thirty-nine highway billboards. In contrast, the content of the ads (that is, brand name, other wording, and notable imagery) could be recognized under the same conditions on more than 95 percent of the billboards. In a similar study of 100 taxicab cigarette ads in New York City, observers were unable to read the health warning in any of the ads but were able to identify the brand name in all ads and notable brand imagery in 95 percent of the ads. The researchers concluded that the Surgeon General's warning is not readable in its current form in the vast majority of billboard and taxicab ads. Factors contributing to unreadability include the small size of the letters, the excessive length of the warnings, the distance between the viewers and the ads, and movement of the viewers in relation to the ads (Davis and Kendrick, 1989).

Another gambit on the part of the cigarette manufacturers to flout tobacco advertising controls is that although the 1970

Public Health Cigarette Smoking Act banned tobacco ads on radio and television, tobacco companies are paying to get exposure in films—"often those aimed at teenagers or even children." Philip Morris paid $150,000 to have Lark cigarettes prominently featured in *License to Kill,* the latest James Bond film, in which the major players light up and a cigarette lighter plays a major part in the plot. Philip Morris also paid $42,500 to have Lois Lane smoke Marlboro cigarettes in *Superman II,* and Liggett paid $30,000 to display Eve cigarettes in *Supergirl.*

Even paid promotion of cigarettes is still common in movies: A recent study found cigarette smoking was shown in 87 percent of PG-rated films. Such movies are seen by little children when they are played on home VCRs. The editor of the *Tobacco and Youth Reporter* comments that "smoking may have been the norm during Hollywood's Golden Age, but today, when smoking is in decline in America, glamorizing smoking is irresponsible. In fact, it's murderous." At the very least, "it is an unfair and deceptive way for tobacco companies to attract children" ("Smoking in Movies . . . ," 1990, p. 3).

Yet the tobacco companies are not about to give up the ghost, because at least they can fight a rearguard action by mobilizing their smokers to fight back. Witness the address by the president of the Retail Tobacco Dealers of America at the association's annual trade show in Chicago in 1989. He said, in part,

> The antismokers are making themselves heard all over the country—from major cities to rural towns. And as we all know, the squeaky wheel gets the grease. So now it's time for us, both as individuals and as retailers who can educate our customers, to speak out—*loud and often.*
>
> I know that you are acutely aware of the general atmosphere concerning tobacco. It might even be appropriate to compare this to the abortion debate—two sides fighting over a highly emotional issue. But if we don't educate smokers about ways to band together to control the governmental

beasts of taxation and regulation, who will? Writing letters to your representative is a great first step, but it is *only* a first step. Talk to the people who come into your shop. Have a sample letter that they can send to their representatives. Most of all, do something, *anything,* to make a difference.

George Bush often talks of a thousand points of light. I'd like to think that those points of light are coming from the glowing ends of cigars, cigarettes, and pipes across the country and symbolize the cornerstone of this nation—tobacco ["Tobacco's Last Gasp," 1990, p. 24].

CHAPTER FOUR

Treating Addiction to Tobacco

Obviously, the primary goal in treatment of addiction to tobacco is to get the addict to stop using it. But tobacco addiction is very stubborn. Segal (1988, p. 376) reports that while three out of four smokers have tried or wished to quit smoking, only one in four do quit before the age of sixty, and fewer than 10 percent limit themselves to intermittent or occasional smoking. The stubbornness of nicotine addiction may seem a little puzzling in comparison with addiction to alcohol or opiates or cocaine, because tobacco is hardly as euphoric as those other substances. Further, the social climate for quitting smoking presumably is much more favorable, now that there has been so much publicity on the high death rates among heavy smokers.

Kozlowski and others (1989) conducted a study that reinforces the general finding of the stubbornness of the smoking habit. About 1,000 persons seeking treatment for alcohol or drug dependence were asked about the difficulty of quitting the use of the substance for which they were seeking treatment (relative to cigarettes), the strength of their strongest urges to use, and the pleasure they derived from use. Fifty-seven percent said that cigarettes would be harder to quit using than their problem substance. Alcohol-dependent persons were about four times more likely than the drug-dependent persons to say that their strongest urges for cigarettes were at least as great as their strongest urges for their problem substance. Cigarettes were generally rated as less pleasurable than alcohol or other drugs. Experts on dependence seem to judge cigarettes as at least as "addictive" as other drug use, but not as pleasurable, indicating important similarities and differences between cigarette dependence and other forms of dependence on psychoactive substances.

Segal (1988, p. 367) discusses four theories as to why people smoke: genetic influences, central nervous system (CNS) effects, psychobiological causes, and social learning. Genetic theories, which have not been tested intensively on a controlled basis, assume that there are genes that predispose some people to smoke. The popularly held CNS model, in common with addiction models for opiates, assumes that certain CNS receptors react to a fall in the level of nicotine in the bloodstream by stimulating a need to smoke in order to restore the addict's nicotine "balance." One psychobiological theory is that of oral gratification, which assumes that smoking brings pleasure from the stimulation of the lips and inner mouth membranes: This theory holds that the smoker will smoke to increase arousal when bored or fatigued or to reduce arousal when tense, and that when neither over- or underaroused, he or she will continue smoking partly because it has become a positive reinforcer (or "habit,"in popular terminology). Social learning theories on smoking assume that once the link between smoking and gratification has been established, the behavior will produce sufficient reinforcement to light up another, and then another.

Segal cites the view of Mangan and Golding (1984) that some of these theories of smoking might be contradictory if we assumed that smokers were a homogeneous group, but there is no reason why different influences should not be especially relevant to certain subgroups, or even the same person at different times and circumstances. Thus with some types of smokers, social learning or oral gratification might be the primary influences, and with others (such as the heavier smokers), we might suspect that central nervous conditioning might be the primary influence. One implication is that much more research is needed in order to identify the primary influences on individual smokers, so as to develop techniques that will help the individual kick his or her own type of smoking habit. It may well be found that lighter smokers who are susceptible to oral gratification may respond well to the chewing of sugarless gum to ward off withdrawal symptoms, while heavier smokers might often require the prescription of nicotine gum, and the "social smoker" might be induced to break the habit by avoiding social-smoking situations. Because of the stubbornness of the smoking habit and the high death rates for heavy smokers, conducting more clinical research on distinguishing different types of smokers and effective treatments for them should yield substantial benefits—particularly in a social climate of high approval for those who manage to quit the habit.

As with the opiates, quitting tobacco can produce strong withdrawal symptoms, although of a different type: craving for tobacco, irritability, drowsiness, and intestinal upsets. While opiate withdrawal symptoms may disappear within a week or so, those for tobacco may last several weeks. It is plausible that this could be expected in a behavior with such frequent reinforcements: Since it is physically possible to smoke at a faster rate than drinking or using opiates, the average smoker goes through many more reinforcement sessions per day than the average alcohol or opiate addict. Also, the linkage between smoking and other frequently recurring activities (such as getting up in the morning or going to bed at night, before or after meals, beginning and completing various tasks) probably tends to trigger the desire to smoke more frequently than is true for drinking or illicit drug use.

Segal (1988, p. 378) notes that the problem of smoking among women deserves special attention, since the rate of deaths from lung cancer between 1950 and 1980 increased among women at a rate almost double that for men, and lung cancer has begun to surpass breast cancer as the most common primary cancer among women. Earlier we have been reminded that while within the last generation the rate of smoking has decreased materially among men, the decrease has been much smaller for women, especially younger women.

There is need for more research to test the likelihood that the weight gain common among those who have just quit smoking may be having some influence on some women's inability to quit smoking permanently. Further, the substantial physiological differences between males and females should be studied to see whether metabolic factors might be interacting with cultural differences to make for the greater difficulty many women have in trying to stop smoking.

Cognitive and motivational factors obviously have a bearing on success in stopping smoking. Wojcik (1988) compared the success over three months of seventy-five smokers who quit through formal treatment programs as compared to seventy-five smokers who quit on their own, finding that a feeling of self-efficacy ("I can do it") was the strongest predictor of success, especially among the self-treatment group. (Persons who attributed greater power to health professionals than to themselves were more likely to relapse.) Similar findings were reported by Reynolds and colleagues (1987) in an analysis of the effects of a self-management program, in which self-confidence in quitting played a key role.

The high rate of relapse into smoking is illustrated in the study of 129 chronic smokers who had successfully completed a smoking-cessation program of behavioral counseling and aversive smoking (Brandon, Tiffany, Obremski, and Baker, 1990). Ninety-two of them reported resuming smoking during the two-year follow-up period. As in the Wojcik study, the return to smoking was found to be related to pretreatment confidence level. This follow-up study also found that it was the *increase* in confidence during the course of treatment that best predicted length of abstinence. Previous research also indicated that *over*confidence can be harmful. The authors believe high initial confidence levels may have reduced subjects' motivation to work harder at quitting. Their reservation: "Clearly, lapse and relapse data are needed from a variety of treatment settings to establish the degree to which the present posttreatment smoking patterns are representative" (Brandon, Tiffany, Obremski, and Baker, 1990, p. 113).

Evaluation of Smoking Cessation Methods

The most definitive recent critique of smoking cessation methods, covering the United States and Canada, is the monograph by Jerome Schwartz (1987) (see the resource). The review covers ten major categories of smoking cessation methods. Some highlights of the findings:

While smoking-cessation evaluations continue to be deficient in design and methodology in general, some methods definitely work better than others. One of the most elaborate large-scale experiments, the MRFIT program, had a validated quit rate of 42 percent for the experimental group of persons at high risk of coronary heart disease, in contrast to 24 percent for the control group of high-risk subjects who did not participate in the extensive treatment but were told to see their own physicians. Schwartz considers the improvement from the experimental program to have been not very cost-effective, but as being methodologically valuable. He found that the highest quit rates for trials with one-year follow-ups were the seventeen with physician intervention with cardiac patients (who obviously tended to be highly motivated) and multiple techniques, which had at least a 33 percent success. Other methods that had at least a 30 percent quit rate after one year were: physician intervention with pulmonary patients, risk factor studies, and rapid smoking and satiation (negative reinforcement) when each were combined with other procedures. Methods with one-year quit rates just below 30 percent were group reinforcements and nicotine chewing gum when combined with behavioral treatment therapy.

Although one-third of the trials of twelve different intervention methods scored at least 33 percent success, Schwartz could not label any one method as the best. He noted that self-help with no professional supervision showed a respectable quit rate of 18 percent (in contrast to a 6 percent increase in quit rate when physicians provided more than brief advice or counseling), concluding that more evaluation of self-help methods is warranted, ostensibly because of their cost-effectiveness.

Schwartz identifies as promising approaches to smoking cessation now being funded by the National Cancer Institute

(NCI): self-help strategies, physician and dentist interventions, mass media programs, and school-based interventions (on the latter, the combined tobacco, alcohol, and other drug strategies instituted under the OSAP-funded campaigns are described in Chapter Two of this book). Targeted for priority intervention by the NCI are heavy smokers, African-Americans and Hispanics, women, youth, and smokeless tobacco users. The NCI is now reassessing the effectiveness of various smoking-cessation methods in the hope that mass application soon of the most effective smoking intervention strategies will have yielded widespread public health benefits by the year 2000.

Various drugs intended to aid in stopping smoking have had mixed success. Clonidine, a drug that was widely touted in 1989 for its apparent success, was found in a study at the University of Rochester not to do significantly better than a placebo (83 percent were smoking again one month later, compared to 87 percent with a placebo) (Edell, 1990). Clonadine also was no better than the placebo in reducing withdrawal symptoms such as tension and hunger. The researchers said that the reason the results were disappointing compared to those for earlier studies may have been the manner of selection: Earlier studies indicating success of Clonadine entailed recruiting of subjects from smoking clinics, and thus the subjects would be more highly motivated to quit. In the Rochester study, patients were those receiving routine care (not necessarily related to smoking problems) at a family clinic. This is one of many instances in clinical experiments of the dangers of bias in selection or assignment of subjects to comparison groups.

The popularity of stop-smoking efforts has boosted the sale of auxiliary drugs considerably (Beckett, 1990). Colgate-Palmolive recently launched a smoking-withdrawal product called "Kick the Habit," with filters that block out cigarette smoke progressively. Another product of another company features nicotine-replacement tablets and motivational tapes; another punctures cigarettes to cut tar and nicotine; there is a "Life Sign" that beeps to let you know when your self-chosen time to smoke has come up; and there is the prescription drug Nicorette of Merrell-Dow, which is supposed to suppress the urge.

As regards Nicorette, a full-page ad in *Time* (April 28, 1990) has the headline, "One medicine and only one has been proven to relieve the agony of quitting," and a full-color illustration of a smoker obviously stressed about his inability to quit. The ad pushes this prescription nicotine gum by saying, *"Why most attempts to quit smoking fail.* Quitting may be one of the hardest things you'll ever do. The reason? Your body's addiction to nicotine. The irritability, jumpiness and anxiety you feel when you try to quit are common. Nicotine addiction can be a serious medical problem. It needs a medical solution."

It is the American Way to count heavily on medicines to bail us out of our behavioral problems. While nicotine gum can help to get some highly stressed smokers over the anxiety of withdrawal symptoms from quitting, it is true that many smokers manage to quit without such props. To emphasize that quitting may be very, very difficult without auxiliary aids like nicotine gum may be serving as a self-fulfilling prophecy of failure by lowering clients' self-confidence. Physicians, pharmacists, and other counselors should be on the alert to build clients' self-confidence in their ability to quit smoking, by making clear that while drugs can tide a former smoker over the first stresses, many people quit without such aids. They should communicate the idea that after all, the most effective factor is the person's belief that he or she can—and will—quit successfully.

Many researchers agree that health professionals can play a much greater role in getting their clients to quit smoking, and at the same time they must be careful to build up the clients' self-confidence that they can quit successfully. One conclusion among physicians (Cummings, Rubin, and Oster, 1989) was that too few physicians routinely counsel smokers to quit. The authors drew up estimates of cost-effectiveness of physician counseling on published reports of randomized trials, using estimates of the average cost of physician office visits. They concluded that the cost-effectiveness of brief advice during routine office visits ranged from $705 to $988 per year of life saved for men and from $1,204 to $2,058 for women, and that follow-up counseling by physicians appears to be similarly cost-effective.

Another study, by Kenney and colleagues (1988), was

conducted among 309 residents in family practice, internal medicine, and pediatrics to determine their practices, knowledge, attitudes, and training in smoking-cessation counseling (SCC). It found that more than 90 percent thought physicians should be responsible for SCC, the majority routinely took smoking histories, and 80 percent said they tried to motivate patients to quit smoking. However, 25 percent or fewer reported discussing obstacles to quitting, setting a quitting date, prescribing nicotine gum, scheduling follow-up visits, or providing self-help materials. Family-practice residents used more SCC techniques than did those in internal medicine or pediatrics. Only 54 percent of the residents in this sample reported recent SCC training and only 13 percent reporting have had formal SCC training; those with recent training used a greater number of counseling techniques. Conclusion: Residents in primary care specialties report holding positive attitudes about smoking-cessation counseling, but indicate inadequate practice and training in the requisite techniques.

Still another physician study, a randomized controlled trial to encourage 112 primary care physicians to help smokers to quit, was reported by Cohen and colleagues (1989). The sample of 1,420 patients who smoked at least one cigarette a day and were recruited without taking into account their interest in quitting smoking was drawn from a general medicine clinic of a city-county teaching hospital. The physicians were randomly assigned to one of four groups: a control group of patients who received a protocol for smoking management and lectures on the consequences and management of smoking, a group to which in addition nicotine gum was freely available, a group with reminder stickers attached to their smokers' charts, and a group with reminder stickers plus ready access to nicotine gum. The percentages of patients who quit smoking before their return visit at six months were small within all four groups: 1.3 percent in the control group, 7.7 percent in the gum group, 7.0 percent in the reminder group, and 6.3 percent in the group getting both gum and reminders. At one year, the percentages were 2.7 percent, 8.8 percent, 15.0 percent, and 9.6 percent, respectively. The conclusions were drawn that the availability of nicotine gum or the labeling of the charts of smokers can help primary care physicians increase their success rates two- to six-fold, and that if all primary care providers used these procedures, they could help an additional two million smokers to quit.

Another approach to helping more people quit smoking is the worksite smoking-cessation intervention or contest, which bears considerable promise, especially at a time when social influences to quit smoking are on the increase. Jason (1990) and colleagues recently reported on one such project, which entailed several components including support groups, incentives, and competition. The workers met on company time and could earn $10 for attending each meeting regardless of their smoking status. After an initial three-week program, participants could earn $1 for each nonsmoking day up to $180, and an extra $30 for every thirty days of continuous abstinence. The program also had such added incentives as prizes for a co-worker "buddy" to help in times of temptation. The combination of incentives and other components increased participation rates to over 80 percent, with 42 percent abstinent at six months compared to 13 percent among a control group.

And there is no end to the variety of popular (if not always well-documented) stop-smoking campaigns directed at the general public. One, advanced by Solomon and Lipton (1989), claims an 85 percent success rate for the following six-step campaign: (1) calculation (smoke one less cigarette a day), (2) stop-smoking diet of regular health foods plus low-calorie munchies such as unsalted sunflower seeds or low-calorie hard candy for fourteen days, (3) biofeedback or relaxation techniques to break up the tension/cigarette cycle, (4) aerobic exercise of twenty to thirty minutes daily, (5) "set yourself up" by telling everyone whose opinion you value that you have made a serious commitment to quit smoking, and (6) stop smoking with some friend, agreeing on a date both of you will quit for good and being supportive of each other in your resolve.

And then there is the annual "Great American Smokeout," described by "Dear Abby" Van Buren (1989) as follows: a one-day campaign to discourage smoking for twenty-four hours, just to prove it can be done. This idea has spread from the United

States to Canada, Great Britain, France, Ireland, Australia, South Africa, Norway, Finland, and Sweden. In 1988, more that 18.4 million quit for the day, or more than 37 percent of the nation's fifty million smokers. She is of the opinion that "quitting 'cold turkey' is the hardest way to quit, but my readers have told me it's the most effective, and in the long run, the easiest way. Cutting down is less traumatic, but the temptation to smoke is often too powerful to resist while smoking just one, two, or three cigarets a day" (p. E12).

Another somewhat better documented televised mass smoking-cessation campaign in Chicago is reported by Flay and colleagues (1989). They compared the relative effectiveness of four different conditions of self-help and social support provided to people attempting to quit smoking in conjunction with a televised cessation program. Smokers ready to quit were told to request free written manuals from hardware stores to accompany the televised program. At many worksites the researchers provided the written manual to all workers. At a random half of the worksites, they also provided training to discussion leaders for smokers attempting to quit. At health maintenance organization sites, the researchers invited smokers who had requested program materials to participate in similar group discussions at health centers. The first-year follow-up results for the above groups were compared to results for a self-help American Lung Association manual alone. Results for the television-plus-manual condition were better than those of past studies (25 percent nonsmoking prevalence and 10 percent continuous cessation one year after the program) and considerably better than with the manual alone. The program did encourage and help over 50,000 Chicago smokers to attempt quitting, 100 times as many as would have done so without the televised program.

There is a consensus among many research specialists that while mass stop-smoking campaigns are making a material contribution to saving many lives, there is need for much additional, and more systematic, effort in which a number of influences are brought to bear to get the most stubbornly addicted smokers and those at greatest risk of cancer or heart disease to stop smoking. The prototype of such human intervention trials is the series directed at Stanford University (Farquhar, Maccoby, and Wood, 1985). As reported by Cullen (1988), the National Cancer Institute (NCI) has undertaken a number of such human intervention trials, with special emphasis placed on chemoprevention, diet, and smoking and other tobacco use.

In 1988, the National Cancer Institute launched large-scale community-based studies through ten U.S. and one Canadian research institutions to encourage smoking cessation, especially among heavy smokers, working toward the NCA's goal of reducing cancer death rates by 50 percent by the year 2000 (Hamm, June 1988). A total of $42.5 million is to be spent over eight years on this Community Intervention Trial for Smoking Cessation (COMMIT) project. The program is enlisting the cooperation of major organizations and social institutions (including media) capable of influencing smoking behavior in large groups of people. Rates of success in experimental communities in quitting smoking will be compared to any changes in rates within control communities not involved in the intensive COMMIT quit-smoking campaigns. The COMMIT campaigns are based on techniques developed through the more than forty-five major studies of smoking control strategies funded in recent years through the National Cancer Institute's Smoking, Tobacco, and Cancer Program (National Cancer Institute, 1988). The NCI will also fund a full-blown follow-up of the COMMIT smoking-cessation model (to be entitled "ASSIST") throughout the country at an estimated cost of about $150 million, in keeping with the NCI's ambitious goal to reduce cancer mortality 50 percent by the year 2000.

To summarize: Great progress has been made in recent years in discouraging people from starting smoking and in getting smokers to kick the habit. Not only has the prevalence of smoking dropped considerably during the last generation, but the public generally has cooperated in complying with many new constraints on smoking in public places, including airplanes, trains, and buses. Special incentives and assistance for employees to quit smoking also have been achieving considerable compliance.

Those working in prevention programs on alcohol and other drug addictions may be able to learn from the successes thus far in diminishing smoking. One point is that health authorities have done an excellent job in driving home the fact that smoking is a clear threat to health and actual survival, not only for the smokers but others close to them. Perhaps the marshaling of more proof of the damage done by alcohol and illicit drugs will convince more users to quit or cut down. But mere proof of damage by itself is unlikely to have much effect on those addicted to alcohol or other drugs, because not only are these substances more immediately reinforcing to the user, but social-psychological influences from the users' peer groups and their negative reactions to moralistic suasions from nonusers tend to make prevention programs for alcohol and other drugs much less effective than is true for tobacco. The next four chapters will discuss the present status of prevention and treatment of addiction to alcohol and other drugs, and how improvements in prevention will continue to be an uphill battle. The situation will only improve when the attitudes and values of the general public change to promote consistent acceptance of constraints on alcohol and other drug use based on fuller awareness on the part of family members and peer groups of the destructiveness that is risked in getting caught up in the trap of addiction.

CHAPTER FIVE

Preventing Alcohol Problems

Prospects for gains in the prevention of alcohol problems are encouraging, not only because of the new concerted research-based campaigns developed by governmental and private agencies (described in the previous chapters), but also because of recent favorable trends in alcohol consumption. Figure 2 shows that in the aggregate, the apparent consumption of alcohol within the United States (which had been rising during the 1960s and 1970s) has been decreasing in recent years. (This is called "apparent" consumption because it is based on alcohol tax records rather than measurement of the consumption by individuals.) The largest decline has been in the consumption of spirits, which has fallen to its lowest level since 1958. Beer consumption has been dropping slightly, but wine consumption has remained fairly steady. The National Institute on Alcohol Abuse and Alcoholism's *Seventh Special Report* (1990, p. 22) speculates that the drop in spirits consumption may be a combination of the aging of the population, a decrease in the acceptability of heavy drinking, increasing concern over overall health and fitness, and the recent appearance of lower-alcohol beverages (such as wine coolers) on the market.

Figure 2. Apparent U.S. Per Capita Consumption of Beer, Wine, and Spirits, 1977–1987.

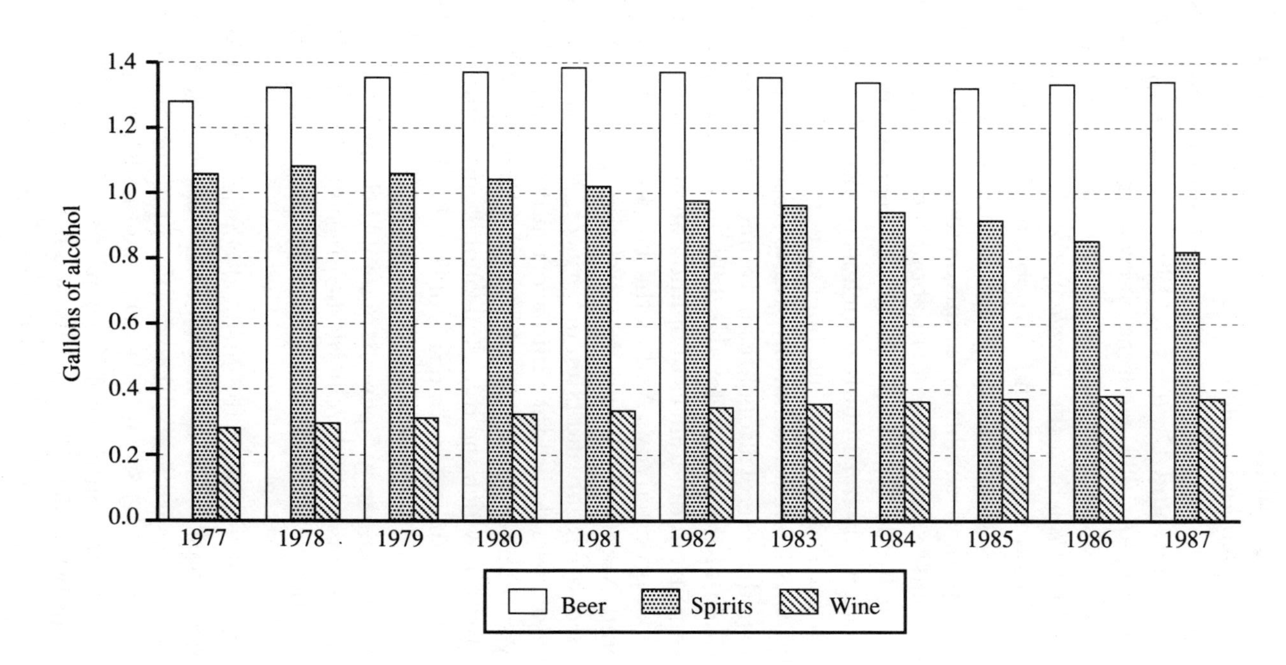

Source: National Institute on Alcohol Abuse and Alcoholism, 1990, p.23.

Authorities differ considerably in their estimates of the total costs of alcohol problems in the United States, including treatment, morbidity and mortality, and lost productivity: Rice, Kelman, Miller, and Dunmeyer (1990) estimate the costs at $85,790 billion for 1988, whereas Harwood and associates' estimate (1984) is considerably higher at $116.7 billion for 1983. And the annual cost cited in the *Seventh Special Report* (National Institute on Alcohol Abuse and Alcoholism, 1990) is estimated to reach $136.3 billion in 1990 and to rise to $150 billion in 1995! Perhaps these conflicting claims on the cost of alcohol problems may cause some amusement about the credibility of some government-funded statistics; but any of the estimates includes some indisputably hard figures, such as the more than $10 billion spent for treatment of alcoholics, more than $2 billion in property losses from alcohol-involved auto crashes, and more than $2 billion in the costs of alcohol-related crime and violence in 1980.

Much of the reason for the difference between the estimates stems from differences of opinion on how to estimate the costs of lost productivity. And as the Director of the Alcohol, Drug, and Mental Health Administration points out (U.S. Department of Health and Human Services, Nov. 6, 1990), such estimates of costs do not take into account the chronic and presumably substantial underreporting of health problems and economic losses in which the role of alcohol is either unrecognized or deliberately concealed. In terms of lives lost because of drinking, Ravenholt (1984) attributes 100,000 deaths to alcohol in 1980, or approximately 5 percent of total U.S. mortality for that year. His finding is reinforced by the latest Centers for Disease Control estimate of 105,045 alcohol-related deaths in 1987 (Lewis, 1990e).

The seriousness of the medical consequences of alcohol abuse is emphasized in the *Seventh Special Report,* especially for chronic liver disease and cirrhosis (the ninth leading cause of death in the United States in 1984), severe effects on the gastrointestinal tract, nutritional deficiencies such as anemia, neuropathy, and Warnicke's disease among heavy drinkers, and the fetal alcohol syndrome resulting from women drinking during pregnancy. Other consequences include cardiac dysfunction (up to 50 percent of excess mortality in alcohol-dependent individuals and heavy users may be attributed to cardiovascular disorders), circulatory dysfunctions, adverse effects on immune, endocrine, and reproductive functions, and such neurological damage as dementia, seizures, hallucinations, and peripheral neuropathy among heavy drinkers.

With respect to the adverse social consequences of drinking in the United States, the *Seventh Special Report* notes that approximately one-half of the 46,386 deaths from auto accidents were alcohol-related, from 20 to 36 percent of suicide victims had histories of alcohol abuse or were drinking shortly before death, and research has shown that alcohol is a major factor in accidental falls, fires, and burns.

However, no clear trends in the levels of drinking *problems* were found between a 1967 national survey (Cahalan, 1970) and a 1979 survey (Clark and Midanik, 1982). A 1984 national survey found that 7 percent of all adults experienced at least moderate levels of alcohol dependence symptoms and 10 percent reported at least moderate levels of adverse social or personal consequences from drinking (Hilton, 1987).

It is indeed true that there has been a recent drop in total alcohol consumption, to a thirty-year low. Per capita consumption of distilled spirits in 1986 was the lowest since 1959 ("Consumption of Liquor Hits 30-Year Low," 1989). However, alcoholic beverages have been around since before 3,000 B.C. (Austin, 1985), and so it is very likely they will still be with us in 3,000 A.D. Again, as Room (1974b) has said, while we talk about "prevention," about the best anyone can hope for is that alcohol problems will be *minimized.* As he commented, "'Minimization' implies a kind of calculus of costs and benefits, and such a terminology might well have the salutary effect of inducing us to recognize and take into account the benefits as well as the costs involved in potentially problem-causing situations. It might be noted that we can readily recognize both the benefits and the problems for the individual in his drinking behavior, but can easily overlook that there are collective and indirect benefits as well as costs from the individual's drinking and behavior while drinking" (p. 13).

While it appears plausible that the mounting chorus of warnings during the last decade from federal sources and the public health community about the dangers in excessive use of alcohol has played some part in the reduction of consumption in recent years, it must be remembered that alcohol consumption throughout history has been found to fluctuate from time to time in "long waves of consumption" (Skog, 1986). Some have suggested that the birth of industrial capitalism may have been responsible for downward trends in drinking because of pressures for productivity, but consumption has gone down in rural areas also. Others have surmised that the long waves of increasing and decreasing consumption that have appeared throughout history may be occurring because after a long period of apparent increases in the harmful effects of drinking, more pressure arises for better control over alcohol. They theorize that it may take several generations before a new growth in consumption can take place, after the concerns over bad effects have died down. Skog (1986, p. 30) tentatively concludes that such social factors—some not too predictable—must play an important role in the long waves of consumption: "The consumption trends are of course related to other macro-level processes such as economic and technological development and so forth, but only within certain limits."

One promising approach to measuring the longer-term effects of societal factors on drinking behavior is the NIAAA-sponsored meta-analytic studies headed by Kaye Fillmore of the University of California at San Francisco. In these, many longitudinal surveys of drinking practices conducted throughout a score of European and North American countries are being pooled together to measure how sociocultural influences affect drinking behavior. In a preliminary analysis in this long-term project, it has been established that *societal* influences have a distinct effect on changes in drinking behavior, over and beyond the individual survey respondents' *personal* characteristics (Fillmore, Johnstone, Leino, and Ager, 1990).

One should note also that political and other social leadership can play a large role in affecting alcohol consumption and attendant problems: witness the Anti-Saloon League's campaign to put across Prohibition (Austin, 1978). Heath (1989, p. 143) interprets the recent drop in drinking as follows: "A long-term rise in drinking by Americans slowed in the 1970s and then reversed; several interest-groups pressed for higher taxes on alcohol, server-liability, severe penalties for drunk-drivers, a higher purchase-age, and many other legislative and regulatory restrictions. Several similar changes are occurring in other countries. A quasi-scientific rationale for reducing alcohol consumption links quantity directly to a wide range of social and individual problems, although the correlation often varies, both cross-culturally and over time in the U.S." Heath then adds the editorial note that "the new temperance movement holds out the false promise of a quick and easy solution to drinking problems, and provides a socially acceptable outlet that allows people to blame alcohol and wrongdoers in a Neo-Victorian complacency."

Alternative Perspectives on Reducing Alcohol Problems

The continuing controversial nature of the prevention or minimization of alcohol problems was commented on by Room (1974a) almost a generation ago. He observed that three governing images of alcohol problems were then [and still are!] affecting discussion of alcohol: that alcohol is a very attractive but dangerous drug, which fits a public health perspective; that alcohol problems belong within the general field of disruptive or compulsive behaviors to be dealt with by social psychiatrists and sociologists; and that alcoholism is a specific disease, which has been the fundamental tenet of the alcoholism movement. He noted that such governing images have distorted and limited discussions of the prevention of alcohol problems. He hoped that some strategies that do not evoke such conflictful governing images might be found to be effective, including measures encouraging nondrinking behaviors, modification of popular images of and reaction to drinking, and insulating drinking behavior from doing social damage.

Segal (1988, pp. 386–387) sees three basic models implicit

in prevention programs in the United States, often operating in conjunction. The first is the distribution-of-consumption model, which assumes a direct relationship between per capita consumption and alcohol abuse (Ledermann, 1956) and assumes that a reduction in the availability of alcohol will result in a reduction of consumption and a decrease in the number and severity of alcohol problems. The second is a social-psychological model that assumes that drinking problems are the result of an interaction between personality and social factors such as peer pressure, the family, and sociocultural and environmental factors, which may be affected through campaigns to change attitudes conducive to overindulgence. The third is a sociocultural model that assumes that alcohol problems result from improper social norms governing the use of alcohol.

The Ledermann distribution-of-consumption model has been interpreted, by many proponents of increasing taxes and other constraints on the availability of alcohol, as supporting the assumption that a reduction of per capita consumption of alcohol can be achieved through reducing its availability, with decrease also in alcohol-related problems. While the alcohol industry is contending that increases in taxes is no solution to alcohol problems, the weight of opinion on the part of many policymakers is leaning toward support of such taxes as a preventive measure, as is the opinion of a growing number of researchers (see Moskowitz, 1989, discussed later). The current trend toward increases in alcohol taxes on both the federal and state levels may well be motivated more by the desire to increase tax revenues than by conviction that higher taxes will help to solve alcohol problems. In any case, the impending alcohol tax increases may provide something in the way of "natural experiments" to test whether both consumption and alcohol problems actually will decrease after their imposition.

A few comments on the social-psychological and sociocultural models and their effects on drinking and alcohol problems are appropriate. There is an abundance of evidence from NIAAA-sponsored national surveys such as those conducted by our Social Research Group (renamed the Alcohol Research Group) at intervals over the last twenty-five years that there are striking differences in consumption and alcohol problems between many subgroups, particularly gender, age, socioeconomic status, urbanization, region, and ethnic origin (Cahalan, Cisin, and Crossley, 1969; Cahalan, 1970; Cahalan and Room, 1974). While those of middle or upper incomes tend to drink frequently but moderately, those of lower status tend to drink less often but to get into more trouble over their drinking. The highest rates of drinking problems involve men under thirty and within certain ethnic groups (such as those of Irish or Hispanic origin; Italians and Jews tend to drink more frequently but more moderately than many other groups).

Particularly in America, the existence of so many quite distinct subcultural groupings and the vast differences in their drinking behavior and its consequences obviously demands the use of prevention programs tailored to the susceptibilities of the various key subgroups in the population, rather than a blanket approach across all groups. Accordingly, a great deal of research is now being conducted on what prevention or minimization measures work best with which subgroups, as discussed throughout this chapter.

Moskowitz, in his landmark critique (1989) of the recent research on the primary prevention of alcohol problems, examined four types of preventive interventions, including (1) policies affecting the physical, economic, and social availability of alcohol (for example, minimum legal drinking age, price, and advertising of alcohol); (2) formal social controls on alcohol-related behavior (for instance, drinking-driving laws); (3) primary prevention informational programs (including school-based alcohol education); and (4) environmental safety measures (such as automobile airbags). He concluded that the research generally supports the efficacy of three alcohol-specific policies: raising the minimum legal drinking age to twenty-one, increasing alcohol taxes, and increasing the enforcement of drinking-driving laws. He concluded that in contrast, little evidence currently exists to support the efficacy of primary prevention programs. However, he notes that a "systems" perspective on prevention suggests that prevention programs may become more efficacious after widespread adoption of prevention policies that lead to shifts in social norms regarding use of beverage alcohol.

There are some signs that such shifts in social norms concerning alcohol may be taking place now in America. As noted earlier, Freedman, in a *Wall Street Journal* article (1989, p. B1), concludes from the results of a survey by Peter B. Hart and the Roper Organization that "alcohol and cigarettes have turned into vices that people want to preserve—but not promote. Although there isn't much grassroots support for outlawing either substance, nowadays half of the nation's consumers would support an outright ban on advertising of all booze and smokes." She notes that marketers have much to fear in the results of the survey, at a time when warning labels on all alcohol containers were just taking effect: About half of the sample supported banning all beer and wine commercials from television and banning celebrities in alcohol ads. Two-thirds favored requiring warnings on containers and advertisements, and 60 percent of those interviewed—including a majority of drinkers—wanted equal time for public health messages to counter alcohol ads.

One strategy for public health–oriented workers in the field of prevention of alcohol problems is to identify alcohol as a *drug*—which, pharmacologically, it clearly is. OSAP no longer uses the term *substance abuse,* even though the words still are contained in the organization's title. Instead, the agency advises adoption of the phrase "alcohol and other drug use." Farhi, in a *Washington Post Weekly Edition* article (1990), says the national Parent-Teacher Association recommends that its local chapters include a reference to alcohol whenever members speak at school meetings about the evils of drugs. Farhi (1990, p. 31) says that "by such subtle rhetorical changes, educators and health organizations say they hope to encourage a profound change in the way Americans think about drug abuse. As the nation confronts the havoc of such illegal drugs as crack cocaine and heroin, these groups promote the notion that alcohol also is a drug, and that any Federal 'war on drugs' must include treatment, education, and legislation to deal with the devastation caused by alcohol abuse."

The author also commented that while few would dispute that alcohol is a drug in the same sense as caffeine and nicotine, the federal authorities and public health people are up against the alcohol industry's $2 billion yearly advertising budget depicting alcohol as suave and sophisticated. They are also trying to deal with the present media emphasis on illicit drugs by reminding us again and again that (according to NCA reports) alcohol is directly or indirectly responsible for at least 97,500 deaths a year, $15 billion a year in medical expense, and $117 billion in lost productivity. Farhi (1990, p. 31) notes that Daniel Beauchamp, currently deputy health commissioner for New York State, says that the current illegal "drug situation is so bleak and independently awful that people's eyes glaze over when you bring up alcohol." Beauchamp, who wrote his doctoral dissertation on Prohibition, says that while no one in the alcohol-is-a-drug school favors prohibiting alcoholic beverages again, labeling alcohol as a drug may still have strong persuasive power from a health and public policy standpoint.

Farhi goes on to note that the alcohol-as-a-drug view is being pushed by the Parent-Teacher Association, NCA (now NCADD), Center for Science in the Public Interest, and a loose coalition of other health advocacy groups. He also points out (1990, p. 32) that President Bush even said at a recent news conference that "we must teach our children [that] alcohol is a drug and that any irresponsible drug use is wrong." All this is alarming the $79 billion-a-year industry that has been fighting declining consumption: This is another public relations problem for them on top of the drunk-driving campaigns. So, August Busch III (Budweiser) has mounted a campaign to shareholders urging them to communicate with their legislators.

Farhi (1990, p. 32) concludes by saying that "although it may be a self-serving notion, those in the alcohol-beverage business say the effort to link drugs and alcohol may end up doing more harm than good. According to this reasoning, equating the two substances lends illegal drugs greater legitimacy in the mind of a child, who sees alcohol widely advertised and being freely used, often safely, by adults."

NIAAA's Special 1990 Report to Congress

The conclusions drawn in NIAAA's *Seventh Special Report to the U.S. Congress* (1990) regarding the relative effects of various types of measures to reduce drinking problems are consistent with Moskowitz's (1989) research review. This is true in that the

NIAAA report sees promise in alcohol tax increases, the recent increase in minimum age in all states, and the application of "per se" laws that establish automatic application of driving-under-the-influence penalties (including automatic suspension of driver's licenses) for exceeding certain blood alcohol limits and mandatory jail or community-service sentences for first offenders. The report also sees some promise in a cognitive-behavioral approach in teaching school-age children how to cope with social pressures to drink, while at the same time conceding that mere distribution of information about the adverse effects of alcohol has not been successful in changing attitudes or behavior.

It is of interest that in its official pronouncements, the NIAAA is gradually focusing increased attention on the many kinds of alcohol problems other than alcoholism, and this *Seventh Special Report* provides much detail about the current revised version of the American Psychiatric Association's *Diagnostic and Statistical Manual of Mental Disorders* (DSM-III-R) (1987) and the World Health Organization's *International Classification of Diseases* (ICD-9) (1978). This may help to clarify the distinction between nondependent problem drinking (defined as "alcohol abuse") and alcohol dependence (alcoholism), through such clarifications as "Alcohol abuse represents a pattern of heavy drinking accompanied by social, psychological, and/or medical problems that are directly related to alcohol use, while alcoholism is characterized by physical and psychological dependence that results in impaired control over drinking. Both diagnostic systems offer specific criteria to guide the diagnostic process and represent a general evolution toward detailed assessment of alcohol use disorders using multiple criteria" (National Institute on Alcohol Abuse and Alcoholism, 1990, p. xxvii).

As for the etiology of alcoholism itself, in the *Seventh Special Report* the NIAAA somewhat distances itself from the heavy credence it gave to genetic effects (Bohman, Sigvardsson, and Cloninger, 1981; Cloninger, Bohman, and Sigvardsson, 1981) in its *Sixth Special Report* by noting that a number of researchers (Peele, 1986; Murray, Clifford, and Gurling, 1983; Fillmore, 1988; Searles, 1988) were challenging on methodological grounds the finding of genetic effects of alcoholism in Swedish studies of identical twins. David Lester (1989) also wrote a well-documented review article (not mentioned in the *Seventh Report*) that was very skeptical of the methodology of past genetic alcohol studies. In the light of NIAAA's very heavy investments in laboratory research, it is understandable that the new report still devotes considerable space to the potential promise of ongoing studies of genetic effects among animals and of biological markers suggesting genetic effects. However, it would be more evenhanded to report that while in principle the possibility of genetic effects should continue to be explored, it is still true that most of the damage to individuals and economic costs from alcohol abuse is attributable to behavior during or after drinking by nonalcoholics. This behavior stems from social influences and other environmental factors that clearly are nongenetic in origin—and much more susceptible to remedial action than any genetic effects. The alcohol industry loves the genetic theory of alcoholism because it can be used to gloss over the fact that much of the problem is in the bottle rather than in the genes.

Still, one very interesting finding on genetic effects in alcoholism comes from new research conducted by medical scientists from the University of California at Los Angeles and the University of Texas (Blum and others, 1990). This research was also covered in feature articles in the *San Francisco Chronicle* (Perlman, 1990) and *Time* (Purvis, 1990). Samples of brain tissue were taken from thirty-five known alcoholics, most of whom had died from the disease, and from thirty-five men and women known not to have been alcoholic who had died from other ailments. In 77 percent of the alcoholics, researchers found a single segment of DNA or gene that commands the brain to produce cells that serve as receptors for a particular type of dopamine. The same gene was absent in 72 percent of the nonalcoholics. (Dopamine is a neurotransmitter that carries impulses across the junctions between nerve cells in the brain and central nervous system; animal studies have shown that it is closely involved in the brain's reward system that produces dependence on cocaine.)

One obvious implication of this finding is that alcohol may be having a special effec. on the "pleasure centers" of the brains of some who have certain genetic characteristics, thus facilitating the addiction process. Of course this intriguing study deserves replication and elaboration. An editorial in the same issue of the *Journal of the American Medical Association* that reported on that study voices enthusiasm over the findings, but suggests that analogous studies could be done on blood samples from live patients (on whom more facts and neurophysiological correlates can be known than in the case of cadavers). It ends (Gordis, Tabakoff, Goldman, and Berg, 1990, p. 2095) on this cautionary note: "Success in research on the genetics of alcoholism would provide insight into the physiology of the disease, suggest new methods of prevention and treatment, and illuminate brain physiology far beyond the issue of alcoholism. Blum and colleagues have added a promising new observation to current genetic research. Genetics accounts for only part of the vulnerability to alcoholism. Understanding how genes and environment interact to produce alcoholism in any individual is the larger challenge to both genetic and psychosocial research."

A more recent study (Bolos and others, 1990) based on live subjects (10 clinically defined alcoholics, 127 nonalcoholic controls, and 2 large families with alcoholic members) failed to find the same genetic link to alcoholism as the study by Blum and others. More research on that issue is pending.

Stanton Peele (1990), a frequent skeptic regarding genetic effects in alcoholism, agrees with the observations of Gordis and his colleagues and also argues that in any case genetic effects cannot account for more than a small fraction of alcoholism in comparison with environmental and individual psychological factors. He also points out that widespread belief in a genetic theory of alcoholism may lead to self-fulfilling prophecy: "In other words, indoctrinating young people with the view that they are likely to become alcoholics *may take them there more quickly than any inherited reaction to alcohol would have.* In fact, a majority of children do not become alcoholic themselves, for whatever reason. No epidemiologic study has ever found that as many as half of such children develop a drinking problem of their own, and most research places the figure at 25 percent or less.",

The *Seventh Special Report* does get around to the topic of *prevention* in the ninth of eleven chapters, although the discussion is rather limited. The topics of biomedical research and the etiology of alcoholism have been the standard bill of fare of NIAAA *Special Reports,* and certainly those topics evoke less controversy than the easily politicized issues of prevention. However, thanks perhaps in large part to the strong backing of some constraints on consumption proposed by the recent Secretaries of Health and Human Services and by former Surgeon General Koop, the new NIAAA *Special Report* goes further toward endorsement of a number of controversial alcohol controls than any prior NIAAA report.

Included among the control approaches NIAAA recognizes as promising is the proposed raising of federal taxes to equalize the rate per ounce of alcohol in alcohol, beer, and wine, citing as justification new studies showing that alcohol-related automobile accidents are correlated with local prices of alcohol (Grossman, Coate, and Arluck, 1987; Coate and Grossman, 1988). As regards possible constraints on alcohol advertising, the NIAAA report noted that research has yet to document a strong relationship between seeing alcohol advertising and drinking, citing Smart's (1988) negative findings and Atkin's (1987) positive findings, and Holder's (1988) discussion of the methodological difficulty of demonstrating effects in the real world. NIAAA evidently accepts Smart's suggestion that with better methods in future studies, experimental studies are most likely to answer questions about the effects of advertising. The report also appears to give credence to the assumption that frequent drinking scenes on television help to create social expectations and norms that drinking is to be approved in all settings.

With respect to the efficacy of drinking-driving laws, this 1990 NIAAA *Special Report* cites approvingly the assessments of Ross (1985) in his review of various deterrents, concluding that increasing the *perceived* certainty of punishment had short-term effectiveness, but *actual* increases in severity of punishment have produced unexpected problems of delay and plea bargaining in the criminal justice system. The report also mentions the findings of Perrine and Sadler (1987) that offenders in California whose driver's licenses were suspended or revoked had fewer crashes afterward than those who were merely assigned to rehabilitation or relearning programs. The report appears to take a favorable view of license suspensions for alcohol-impaired driving, with reeducation of offenders being more appropriate as a supplement than as an alternative to revocation or suspension of licenses.

The NIAAA *Special Report* concurs with Rootman's (1985) conclusion that mass media campaigns can increase awareness, change attitudes, and provide a context in which other strategies can succeed. The report also notes that the apparent success of social learning approaches with *smoking* prevention may be related to recent changes in the current social climate resulting in the general belief that people should not smoke. It suggests that if somehow we could change the prevailing messages about alcohol similarly, social learning might work also in reducing alcohol problems. However, this report limited itself primarily to presenting pro-and-con research findings rather than drawing the conclusions voiced publicly by the present and last Secretaries of Health and Human Services—that to effect a change in the social climate of drinking, it is advisable to set constraints on alcohol advertising and to have a great deal more publicity on the high toll on public health and human relations occasioned by heavy drinking.

New Prevention and Research Opportunities Report

Another new landmark NIAAA-supported report bearing on the prevention of alcohol problems is the Institute of Medicine's monograph *Prevention and Treatment of Alcohol Problems: Research Opportunities* (1989). This report completed the second stage of the Institute of Medicine's mission to study alcohol research progress and needs, the first being fulfilled in the IOM report on the causes and consequences of the misuse of alcohol (Institute of Medicine, 1987). (See the resource for a list of recent additional IOM NIAAA-sponsored alcohol research and treatment policy reports.)

For the IOM prevention and treatment report, there was an overall steering committee of ten established scientists in the alcohol field, and separate panels for each of the two aspects, each representing a broad array of biomedical or behavioral research or treatment institutions. The prevention section of the report deals with the epidemiology of alcohol-related problems, individual-environment interactions, life-course development, genetic determinants of risk, and community perspectives from other health fields (such as community risk factors in cardiovascular disease, drawing heavily on the Stanford studies) (Farquhar, Maccoby, and Wood, 1985).

Since the prevention committee's summary of recommendations for future alcohol prevention research is so brief, it is included here in full:

- Findings from biomedical research should be integrated with theories from the social sciences that seek to explain alcohol use and abuse. Integrated models can then be used to guide the development of prevention interventions.
- Theory-driven research should be promoted. Its development can be aided by borrowing theory-based analogues from studies in other health fields.
- Life-span considerations and developmental factors should be incorporated into comprehensive theories of research that draw on work in any of the fields applicable to alcohol problem prevention. If specific interactions between individual characteristics and environmental or cultural demands are predicted to produce a group at risk, such predictions can be used to plan and test preventive strategies.
- Collaboration among scholars from diverse fields should be encouraged in theory development. These fields might include the biomedical sciences, psychology, sociology, anthropology, clinical epidemiology, education, econometrics, and any other disciplines shown to be relevant.

- Program planning and implementation should be integrated with evaluation. Pilot studies of untested components of programs (formative research) should be increased. One barrier to community prevention research has been the cost of collecting the data necessary to measure whether an intervention was effective. NIAAA may want to encourage local and county agencies to develop information management systems that can serve as data bases.
- Long-term community trials of prevention strategies should be instituted.
- Prevention research should inform policy formation. In particular, prevention research must develop the necessary methods and techniques to help prevention planners estimate the potential effects of various interventions, based on the best available research.
- Prevention research should include a consideration of cost-effectiveness in evaluations of interventions [Institute of Medicine, 1989, pp. 8–9].

Applied and Basic Prevention Research Developments

Concurrent with the IOM report just discussed, Harold Holder, a member of the prevention panel and director of the Prevention Research Center (PRC) of Berkeley (the only one of the dozen NIAAA-funded Alcohol Research Centers devoted specifically to prevention studies), wrote an insightful article for the NIAAA's quarterly *Alcohol Health and Research World* (1989). This article provides an excellent history of the emergence of increased emphasis on preventive theory and research since its almost complete neglect in the early days of the NIAAA, whose major constituencies were then preoccupied with getting alcoholics better treatment. He relates how the PRC, founded in 1983 under a mandate by Congress, in its research emphasizes a public health systems model stressing reciprocal interaction between the agent (alcohol), the host (the individual drinker), and the environment (the social and physical drinking context). The PRC conducts two types of prevention studies, *basic* (on factors that influence risks, such as individual characteristics like age and gender, and within environments, such as family interactions and workplace phenomena); and *applied* (evaluating the effectiveness of efforts to reduce drinking problems within test localities).

Concerning the importance of media studies, he reminds us that American children spend an average of twenty-seven hours per week watching television, and that by age twelve they watch primarily adult programs where alcohol use is heavy (Wallack, Breed, and Cruz, 1987). The PRC is undertaking a five-year longitudinal study to evaluate adolescents' exposure to prime-time television and its relationship to seeing alcohol ads, and how this interacts with other influences—such as peer group and parental behavior—that influence drinking decisions.

Concerning promotion of traffic safety, the PRC found a six-year decline of up to 16 percent in single-vehicle night-time crashes among eighteen-to twenty-year-olds in states that had raised the minimum age to twenty-one (Wagenaar, 1986; Wagenaar and Maybee, 1986). A later time-series analysis by O'Malley and Wagenaar (forthcoming) on the apparent effects of increases in minimum drinking age in several states on rates of fatal crashes found that higher age minimums were associated with lower levels of alcohol use among high school seniors and recent graduates. The study also found that the lower levels of use persisted into the early twenties after all respondents were of legal age, and that lowered involvement in alcohol-related fatal crashes among drivers under twenty-one appeared to be due to lower alcohol consumption rates—in particular, less drinking in bars or taverns. Such findings have been ventilated in public debates leading to national legislation to provide incentives for states to raise their drinking ages, and the minimum age in all states is now twenty-one.

On evaluation of alcohol server intervention, a PRC experiment demonstrated that with training of servers, the number of patrons leaving the establishment legally intoxicated was reduced by up to 50 percent (Saltz, 1988). This was a study on service of alcohol in clubs on a naval base. A different study, conducted by the Marin Institute later with the collaboration of Robert Saltz of the PRC (who conducted the naval-base study), focused on server training in civilian facilities in two Southern California communities. It showed that a modest but statistically significant reduction of intoxication in bar patrons was achieved in one community in which both the citizenry and the managers of drinking places were involved in the project, but no reduction in the other community where there was little citizen and managerial interest (Mosher, Delewski, Saltz, and Hennessy, 1989). In a subsequent discussion of principles of community organization to reduce alcohol and other drug problems in general, members of a Marin Institute team that is developing such programs emphasized that to be successful, the organizing process must be focused on the vital interests of the community rather than the desires of the organizers, and that the organizers should primarily play the role of facilitators rather than managers, putting strong emphasis on strengthening the bonds within and between community members that can increase their power to achieve mutually rewarding goals (Greenfield, Huff, Jones, and Wechsler, 1990).

The PRC's efforts with respect to community alcohol problem control issues should also be mentioned. It used computer simulations to forecast for Alameda County, California, the effect of four strategies on alcohol-involved crashes: community education, increases in alcohol price, community education along with price increases, and increased enforcement of drinking and driving laws along with increased conviction rates. It found that the combination of community education and a price increase would have the greatest long-term effect compared to the other strategies (Holder and Blose, 1987).

The PRC's ongoing workplace and family studies are finding that the workplace can be supporting a heavy-drinking subculture through alienation and boredom (Ames and Janes, 1985, 1987). In addition, the PRC is focusing observational studies of drinking behavior within special populations such as Mexican-American families, and studies of correlates of problem drinking for women that are not commonly emphasized in studies of male drinking (such as physical appearance and self-presentation, and social and personal relationships).

Holder (1989) sums up his estimate of promising future directions in prevention research, recognizing that thus far most alcohol problem prevention programs have not caused a substantial reduction in problems. He sees a special need to study *interactions* of preventive measures—that is, education coupled with restrictions on alcohol availability—and enforcement of drinking-driving penalties coupled with counseling, treatment, and early identification. In the future, he expects there will be more emphasis on longitudinal instead of cross-sectional studies, and utilization of more sensitive and complex tools including econometric models and computer simulations. He ends by saying (1989, p. 342), "NIAAA-funded research supports the tools not only to evaluate ongoing strategies, but also to develop the basic research that can be used in the direct design and creation of more effective prevention strategies."

Holder and Stoil (an associate editor of the NIAAA research quarterly) discussed in more detail some of the potentials for prevention research and action programs in a later issue of *Alcohol Health and Research World* (1988), making the following points:

Key elements in the public health perspective on prevention during the last fifteen years have been the recognition that alcohol is a drug with considerable risks, that destructive drinking in any situation may be termed "alcohol abuse," that alcohol abuse affects all citizens and thus raises public health concerns, that reducing alcohol problems requires intervention both in individual lives and the environment, and that there is need to apply a number of strategies. These include public information and education, changes in the social contexts of drinking, and limits on the availability of alcoholic beverages. Restrictions may be based on minimum age of purchase or use, manipulation of the price relative to other beverages, limitations on the location and hours of sale, and the strengthening of law enforcement against such dangerous use as drinking before driving. Holder and Stoil review the limitations of the

Anti-Saloon League's drive early in this century to bring about Prohibition, in which the strategy was to blame the saloon rather than blaming consumption for alcohol abuse, and they note how the repeal of Prohibition was accompanied by another limited strategy: to focus increased attention on the individual drinker, with most tipplers being considered "social drinkers" and only a few being the "alcoholics."

A change came about in the 1950s when Ledermann (1956) questioned "alcoholism" as a driving force in drinking problems, arguing that problematic drinking was sensitive to supply and demand. And finally in the early 1970s, the public health perspective on alcohol problems really began to come into its own when a consortium of colleagues in Scandinavia, Canada, and the United States concluded that overall consumption had an impact on cirrhosis, accidents, and certain cancers and that thus overall consumption would have to be reduced in order to bring down the level of drinking problems (Bruun and others, 1975). Holder and Stoil (1988, p. 295) note that Moore and Gerstein's (1981) report of a panel sponsored by the National Research Council of the National Academy of Sciences "held that NIAAA had become the primary institutional base for the perspective that prevention of alcohol abuse was dependent on treatment of alcoholism," citing that report as follows: "'The emphasis of NIAAA, AA, and a host of related institutions has been on refinement, financing, and legitimation of the treatment of alcoholism . . . . It is also notable that this governing idea, projecting the concept of vulnerability onto a small part of the population, has been able to establish and maintain support from the alcohol industry.'"

Holder and Stoil (1988, p. 295) conclude that " the panel report and observations in research papers commissioned by the NIAAA-funded effort provided strong evidence that emphasis on alcoholism is not a sufficient response to alcohol abuse, in part because such abuse occurs among individuals other than alcoholics." But they credit NIAAA with taking other prevention initiatives, including the commissioning of the Prevention Research Center and support for environmental studies such as the role of the workplace in alcohol problems. However, they see several barriers to producing sufficient prevention research of a level convincing to policymakers, one being that most support in the alcohol field emphasizes biochemical and treatment research, consistent with the long-held view that susceptible individuals are the ones responsible for alcohol abuse. They also feel that there is need for more of a public health perspective emphasizing epidemiologic, legal, and cultural research on the behavior of populations and groups relating to drinking and alcohol misuse.

Public Health and Alcohol Advertising

In a monograph on a symposium on control issues in alcohol abuse prevention, Wallack made these observations about public health and alcohol advertising: He said that public health traditionally has highlighted system-level rather than individual-level failures as the principal determinants of disease. However, it often seems that commitment to prevention is only high when powerful vested interests are not threatened, and that as a result, prevention policies and programs are almost certain to be severely handicapped in attaining desired outcomes. "Rather than being potent agents for change, prevention programs often run the risk of reinforcing existing arrangements that run counter to public health goals" (Wallack, 1984a, p. 96).

Wallack notes that alcohol and tobacco advertisers rely on persuasive measures that have little or nothing to do with the product. Public health cautions on the negative effects of excessive drinking are seldom mentioned.

Wallack says that the fallacy inherent in examining the question of whether there is a proven relationship between alcohol advertising and consumption is: It is also the case that it cannot be proven that advertising does *not* lead to increased consumption. He points out that it is often heard that we need a tightly controlled experimental study, presumably in a natural setting, to get conclusive findings, but this sets up an impossible situation whereby any effects are easily dismissible because of methodological deficiencies in the study.

He points out that in the early 1980s NIAAA was spending

about $11.4 million to provide accurate information about alcohol to the general public, and if we assume that each state spends about $1 million on prevention-related activities, the total of governmental prevention spending would be only one-half of the 1978 advertising budget of either Anheuser-Busch or Miller Brewing companies. This is "only a bare pittance compared to the more than 1 billion tax-deductible dollars spent on alcoholic beverage advertising this year" (Wallack, 1984a, p. 99).

Wallack also criticizes the Bureau of Alcohol, Tobacco, and Firearms for not fulfilling its obligation to prohibit misleading alcohol advertising, and for its rejection of the 99 percent of invited comments on rule making that generally favored a ban on all alcoholic beverage advertisements. In addition, he points to the ineffectual policing of the ban on associating drinking with athletes and athletic events, contending that the BATF will consider only specific cases of deception even though its charge is clearly to assess the overall impression of the advertisement. Further, Wallack contends that advertisements are not fully protected by the First Amendment where there is potential for consumer deception, citing a Supreme Court ruling that commercial speech is only protected when it provides *accurate* consumer information. He contends (1984a, p. 103) "if society is truly concerned about alcohol-related problems, this concern should be reflected in public policy. The regulation of alcoholic beverage advertising should be an important component in the design of such a policy."

Another criticism of the BATF points out that more than half of the 145,000 injury deaths in the United States in 1985 were directly associated with alcohol, tobacco, or firearms. Although we have government agencies (like BATF) responsible for maintaining compliance with tax laws that bring in revenue from these products, the responsibility for mitigating the health hazards of these products is really *not* being undertaken competently by any regulatory agency (McLoughlin and Wang, 1989).

Alcohol advertising continues to be under increasing attack from advocacy groups. A coalition of twenty-two African-

American, Latino, and health organizations urged Health and Human Services Secretary Sullivan to demand that beer companies stop targeting high-alcohol malt liquor to African-Americans and Latinos and to limit the alcohol content of malt liquor to 5 percent. Michael Jacobson, director of the Center for Science in the Public Interest (CSPI), who coordinated that news conference in the fall of 1989,said that the ads stressed strength and power and thus appeared to violate the federal law prohibiting such words as *full-strength.* Noted were such ads as Colt 45 saying that malt liquor "works every time" in seducing women (Lewis, 1989).

Soon thereafter, the mayor of Baltimore reported that an advertising company had agreed to take down by the following summer 450 ads advertising tobacco and alcohol that were located in primarily African-American communities. A study by the Abell Foundation had shown that of 2,015 billboards surveyed in Baltimore, about 70 percent were located in poor, inner-city neighborhoods. Of these, 76 percent were advertising liquor or cigarettes. (The Institute of Outdoor Advertising reports that combined contracts from alcohol and tobacco companies accounted for one-third of 1988 outdoor advertising contracts, for a total of $471.5 million.) This news article cited a 1987 CSPI study that found that African-American men have a 70 percent higher death rate from cirrhosis than white males. Also, according to a Health and Human Services report (Glaser, 1989), 40.6 percent of African-American men age twenty or older smoke, compared to 31.8 percent of white men, and 31.8 percent of African-American women smoke compared with 28.3 percent of white women.

After repeated delays, the BATF finally agreed in February 1989 to promulgate temporary rules requiring warning labels on alcoholic beverages. However, the National Council on Alcoholism (NCA) almost immediately charged that the BATF implementation regulations circumvented the spirit of the law by allowing alcoholic beverage producers broad latitude to make the labels too hard to read, at disservice to alcoholic beverage consumers and the public's health. BATF had proposed two type sizes for labels, one of one millimeter (thin as a dime) for containers of less than eight fluid ounces, and one of two millimeters for larger containers. NCA said the type was too small and that there should be a third size for containers larger than 750 millimeters. NCA also recommended that labels be placed on the fronts of containers rather than on the side, and that typefaces should be boxed or boldfaced for emphasis. NCA noted that it had been pushing for health warning labels since 1981, and that BATF had resisted at every turn the exercising of its authority to impose such labels (Lewis, 1989b). After continued haggling between the BATF and public health advocacy groups, the final regulations called for "GOVERNMENT WARNING" in boldface, with a statement that women should not drink when pregnant because of the risk of birth defects, and that the consumption of alcoholic beverages impairs ability to drive an automobile or operate machinery and may cause health problems (Lewis, 1990b).

Almost one-fourth of all the alcohol consumed in America is supplied by Anheuser-Busch, and the next four companies furnish another fourth of the total consumption, according to a report released by CSPI Director Michael Jacobson. Jacobson said that "the more alcohol a company produces, the more drunk-driving, social problems, and deaths for which it must share responsibility" (Lewis, 1989d, p. 4). The report stated that beer provides 58 percent of the alcohol Americans consume, liquor 29 percent, and wine 13 percent.

Advocates of more control over alcohol marketing and advertising are clearly using the history of the recent rather effective campaigns to put further controls over cigarette advertising. In response to appeals from advocacy groups, Senator Albert Gore and Representative Joseph Kennedy have proposed legislation that would require health and safety messages on printed, television, and radio advertising for alcoholic beverages. Members of the advertising and alcohol industry are opposing the legislation, emphasizing their fear of greater congressional regulation of advertising content in general. But Senator Gore contended that "labels on bottles and cans simply do not provide an adequate-enough warning," noting that tens of thousands of newborn babies each year suffer from fetal alcohol syndrome or other serious alcohol-related birth defects. Representative Kennedy said that warnings are needed to balance the industry's message that drinking is glamorous and acceptable. The Association of National Advertisers warned that the labels "would be an onerous burden" for advertisers when producing and distributing print advertising and "would be virtually impossible for viewers of outdoor advertising to read and absorb" ("Lawmakers Want Liquor Ads to Carry Health Warnings," 1990). This rearguard defense is consistent with the communications industry's legendary reluctance to carry print or broadcast stories about the dangers in the two products, tobacco and alcohol, from which they have derived such a large share of their advertising revenues.

Meanwhile the evidence is mounting that alcohol advertising will continue to offer strong pro-drinking inducements to youth that can be especially seductive within the American culture in the relative absence of warnings about alcohol's dangers:

The research paper presented by Wallack during hearings on H.R. 4493 (the House version of the Gore-Kennedy bill that would require rotating health and safety messages on the risks associated with alcohol use) on July 18, 1990, reported the results of his recent study of a representative sample of youths aged ten to thirteen. He found that the more alcoholic beverage commercials that children can recognize, the more likely they are to say that they will drink when they become adults, and that those able to identify three or more brands from commercials are almost twice as likely to have a high expectation about drinking as an adult as the children who could not identify that many brands. The gist of his study (1990b, p. 4) is that "*the relationship between seeing, attending to, and remembering beer commercials with beliefs and expectation to drink is consistent and statistically significant.* While this study is correlational rather than causal, it would be difficult to justify an explanation that suggests that beliefs and expectations to drink precede rather than follow exposure and attention to advertising."

A paper presented by Jean Kilbourne at the same session reviewed the evidence on the magnitude of alcohol advertising targeted toward the young. She drew (1990, p. 19) the following conclusion: "One doesn't even have to enter into the argument about whether such advertising increases consumption.

At the very least, it drastically inhibits honest public discussion of the problem in the media and creates a climate in which advertising is seen as entirely benign. Health and safety messages on the ads would provide more free speech, not less."

Another attack on alcohol marketing practices appears in a report prepared for the American Automobile Association's Foundation for Traffic Safety by the Marin Institute (Buchanan and Lev, 1990). It gives many illustrations of how the beer industry caters to the risk-taking tastes of young blue-collar men by heavy sponsorship of sports car races and rallies. Young men eighteen to twenty-four drink more beer than any other group: Miller Brewing even dedicated a book "to that twenty percent of beer drinkers who drink eighty percent of the beer." The report cites evidence that beer drinkers typically drink to higher levels of intoxication, are more likely to drive after drinking, and consider driving while intoxicated less serious than do others.

Prevention on the Community Level

The Marin Institute in San Rafael, California, has worked closely with the Trauma Foundation of San Francisco General Hospital in public advocacy of a broad range of prevention objectives concerning alcohol. One illustration is the preparation of a handbook for action on the part of community groups for better control over the licensing and supervision of alcoholic beverage sales outlets. Sponsored by the California State Department of Alcohol and Drug Problems, this illustrated report (Mosher and Colman, 1989) presents much of the collected evidence on the shortcomings of the typical state alcoholic beverage control system, which it says caters to the industry rather than to the general public. To encourage more local input into alcohol outlet permits and zoning, the report helps to clarify the myriad of ABC laws and regulations. It also describes how to bring about more local input in protesting additional liquor licenses and stiffening shop laws, and on how to work through the injunctive and regulatory processes.

Another instance of collaboration between the hospital-based Trauma Foundation and the Marin Institute is seen in an article (Jernigan, Mosher, and Reed, 1989) on how public hospitals can make a substantial contribution to the prevention of alcohol problems. The report contends that general hospitals should have a special incentive to take the initiative in prevention because research has shown that the bulk of alcohol problems are not caused by alcoholics, but by "normal" so-called moderate and heavy drinkers—many of whom show up in hospital emergency rooms. Jernigan, Mosher, and Reed note that trauma patients in the United States spend an estimated nineteen million days per year in hospitals—more than for all heart patients, and four times that for cancer patients. A very heavy proportion of the injured have high blood alcohol levels (BAL)—but only 42 percent of all drivers in fatal motor vehicle accidents are tested for BAL, and only 80 percent of those tested are actually reported. Alcohol is involved in 11 percent of all motor vehicle crashes, 16 percent of all injury-producing crashes, 29 percent of serious-injury crashes, and close to half of all fatal crashes. The article emphasizes the need for more testing of BAL in hospital emergency rooms, and also finding out the locus of the last drink and other data on pinpointing the environments related to high BALs. Emergency rooms can be used to detect and treat alcohol problems and refer patients for follow-up treatment. But for prevention programs to work, more adequate training of hospital staffs on alcohol problems must become routine practice.

Jernigan, Mosher, and Reed also describe how public hospitals can help in victim assistance and help the families of problem drinkers. The authors think general-hospital staffs and administrations should become involved in such preventive issues as motorcycle helmet laws (many injured cyclists have high BALs), warning labels, and local zoning and other alcohol regulatory action programs: that the high credibility of the medical community can have a major impact on community norms, attitudes, and activities if properly exercised.

Increasing Taxes on Alcohol

The long-term campaign by a consortium of advocacy groups to get Congress to raise the taxes on alcoholic beverages was given a strong boost by public support from Everett Koop, the Surgeon General throughout most of the 1980s. In his testimony before Senator John Glenn's Government Affairs Committee in 1989, Koop urged congressional adoption of nine points, practically all of which had been proposed to him shortly before by the Surgeon General's Workshop on Drunk Driving (see Chapter One).

Koop conceded that there was no compelling scientific evidence that advertising influences consumption and the nature and level of alcohol-related problems. "There may never be [such evidence] because of methodological difficulties in designing research studies," Koop (1989, p. 2) said, adding, "What we do have are observation, common sense, and logic. They have served us well with smoking since 1964 when members of Congress, the public health and medical communities, and citizen's groups embarked upon a program to end America's high-risk romance with tobacco."

Koop's recommendations were bolstered by the findings of his workshop, including these summarized by Wallack (1989). Wallack noted that 100,000 Americans would be dying in 1989 of causes directly related to alcohol, at a cost to society of more than $120 billion, and that alcohol-impaired driving would account for approximately one-quarter of these deaths and be the leading killer for youth age eighteen to twenty-four. Wallack also pointed out that before retiring as Surgeon General, Koop had called for increases in federal and state excise taxes on alcoholic beverages and called on the industry to stop advertising to youth. Wallack (1989, pp. 4–5) stated that "research conducted by the National Academy of Sciences and the National Bureau for Economic Research strongly supports the Surgeon General's position on excise taxes. Economic research suggests that a 'nickel a drink' increase would reduce both consumption and alcohol-related traffic fatalities. The effect on youth would be even greater. It is estimated that 8,000 to 11,000 highway deaths per year could be prevented, and $20 billion annually in Federal revenues generated, if Dr. Koop's tax recommendations are implemented. A tax hike would save lives and reduce the deficit. It is good public policy and good public health."

Wallack also cited a *Fortune*/CNN poll in December 1988 of 225 Fortune 1,000 chief executive officers that found that 88 percent wanted to increase alcohol excise taxes to reduce the federal deficit. In 1986, seventy-eight economists, including four Nobel Laureates, signed a petition calling for reduction of public health and other costs through substantial excise taxes on alcoholic beverages. Moreover, a February 1989 Gallup poll found that 69 percent of the general public wanted to raise the tax on beer and wine to the same rate as taxes on distilled spirits.

These findings are consistent with analyses of polls by Wagenaar and Streff (1990), who found that Michigan adults expressed high levels of public support for raising alcohol excise taxes (82 percent), prohibiting concurrent sales of alcohol and gasoline (74 percent), administratively suspending driver's licenses of those above the legal alcohol limit (67 percent), limiting the number of alcohol outlets via government regulation (63 percent), and lowering the legal limit for drivers to .005 (55 percent). The authors also cited eleven of fourteen national surveys between 1986 and 1989 as finding that three-fourths of respondents favored a tax increase. In addition, a 1986 survey indicated that 56 percent favored a thirty-day license suspension or an even more severe penalty for being caught while drunk driving.

Koop's (1989, p. 4) closing remarks to the drunk driving task force were:

> In this matter of drunk driving, the Surgeon General's role is virtually nothing more—but certainly nothing less—than public education. And by "the public," I include not only lay citizens but also my colleagues at all levels of government—Federal, State, and local—and my fellow citizens in the private sector, both in profit and nonprofit activities.
>
> As Surgeon General, I have a responsibility to speak to them *all.* And I intend to, whether they are comfortable with what I have to say or not.

He had some candid final words about the negative behavior of the broadcasters and advertising association representatives whom he had invited to participate; they had declined and suggested that the workshop be canceled. He said (1989, p. 97) that "I don't wish to dwell on the NAB's [National Association of Broadcasters] criticism because it may be nothing more than an early and predictable phase in the industry's learning process. . . . I respectfully suggest that Mr. Fritts, Mr. O'Toole, and Mr. Helm—and their colleagues—review the history as I did, because the American people may now be—in terms of alcohol—where we were 25 years ago in terms of tobacco."

He also took to task the chairman of the National Commission Against Drunk Driving, who asked him to postpone the meeting and also asked that all panelists be notified that the Department of Transportation had given $100,000 to the commission to do a sixteen-month assessment of drinking-driving initiatives. The chairman was invited to speak, but the day before the workshop opened, he sent a fax to Koop demanding that in return for that speech, Koop would not release conclusions or recommendations of two of the panels until the sixteen months beyond whenever the commission started its inquiry. Of course Koop found this unacceptable. The meeting managed to do rather well without the presence of either the media association representatives or those of the alcohol-industry-subsidized National Commission Against Drunk Driving.

It is almost inevitable that federal taxes on alcohol will soon increase sharply, not only because of public health–oriented campaigns to cut consumption through such increases, but because the administration and Congress are seeking every politcally acceptable avenue to reduce the crushing burden of public debt. The current administration-sponsored plan for increases in excise taxes on wine and beer to bring in as much as $3 billion more per year (McNicholas, 1990) is being fought vigorously by the National Wine Coalition, which estimates that the proposed tax increases would result in the loss of 94,000 wine-industry jobs and $6 billion in business activity. However, the pressure to raise more federal funds to reduce the deficit was so strong that the 1991 budget now calls for an increase in taxes from the current 16 cents per six-pack of beer to 32 cents, from 3 cents per 750 milliliter bottle of wine to 21 cents, and from $12.50 per 100-proof gallon on spirits to $13.50. These federal alcohol tax increases will raise an estimated $8.8 billion in additional taxes over the next five years.

The Washington-based Center for Science in the Public Interest (CSPI) (1990) has conducted case studies of potential alcohol tax revenues for fourteen states and the District of Columbia, finding that those jurisdictions alone could raise more than $1.3 billion in new revenues by increasing excise taxes (or "user fees") a nickel a drink, as recommended for all states in 1989 by outgoing Surgeon General Koop as a means of reducing drinking-driving and other alcohol problems. The CSPI analysis found that for the fifteen jurisdictions, inflation since 1966 had reduced the relative cost of alcoholic beverages by 50 percent or more. The CSPI also recommended that alcohol tax rates per unit of alcohol be equalized for beer, wine, and liquor (in most states, wine and beer are still taxed at lower rates than liquor).

In 1990, more than thirty states considered bills to increase alcohol taxes, which were passed in seven states; but California turned down the initiatives to raise alcohol taxes a "nickel-a-drink." The estimated $800 million that would have been raised by the initiative was to have been spent to finance health and safety programs currently burdened by costs associated with alcohol and other drugs: 25 percent for trauma treatment, 24 percent for treatment and prevention of alcohol and drug abuse, 21 percent for law enforcement, and 15 percent each for mental health programs and aid to victims of alcohol abuse (Campbell, 1990). While the initiative raised more than 1,150,000 signatures in getting on the ballot, it received only 31 percent of the votes in the election. The alcohol industry, which spent more than $27 million to fight the nickel-a-drink initiative, sponsored a competitive initiative that would have raised less than $200 million in taxes; and it too was defeated.

Other factors that defeated the nickel-a-drink initiative included additional competition from twenty-six non-alcohol-related initiatives (only two of them requiring any public funding were approved in that recession-anxiety atmosphere), some public reluctance to earmarking of tax funds for special purposes instead of for the general fund, and the fact that Congress had just approved additional federal taxes on alcohol (see earlier). It is likely that some nickel-a-drink tax proposals will come up again soon in California, although perhaps through a regular legislative bill rather than via the apparently even more equivocal initiative route.

The Alcohol Industry's Defensive Tactics

The Wine Institute of San Francisco has been one of the industry's leaders in rearguard damage control, in part by somewhat dissociating wine from beer as being an adjunct of gracious living rather than an intoxicant. At a meeting of thirty California winemakers who came to Washington to meet with legislators, agency and administration officials, allied associations, and the media during their annual Washington Week, Wine Institute President John De Luca announced the formation of a "National Wine Coalition" "to educate the American public about the positive aspects of wine." It will be headquartered in New York, with offices in Washington, and will bring together growers, suppliers, wholesalers, and wine consumers, as well as winemakers, in programs of public education and promotion. Allied industries such as restaurants, hotels, food commodities, and anti–alcohol abuse groups are being invited to join.

The Wine Institute's director of industry affairs, Jerry Vorpahl, who will head up the coalition, said, "We're going to broadcast the story of wine's contribution to culture and society for thousands of years in religion, art, diplomacy, and at the dinner table. With the plethora or warning labels, signs, and unsubstantiated claims by an assortment of reform-minded organizations, the consumer has a right to know the values and pleasures of wine when used intelligently and in moderation" (Lewis, 1989e, p. 7). Patricia Schneider, formerly with the Wine Institute, is executive director of the new American Wine Alliance for Research and Education (AWARE) in San Francisco. Chairman Allen Shoup announced that the organization would engage in research and public education "to provide a balanced view about wine's cultural values and proper role in society," with plans to "support the development and distribution of objective information and to work with various organizations on effective programs to reduce alcohol misuse" (Lewis, 1989i, p. 7).

The Wine Institute more recently widely circulated a seven-page glossy pamphlet entitled *A Scientific Look at Wine* to combat what the industry calls the "neoprohibitionists" who have made alcohol the target of higher taxes, warning signs in restaurants, and health warnings on bottles, and have blamed it as a major cause of highway deaths. The pamphlet cites an old study that indicated that those who drink up to one or two drinks a day may derive health benefits from wine, since they tend to live longer than total abstainers. It contended that moderate use of wine is good for the elderly and has social value in terms of feelings of worth and competence: that over half of large-city hospitals found that offering a wine service to their patients improved their morale. The pamphlet tried to distance wine from beer and spirits by claiming that only 2 percent of the people arrested for drunk driving drank only wine, and that Italians drink about ten times as much wine as Americans and yet have one of the lowest rates of alcoholism (Schreibman, 1990).

In refutation of the claim that moderate consumption of wine is healthier than abstention, the *Harvard Medical School Health Letter* ("Alcohol, Heart Disease, and Mortality," 1989) published the results of a British study in which nearly 8,000 men age forty to fifty-nine were examined and questioned about their health and habits. They were then followed for an average of seven and a half years to monitor their deaths and causes of death. This study also confirmed the U-shaped curve on alcohol consumption and mortality, *but* it found that this U-shaped curve only held for those *who already had heart disease!* Many of the men in this group were giving up drinking in response to their illness: Low intake was a response to heart disease, not the cause of it.

Congruent findings emerged from our first national survey of the drinking practices of those twenty-one or older (Cahalan, Cisin, and Crossley, 1969), in which one-third of the abstainers reported being former drinkers. One of their leading reasons for quitting drinking was "poor health." Furthermore, abstainers as a group are in poorer condition than moderate drinkers economically and psychologically, as detailed in our 1969 book and also in my article in *Circulation* (Cahalan, 1981). In the 1981 article I pointed out that while research has shown moderate drinkers to have lower blood pressure and harmful cholesterol levels, there are many life-style reasons other than the salubrious effects of alcohol why moderate drinkers have better health than either abstainers or heavier drinkers. These include the likelihood of moderation in a host of other life-style behaviors on the part of those who drink fairly often but always in small quantities. Yet the alcohol industry still continues to give a high priority to publicizing the story that moderate drinking has been medically proven to be good for health.

The beer and distillery industries also have continued to fight hard to maintain their markets and their political influence. In attempting to offset the decline in alcohol sales that began in the 1980s, beer companies are intensifying their campaign to make beer drinkers out of women, with such advertising themes as, "You don't have to be a man to appreciate a great beer." Laurie Lieber (University of California at San Diego, 1990a, 6–7) of the Trauma Foundation of San Francisco, who monitors alcohol advertising themes, points out that the messages aimed at women in television commercials, billboards, and magazine and newspaper ads are only part of the problem. Beverage advertisers appear to be "buying silence" in the media—using their economic clout to inhibit publication of articles directed to women about the dangers of more than small quantities of alcohol.

As noted in the same article, William Montague's comments in the *Chronicle of Philanthropy* state that some of this buying of silence is through contributions by the alcohol industry to agencies to forestall actions against its interests. The anti-drunk driving group Remove Intoxicated Drivers, the National Council on Alcoholism, and Mothers Against Drunk Driving used to accept industry contributions but no longer do so, although Students Against Drunk Driving (SADD) still is heavily subsidized by Anheuser-Busch. The National Commission Against Drunk Driving, the American Council on Alcoholism, and the Health Education Foundation of Washington, the Alcohol Policy Council, the Congressional Black Caucus Foundation, and BACCHUS all get substantial support from the beer and spirits industries. U.S. and Canadian brewing companies support an Alcoholic Beverage Medical Research Foundation, which since 1982 has channeled nearly $9 million to fund medical and social science researchers who are sympathetic to industry interests. The University of California at San Francisco has received more than $900,000 from the Gallo wine interests, Seagram recently gave $4 million to Harvard for alcohol research, and Anheuser-Busch supports the journal *Alcohol, Drugs, and Driving* published by the University of California at Los Angeles. As Ernest P. Noble, former director of the NIAAA and now a professor of alcohol studies at the University of California at Los Angeles, comments, "When I see scientists being funded by the industry, I like to know if they have complete freedom to interpret their research. My guess is that if they interpret it against the industry's interests then they are not going to be funded in the future. That's not always the case, but it happens" (University of California at San Diego, 1990d, p. 15).

The industry also is trying hard to cope with the present trend on the part of advocacy agencies and some professional health-oriented associations to link alcohol with other drugs. "Is alcohol a drug? Alcohol companies are working feverishly to keep their products out of the nation's drug strategy," is the opening line of a CSPI article in the initial number of the periodical *Booze News* (Center for Science in the Public Interest, 1989, p. 1). Wine trade associations are promoting wine as an agricultural/food product and attempting to move jurisdiction from the Bureau of Alcohol, Tobacco, and Firearms to the Department of Agriculture. Beer producers, under the leadership of August Busch, III, are decrying the linkage of beer with drugs. New moderation messages paid for by the industry are airing on television and are sent to members of Congress. But even alcohol industry allies like Edward Fitts, president of the National Association of Broadcasters, believe these messages fail to address the strong level of public concern. He told a recent Beer Wholesalers convention that "there is an ill wind blowing" and that their ads portraying sexy and youthful life-styles are the most problematic (Center for Science in the Public Interest, 1989, p. 1).

To sum up the current status of alcohol-problem primary prevention: Although substantial inroads have been made recently, constant vigilance and steady campaigning (without overzealousness with consequent risk of a backlash) will be needed by social agencies in order to prevail over the very determined opposition of the well-financed alcohol industry. As Mosher and Jernigan (1989, p. 245) put it,

> An exciting drama is unfolding in the public health field today. . . . A new consensus is emerging regarding the prevention of alcohol-related problems, one of our most serious health issues. Built on public health policy and experience, this new alcohol policy movement offers the entire public health field the opportunity to reach new constituencies. In keeping with the nature of the problems it is designed to prevent, the approach cuts across ideological, racial, ethnic, and socioeconomic divisions in our society and provides the means to build a coalition for broad social change in regard to health policy.
>
> As was the case with the anti-smoking and other public health movements that preceded it, this new alcohol policy movement is opposed by powerful economic and political interests. Classic tactics to divert and blunt health policy reform are now a familiar part of the alcohol field—industry denials of health risks associated with their product; industry-financed research designed to cast doubt on studies documenting adverse consequences of its use; strong-arm lobbying at local, State, and Federal levels, including massive contributions to legislators; industry "donations" to a variety of social groups to deter their participation in the reform movement; massive advertising budgets that are used to silence and shape media attention to alcohol problems; and much more. That the tactics have a familiar ring is no coincidence: many alcohol companies are owned by tobacco conglomerates, and draw on that industry's experience in conducting a

> sophisticated and heavily financed campaign to blunt efforts to prevent alcohol-related disease.

In Chapter Six, we will summarize some of the recent developments in the treatment of alcoholism that are most relevant in improving the effectiveness of secondary and tertiary prevention of the recurrence of alcohol problems.

CHAPTER SIX

Improving the Treatment of Alcoholism

This chapter focuses primarily on alcoholism treatment issues that have implications for prevention practices or policies, and thus does not attempt to provide a detailed discussion of all of the various modes of treatment of alcoholism as currently practiced in the United States. One helpful discussion of treatment is Segal (1988). My book *Understanding America's Drinking Problem: How to Combat the Hazards of Alcohol* (1987) also summarizes recent trends in treatment philosophies, politics, and economics.

Alcoholism treatment has become big business in this era of increased third-party coverage under various types of health plans and the expenditure of many millions of dollars in treatment costs each year through city, state, and federal programs. According to the 1987 NDATUS survey jointly commissioned by NIAAA and NIDA, the total financing of treatment in 1987 for alcohol and drugs was estimated at $3,020,077,000, of which about $1.7 billion was for alcohol and $1.3 billion for drugs (Lewis, 1989a, p. 3). The largest share of these costs was third-party payments (including Blue Cross/Blue Shield, Health Maintenance Organizations, and other insurance carriers) totaling $939,410,000, of which alcoholism treatment funding was $592,447,000 of private third-party payments, and drug abuse was reported at $346,963,000. The second largest funding source for alcoholism was state governments (including federal block grants administered by ADAMHA), totaling $345,023,000. Client fees for alcoholism treatment amounted to $236,531,000.

Alcohol-only facilities decreased from 2,729 in 1982 to 1,708 in the 1987 National Drug and Alcohol Treatment Unit Survey, a 37 percent decline. Drug-only treatment units experienced a lesser decline, from 1,514 to 1,075, which represented a 29 percent drop. Combined alcohol and drug treatment units rose dramatically from 1,504 in 1982 to 4,083 in 1987, for a jump of 171 percent (Lewis, 1989a).

Over recent years, there has been mounting professional uneasiness over the growing costs of alcoholism treatments but without any apparent diminution of severe drinking problems and without effective measures of the efficacy of treatment. As Miller and Hester (1986, pp. 162–163) put it, "American treatment of alcoholism follows a standard formula that appears to be impervious to emerging research evidence, and has not changed significantly for at least two decades." The standard treatment is to resort to Alcoholics Anonymous, alcoholism education, confrontation, perhaps disulfiram, group therapy, and a little individual counseling. In their review of treatment methods, Miller and Hester pointed to a different set of practices as being of demonstrated effectiveness: aversion therapies, behavioral self-control training, community reinforcement, marital and family therapy, social skills training, and stress treatment. They concluded that any treatment should have a proven track record for effectiveness. They also urged that clients be matched to interventions proven to be optimal for persons with their characteristics, and that clients be informed and active participants in their own treatment programs.

While the average actual treatment regimen may not have advanced very much during the last generation, just during the last few years there have been some promising steps in the directions advanced by Miller and Hester. As will be discussed later, the NIAAA has now been accorded the funds to act on the recommendations from a series of several large-scale inquires by the Institute of Medicine into needed reforms in alcoholism treatment and research into cost-effectiveness.

It can be argued that almost every aspect of alcoholism treatment—except perhaps the detoxification process—can play a material role at least in tertiary prevention (helping to keep the problem from becoming any worse) and certainly in secondary prevention (helping to stop or minimize drinking problems that already exist), because the real definition of "effective treatment" is that which helps the client to avoid relapsing into drinking problems. And even the way alcoholism and other alcohol problems are defined and described by authority figures in the treatment field can play a material part in primary prevention. For example, the disease model of alcoholism, popularized during the last fifty years with the best of intentions for getting alcoholics more humane treatment, may have had the side effect of contributing to the denial process among problem drinkers. They tend to fasten on an either/or disease model to protest that they are "not there yet": "—I ain't what you'd call a real alcoholic."

Heather and Robertson, British behavioral psychologists, in their book *Problem Drinking* (1989), make common cause with Miller and Hester (1986) both in their extensive documentation of the effectiveness of behavioral methods compared to disease-model treatment of alcohol problems, and in their conviction that the disease theory of alcoholism does not fit in well with prevention programs because its either-or nature encourages denial of early-stage drinking problems instead of encouraging behavioral and environmental learning changes.

The Disease Theory

Such cautions are voiced by Fingarette (1988, pp. 4–5):

> Many knowledgeable people are greatly disturbed by criticism of the disease concept. They argue that the labeling of alcoholism as a disease frees alcohol abusers from feeling guilty or ashamed of their drinking, and thereby makes it easier for them to

> seek treatment. This has the ring of plausibility, and yet reports suggest that the disease concept does not always have this effect. Many heavy drinkers view the label "diseased" and "alcoholic" as stigmatizing, and so they reject help under such terms. Furthermore, the notion that this disease causes people to lose the ability to control their drinking may discourage a heavy drinker from trying to stop in the (false) belief that it's hopeless. Then, too, some drinkers will not seek help if they believe that lifelong abstinence is the only "remedy" for uncontrolled heavy drinking; the thought of never being able to have even an occasional social drink is too disheartening. Finally, proponents of arguments for retaining the disease concept as a useful tool take it for granted that getting the drinker into alcoholism treatment will make a big difference—an assumption that is not supported by the scientific evidence . . . .
>
> The litany of excuses and denials is endless. These people deny the significance of their heavy drinking by showing, often quite correctly, that in one respect or another they do not fit the profile of symptoms of the so-called disease. In this way, the prevalence of the disease concept narrows the scope of inquiry, concern, and help.

Another writer skeptical about the implications of the disease theory is Peele (1987), who has been a frequent critic of the contention accompanying the disease model that those who are true alcoholics never are able to resume normal drinking. He reports that many variations have been found in the reported rates of controlled drinking by former alcoholics. Reports of such outcomes were common for a brief period ending in the middle to late 1970s, but by the early 1980s, a consensus had emerged in the United States that severely alcoholic subjects and patients could *not* resume moderate drinking. But then (Peale contends) in the mid 1980s when the rejection of the possibility of a return to controlled drinking appeared to be unanimous, a new series of studies reported resumption of controlled drinking was quite plausible and did not depend on the initial severity of alcoholics' drinking problems. As he sees it, variations in controlled-drinking outcomes—and in views about the possibility of such outcomes—are susceptible to changes in the scientific climate and differences in individual and cultural outlooks, and such cultural factors have considerable clinical implications.

As discussed in Chapter Seven of my 1987 book and by many other authors, much heat and emotion have been generated within the last generation over the validity of the disease concept, with many Alcoholics Anonymous–oriented advocates contending bitterly that those who question the reality of alcoholism as a disease are encouraging alcoholics to kill themselves by resuming drinking. Fortunately for long-term medical and scientific progress, more and more specialists in clinical practice or research have become tired of that Aristotelian either/or battle and have been advocating an eclectic approach in which it is made clear to treatment clients that once someone has a recurrent drinking problem, it is indeed courting disaster to try to resume drinking. On the other hand, the person will be accepted for treatment if he or she agrees to *consider* abstinence as a worthwhile ultimate goal.

Recent advocates of a rapprochement between believers and skeptics of the disease model include Nathan and McCrady (1987, p. 109), who say that "behavioral treatment with abstinence as a goal and behavioral treatment methods with moderation as a goal share important theoretical, historical, and methodological assumptions, even as they differ in strategy, tactics, and ultimate goals." Miller (1987, p. 147) ends an article with this plea for tolerance in treatment goals: "In the heat of 'abstinence versus controlled drinking goal' debates it is easy to lose sight of the fact that our ultimate goal is always the same: to alleviate problems and suffering related to alcohol use, and to prevent such problems from reemerging. No one approach can truthfully claim preeminence as a means to this end. Both abstinent and problem-free drinking outcomes occur (with and without intervention), and both are to be regarded as successful realizations of the common goal. A worthy search now is for greater knowledge of what methods work best with which individuals, and for better methods to motivate at-risk drinkers to alter their hazardous use patterns before inflicting greater damage upon themselves and others."

The trend toward prevention-mindedness in the alcoholism field is evident in the comments of Peter Nathan (1988), a clinical psychologist who was then the director of the Rutgers Center for Alcohol Studies, an organization once completely dedicated to the Alcoholics Anonymous abstinence-only point of view. He says that current data on efforts to prevent alcoholism indicate that we are better able to prevent some of the consequences of alcohol misuse, such as alcohol-related car crashes and fetal alcohol syndrome, than chronic alcohol dependence itself. He also points out that a review of outcomes of treatment for long-term alcohol dependence indicates that nine out of ten alcohol-dependent persons receive no treatment for the disorder in any given year, and that when treatment is provided for long-term alcohol-dependent persons, it has only slightly positive effects. He observes (1988, p. 683) that "as a result, many clinicians and researchers have concluded that rather than exclusive preoccupation with long-term alcoholics, early intervention with persons who are just beginning to abuse alcohol may be a more effective use of resources."

New Perspectives in NIAAA

Indeed, NIAAA officials as well as a wide range of clinical and research specialists are now taking an increasingly eclectic view on the necessity to keep many treatment options open in dealing with such a complex phenomenon as alcohol problems. This is especially evident in three recent weighty reports on the status of alcoholism treatment that have been sponsored by the NIAAA, two of which have been dealt with in the preceding chapter.

One of these is the NIAAA's *Seventh Special Report to the U.S. Congress on Alcohol and Health* (1990). In its eighth chapter, special approval is accorded to the diagnostic criteria in the *Diagnostic and Statistical Manual of Mental Disorders* (DSM-III-R) of the American Psychiatric Association and the *International Classification of Diseases* (ICD-9) of the World Health Organization, both of which differentiate nondependent problem drinking (there called "alcohol abuse") from alcohol dependence (alcoholism). These conditions are summarized as follows: "Alcohol abuse represents a pattern of heavy drinking accompanied by social, psychological, and/or medical problems that are directly related to alcohol use, while alcoholism is characterized by physical and psychological dependence that results in impaired control over drinking. Both diagnostic systems offer specific criteria to guide the diagnostic process and represent a general evolution toward detailed assessment of alcohol use disorders using multiple criteria" (National Institute on Alcohol Abuse and Alcoholism, 1990, p. xxvii). The use of multiple criteria and avoidance of simplistic diagnoses in the treatment of alcoholism have long been advocated by such clinical specialists as Schuckit (1973) and Pattison (1974). In addition, as discussed later, careful attention to the individual client's social and other environmental characteristics is beginning to receive more emphasis in research on the treatment of alcohol problems.

The report even goes so far as to say that while controlled drinking is not an appropriate treatment goal for alcoholics, alcohol abusers (that is, individuals who are not dependent) may benefit from interventions aimed at moderating their consumption, with behavioral self-control training being the most frequently used approach. But it cautions (1990, p. xxix) that "research concerning its effectiveness is limited and has thus far produced mixed results." The idea that clients' backgrounds need to be carefully differentiated is again emphasized in the case of driving-while-impaired (DWI) individuals. The report cites research showing that drivers at risk of DWI offenses should be assessed for their general propensity to engage in risky behavior, heavy alcohol consumption, and their skills at estimating their own blood alcohol concentration.

As to who should have the prime responsibility for diagnosing the alcohol-abuse/alcoholism status of patients: The report says that the primary care physician is in a key position to make early diagnosis, but that many of these physicians are poorly trained about alcohol. Schuckit (1987) notes that many have erroneous stereotypes of most alcoholics as having antisocial personality disorders. Among 294 adult patients, primary care physicians identified only 40 percent of those carefully diagnosed as being alcoholics. Alcoholic patients who were not identified as such were more likely to have a coexisting depressive disorder (Coulehan and others, 1987).

The report speaks approvingly of behavioral approaches to early intervention, stating that there is growing evidence that brief interventions utilizing advice or counseling should cover a period of time. Miller and associates found that minimal intervention of three hours of assessment, advice, and encouragement and a self-help manual based on behavioral self-control training got the same results as six to eighteen weeks of individual behavioral self-control training therapy; all groups showed significant reduction in consumption (Miller and Taylor, 1980; Miller, Taylor, and West, 1980; Miller, Gribskov, and Mortell, 1981; Miller and Baca, 1983).

The NIAAA 1990 *Special Report* noted that *relapse prevention* is a behavioral approach that has been getting increasing research attention. It cites a model proposed by Marlatt (1985) suggesting that drinking episodes can be analyzed according to five major variables: exposure to situations that hold high risk for drinking, use or nonuse of successful coping responses in such situations, enhanced self-efficacy for coping or reduced self-efficacy for noncoping, expectancies about the effects of alcohol in the situation, and the abstinence-violation effect (the person's cognitive and emotional reaction on his or her drinking of alcohol).

The NIAAA *Special Report* further emphasizes the growing attention to the individual characteristics of clients in its comments on Miller's (1989) self-matching approach, in which each client is presented with a list of carefully described options and is encouraged to choose the approach that seems most appropriate for him or her. The self-chosen option may be more likely to be followed, thereby improving the chances for more rapid recovery.

Some Newer Perspectives on Improving Treatment

The Institute of Medicines NIAAA-sponsored study, *Prevention and Treatment of Alcohol Problems: Research Opportunities* (1989), which was released while the NIAAA's *Seventh Special Report* was in preparation, offered many perspectives about treatment research that dovetailed with the NIAAA's own report. These include the following:

The summary on research opportunities in treatment notes that NIAAA, after supporting mainly biomedical and psychosocial research, has now created a Division of Clinical and Prevention Research and is making funds available for new research projects. This section commented that the maturing of the baby boom population means that an increasingly large number is now passing through the peak prevalence of abuse and dependence in the ages of thiry-five to forty-five, and that other trends that may influence the demand for treatment services include changes in the nuclear family, increases in the number of homeless persons, the aging of the population, and the deinstitutionalization of psychiatric patients.

In commenting on studies of the effectiveness of various treatment modalities, the report noted that since 1980, more than 250 new studies have been published on the outcomes of a wide variety of modes of treatment, including pharmacotherapy, aversion techniques, psychotherapy and counseling, didactic approaches, mutual-help groups, behavioral self-control, conjoint therapies, broad-spectrum treatment, and relapse prevention. Behavioral self-control has been the single most studied modality since 1980, but evidence for its effectiveness is mixed. Some promise has been found in conjoint family efforts, particularly when tied in with family problems other than alcohol as such. Combinations of modalities enjoying relatively high success rates include detoxification and health care, Alcoholics Anonymous, lectures and films, group therapy, individual counseling, recreational and occupational therapy, medication, and aftercare group meetings. In many of the studies the absence of random assignment and control groups means that absolute effectiveness cannot be assumed, but the authors of the report expressed confidence that continued research on program effectiveness will pay off in the long run.

The IOM Research Opportunities authors speculated that much might be learned from research on the common processes operating both in alcohol and other psychoactive substance use disorders, including nicotine.

One of the major conclusions in the IOM report was that within the past ten years, matching patients with *individualized* treatments has shown possibilities for improvement in the effectiveness of treatment. Four patient variables appear to be especially predictive of improvement: social stability and social supports, psychiatric diagnosis, severity of alcohol use or dependence, and presence of antisocial personality disorders. "Matching" programs permit patients to select among alternative treatments, employ feedback designs assigning patients on the basis of statistical hunches as to the effectiveness of particular treatment, and permit testing the effects of elements provided in addition to the usual treatment. Obviously, for the matching process to be effective, it is necessary to have clear specifications for both the characteristics of individuals and the components of particular treatment approaches. The IOM report authors emphasized that there is urgent need for a great deal more research on treatment effectiveness, and concrete steps toward implementing this goal are being taken, following the recommendations in yet another (and even more recent) IOM study, to be discussed later. This IOM research opportunities report notes that multisite studies will be needed because of local scarcities of certain relatively rare conditions, for example, pancreatitis. This recommendation was an opening wedge for the multisite nature of the "patient matching" NIAAA project described later.

The report called for much more research into treatment costs, benefits, and cost offsets as a guide for treatment policy in the future. Costs of treatment should be considered within effectiveness. "Cost offset studies [properly should] measure post-treatment health care costs (including the cost of ongoing alcohol treatment) and compare them with total health care costs this group would have incurred if no alcohol treatment has been received" (Institute of Medicine, 1989, p. 15). While available studies have many flaws, they do suggest that treatment contributes to sustained reductions in costs. "A question of great interest is the extent to which coverage for alcohol treatment might actually stimulate the use of other health care services, thereby improving the patient's condition and reducing his overall use of general medical services in the long run" (pp. 15–16).

The report also called for intensified studies of the effects of various insurance or other payment modes, and on whether private expenditures for treatment may result in reduced public costs in such things as less crime and accidents.

In discussing the funding mechanisms for research, the report said that "in particular, the use of prevention trials to evaluate intervention effectiveness should become an established tradition at NIAAA. Significant opportunities now exist for NIAAA/NAtional Institute on Drug Abuse (NIDA), and the Office of Substance Abuse Programs [Prevention] (OSAP) to conduct controlled prevention demonstration projects with well-designed prevention components" (p. 17).

The report noted that when NIAAA created its new Division of Clinical and Prevention Research in 1988, treatment research was accorded more stature. However, only one of NIAAA's twelve research centers currently conducts alcoholism treatment research; it is suggested that NIAAA might consider funding additional centers for such research in collaboration with another federal agency, and that NIAAA might also expand treatment research in the existing centers.

Further, "the committee commends the recent designation of set-aside funds within block grants for use in evaluating alcohol and drug abuse treatment programs and in assessing the quality of various forms of treatment. The policy could well encourage linkages among university-affiliated researchers, state agencies, and treatment facilities" (p. 18).

The IOM report summary observed that NIAAA's operating mechanisms appear to be sufficiently flexible to permit the implementation of most of the expanded research activities recommended, and that "by coordinating activities among such interest groups as research centers, pharmaceutical companies, hospital chains, insurance companies, and state and federal agencies, NIAAA may be able to guide treatment research on alcohol problems along an increasingly coherent and productive path" (p. 18).

Shortly after the IOM report recommendations were presented, NIAAA took steps to fund a new, long-term patient-matching treatment initiative that will involve NIAAA in-house staff researchers and clinicians, eight extramural research sites, and a data processing and coordinating center. Private as well as public treatment programs will work with university- and hospital-affiliated treatment research specialists to investigate which are the most effective strategies for patient-treatment matching, which will entail study of such variables as different psychological and behavioral characteristics, severity of alcohol dependence, and such demographic characteristics as age, gender, ethnic group, and family history of alcoholism.

The project was funded for $2 million for fiscal 1990. The eight extramural research sites include the University of Connecticut; the Center for Alcohol and Addiction Studies in Providence, Rhode Island; the University of Washington; the Research Institute on Alcoholism in Buffalo, New York; the University of Houston; the Veterans Administration Medical Center in Charleston, South Carolina; the University of New Mexico; and the University of Wisconsin at Milwaukee (Doria, 1990).

Still another massive Congress-initiated Institute of Medicine study has been released, entitled *Broadening the Base of Treatment for Alcohol Problems* (1990). This study was authorized in 1986 and charged with the tasks of critically reviewing available research knowledge in the United States and other countries regarding alternative approaches for treatment and rehabilitative services for alcoholism and alcohol abuse, assessing comparative cost-effectiveness of such services, reviewing financing alternatives available to the public, and making recommendations for policies and programs of research, planning, administration, and reimbursement for treatment.

The Committee for the Study of Treatment and Rehabilitation Services for Alcoholism and Alcohol Abuse consisted of sixteen persons with a wide variety of professional experience in treatment, counseling, and research into the economics and cultural aspects of alcohol. The committee's objectives were carried out by an experienced IOM staff, with review of the final report by members of the National Academy of Sciences, the National Academy of Engineering, and the Institute of Medicine itself.

At the outset of the report, it was emphasized that in keeping with its legislative charge, the objective of the inquiry was to focus largely on treatment rather than prevention. (While prevention and treatment are inextricably bound together, prevention was to be covered intensively in a separate, concurrent IOM research inquiry, discussed previously.) The report is indeed a weighty tome, both physically—more than 600 pages set in small type—and in content. It is hard to imagine many congresspeople struggling through it, even though it is obviously full of important implications for public policy, so it is presumed that brief action-oriented summaries are being prepared by congressional staffs. The following brief summary merely attempts to sketch out a few hints as to its contents.

The central principle on which the inquiry was founded was that any viable treatment system has to entail both a broad communitywide treatment effort (to identify individuals with alcohol problems through early intervention and refer them for treatment) and specialized treatment resources (with provision for comprehensive pretreatment assessment, the matching of particular individuals to specific treatment services, and careful assessment of the outcome of treatment).

Who is to be treated is defined as not only those with severe problems, but also others who would benefit from some intervention. As the report says (Institute of Medicine, 1990, p. 7), "'Alcohol problems' is felt to be a more inclusive definition of the object of treatment than such current alternatives as 'alcoholism' or 'alcohol dependence syndrome,' but it is nevertheless compatible with these widely used conceptual frameworks." As to *who provides treatment,* the report has a good word for Alcoholics Anonymous as the best-known source of care, but there is need for expanded efforts to obtain more detailed research on exactly what is involved in the various types of treatment. And as to whether treatment really *works,* the overseeing committee expresses a qualified "yes," but emphasizes that some improve without treatment and that some treatment can be harmful. The commttee was especially concerned over whether the growing use of coercion in bringing individuals in for treatment is doing harm.

On *availability* of treatment, the report found wide differences throughout the country. Private health insurance is now the largest single source of funding, followed by state and local government-funded programs with the newly augmented federal alcohol, drug abuse, and mental health block grants becoming a substantial component of state funding.

Because it is evident that a relatively small proportion of those with alcohol problems are in need of expensive specialized care, the report recommends that communities should provide intervention capabilities that can work efficiently in referring individuals to the types of services they really need. It also urges that the assessment of the individual's needs be carried out prior to assignment to a specific treatment intervention. "Care needs to be taken to insure that the assessment process is a positive experience and that its objectivity is maximized. In addition to its benefits for the individual entering treatment, the gathering of compatible assessment data across treatment setting would contribute greatly to our understanding of many aspects of the treatment process" (p. 8).

As with the IOM Research Opportunities study that preceded it (discussed earlier), the report devoted much attention to the necessity for *matching* the individual client to appropriate treatments. It also emphasized that there is need to ensure independent assessments of treatment outcomes by those not connected with providing the treatment. Obviously alluding to the NIAAA's plans for setting up several cooperative centers for a long-term integrated treatment matching program (implemented while this report's final draft was being reviewed), "The committee recommends that four or five model comprehensive treatment systems be implemented as demonstration projects in the immediate future, with provision for full, objective evaluation of all aspects of their functioning and of their treatment outcomes" (p. 9).

As for *payment* systems, the report stressed the necessity for the development of flexible benefit plans, whether public or private, that cover effective care that is assessed to be worth its cost. While the committee did not yet have on hand the data that prove that broadening the coverage for alcohol problems will result in lessened health costs in the long run, it hoped that this possibility would be considered. The report said that "should a net increase in the cost of treatment ensue, the committee is confident that it would not be excessive and that the total costs of treatment would continue to represent only a small fraction of the social costs of alcohol problems" (p. 12).

Appendix D to that report presents a systematic discussion of the growing prevalence (and problems) in *coercion* in alcohol treatment: the appendix was prepared by Constance Weisner, one of the members of the study's central committee. In it she defines coercion as a form of institutionalized pressure (with negative consequences as an alternative) that causes an individual to enter treatment, including familial pressure involving some institutional contact. She covers many types of coercion: civil commitments, diversion from the criminal justice system (as in drunk driving remedial treatment programs), workplace referrals, and family intervention programs. She notes that the type of coercion and its intensity vary greatly from one individual to another, but that there is general agreement that there is at least some form of coercion in most entries into treatment. However, there is little research on how effective or harmful coercion is, and under what circumstances. In an earlier paper, Weisner (1987) reminded us that the *majority* of clients in public alcoholism treatment programs now come from criminal justice or other coercive systems. She also noted (1986) that compulsory rehabilitation of the drinking driver has taken over much of the alcoholism treatment agenda throughout California in recent years: Only 28 percent of the caseload of three outpatient programs consisted of mandatory clients in 1979–80, but that figure reached 80 percent in 1983–84, when first violators of stiffened driving-under-the-influence laws were dumped into the alcoholism treatment load by the courts and probation officers. Recovery homes are also affected by this practice, because of the temptation to accept fee-paying DUI clients rather than often-indigent voluntary clients.

In summary: The current treatment of alcohol problems tends to be costly and inefficient, in part because heavy alcohol consumption usually is accompanied by a very stubborn addiction, in part because our culture has teetered between libertarian and moralistic attitudes concerning what really should be dealt with as a mammoth public health problem, and in part because institutional market factors have led to an overemphasis on late but very expensive treatment of alcohol addiction. However, there now appears to be an emerging emphasis within NIAAA and among professional alcohol specialists toward applying earlier and more effective primary and secondary prevention measures. It is hoped that the newer approaches toward evaluation of treatment regimens described earlier will help to lessen the prevalence of alcohol problems within the next few years.

PART THREE

Coping with Illicit Drugs

CHAPTER SEVEN

Have We Lost This War on Drugs?

The nation's experience of the last several years with the so-called "War on Drugs," as well as with several sporadic antidrug crusades of the past, raises the question of whether the declaration of such a war is not an almost certain recipe for losing it. A declaration of "war" carries much counterproductive surplus baggage, such as emotional political bombast that assumes there is a distinct, personalized foe to be crushed and that some quick, massive attack can defeat the foe. Personalizing the foe contributes to the risk of making it a war against distinctive minority groups reputed to be high in drug use, such as young African-American males. The term "war" implies military or paramilitary force, which fits in rather nicely (but rather counterproductively) with both the demand in some federal quarters for building many new huge prisons or concentration camps for the detention of the drug-using enemy within our midst, and also paramilitary incursions into Latin American countries to try to wipe out drugs at the source. If such a "war" is not won decisively after massive expenditures over a few years, there is a risk that disillusionment will lead to analogies with our dismal experience with our war in Vietnam.

It is ironic that the amount of federal resources spent on dealing with tobacco, alcohol, and other drug problems is sadly out of joint with the number of deaths attributable to those three types of substances. As reported by Ravenholt (1984), deaths from drugs other than tobacco or alcohol in 1980 totaled about 30,000 for the whole United States, or between 1 and 2 percent of total mortality. But the War on Drugs now gets the largest budget. Corresponding 1980 deaths from alcohol totaled about 100,000, and deaths from cigarettes probably totaled more than a half million—yet coping with tobacco got the smallest budget of the three.

The issue of "drugs" in 1989 became the single issue most frequently cited in national surveys by the U.S. public, both adults and teenagers, as the most important problem facing the country. Among teenagers, the same question was asked at intervals for a decade, with finding drugs "most important"ranged from only 2 percent in November-December 1982 to 57 percent in March-April 1990. Among adults, drugs were not rated as "most important" in surveys from 1977 until September 1989, when 63 percent selected drugs in first place, but it dropped sharply to 30 percent in April 1990 (Bezilla and Gallup, 1990).

Hypotheses ventured by Bezilla and Gallup for the sudden jump in attention to drugs as a public issue included: actual perception of the pervasiveness of drug use in respondents' areas increased; the lessening of the salience of other issues (such as international tensions, economic problems) from the standpoint of both the media and the general public permitted "drugs" to emerge as the "most important" issue; President Bush and Drug Czar Bennett had heavily publicized the War on Drugs recently; and the well-publicized drug-caused deaths of actor John Belushi and basketball star Len Bias may have been a factor (the last survey found 93 percent of adults and 97 percent of teenagers rating cocaine a "very dangerous" substance).

Certainly the United States would appear to have a mammoth drug problem. As Arnold Washton (in Debussmann, 1989, p. 1) said, Americans are only 2 percent of the world population, but consume 60 percent of the world's illicit drugs. In addition, millions abuse prescription drugs from tranquilizers to sleeping pills, and alcohol and tobacco also cause at least 450,000 deaths a year. Washton noted that "we are not only talking about cocaine or crack. We are now seeing high school kids who are getting high from typewriter correction fluid. We are becoming a nation of compulsive drug users."

Drug Wars Come and Go

The federal budget for the War on Drugs is now more than $8 billion a year, with Congress and the administration vying with each other to raise the ante. Yet a growing number of social scientists see it as a battle that is destined for failure. A heavily documented analysis by Morgan, Wallack, and Buchanan (1988) began by saying,

> The battle cry is "just say No." The ammunition combines a massive media campaign with billions of dollars of law enforcement hardware to battle the supply side of the problem. Furthermore, millions of Americans have been enlisted as foot soldiers to fight both dealers and users. It is the latest drug war and it is causing havoc and disarray almost equal to the drug use it battles.
>
> The rationale behind this latest drug war, like others before it, is to do away with substances which harm people. The ultimate purpose is to keep individuals from harming themselves. But is this the best way to prevent the harmful consequences of drug use? Why is the banner of morality and not health and welfare raised to spur action? What social, economic and political incentives lead a government to wage war on the personal habits of its citizens? Additionally, what are the implications for the prevention of harmful drug use in such an atmosphere?

In their historical review, the authors cited Makela and Viikari (1977) and Morgan (1978), who said that the state's interest in drugs entails four principal (and often conflicting) concerns: fiscal, economic, health and welfare, and public order. But how a government says it wants to deal with drug problems may reveal more about current political needs than about its intrinsic concerns about drugs. If a government puts greater value on the worth of its less powerful or fortunate citizens, it will look for a health and welfare solution, but it will go for a public-order solution if it places less value on the less fortunate than on the more fortunate. Morgan, Wallack, and Buchanan also contended that our government is acting as though it does not care much for the lower ranks in our society.

The use of the term "war" is seen as fostering a climate that is dividing our society, promoting a picture of an "enemy" in a self-righteous battle that will be morally and politically acceptable even if it is destined to be a losing one.

The authors documented how this drug war has much in common with other drug wars over the past 100 years, including the first anticocaine war against African-Americans just after the Civil War, the anti-Chinese war against opium dens in the 1870s, and the anti-Mexican marijuana war of the 1930s under Harry Anslinger. The common elements in such drug wars include the fostering of the notion of a new public menace, the introduction of antidrug legislation with hidden political agendas, and immediate emphasis on a harsh punitive criminal justice response instead of public health remedial measures.

Morgan, Wallack, and Buchanan described the current drug war as relying on four basic strategies: increased interdiction of drug supplies, increased penalties for drug users, increased detection and surveillance, and increased dissemination of proscriptive or negative norms ("just say no"). These strategies were not seen by the authors as likely to work, because interdiction leads to innovations in new drugs in more potent forms (for example, crack cocaine) that are easier to conceal; increased penalties are overcrowding our prisons and mixing drug users in with more violent criminals to emulate; increased surveillance in such forms as urine testing ("jar wars") is resulting in more cynicism and damage to civil rights; and the "just say no" symbolic crusade is likely to create much resentment and resistance among adolescents who really need positive rather than negative guidance.

Among the longer-term remedies to minimize drug use, Morgan, Wallack, and Buchanan saw more promise in the following: availability of contraceptive services to reduce teenage pregnancy and disease; expanded prenatal outreach and support programs; affordable pediatric and day care for all children; much better schools, and "clear and unmistakable ties between the world of school and the world of rewarding, worthwhile work." As they said, "Finally, drug problems will need to be seen as *socially generated public health problems* (1988, p. 124). This will result in a focus on policies that highlight the social and health sector or the community rather than the criminal justice system."

Readers who feel they need a refresher course on the history of psychoactive drug use in America should scan two classics in the field, Brecher (1972) and Musto (1987). Both have similar views on what they consider to be the politicized pattern of antidrug "wars" in the past, although they have somewhat different views as regards the dangers of different drugs.

Writing a generation ago, Brecher presented an outstanding summary of the history of the use of narcotics, tobacco (especially Freud's addiction), cocaine and stimulants like amphetamines, and marijuana. He had a much more permissive attitude about narcotics than the common view today, blaming them mostly because they are addictive rather than intrinsically harmful. But, as many contend today, he said that the only way to "solve" the problem of drugs is to deal with the demand. Amphetamines he considered not too dangerous in small doses, except if taken intravenously (this was before the days of "ice" and other designer amphetamines). He considered barbiturates and alcohol in the same league, recommended prohibition of advertising and the promotion of use of alcohol, and advocated warning labels. He was strongly opposed to nicotine because of its addictive properties and damage to health, and favored banning all cigarette advertising, point-of-sale promotion, and vending machines. On marijuana, he felt states should be left free to devise their own systems of control under a state-run monopoly, either private or public.

Musto (1987) noted that our memories are all too short about the big drug scares of the past that have come and gone, and that the national anxiety-born militancy about drugs is leading to even more intolerance of minorities and other poor people in the inner cities. In an interview in the *New York Times* (Kerr, 1987), Musto saw essentially two drug problems—one in middle-class America that may be waning after a twenty-year dalliance with illegal drugs, and the other among the poor. Of the latter, he said, "The question we must be asking now is not why people take drugs, but why do people stop. In the inner city, the factors that counterbalance drug use—family, employment, status within the community—often are not there. It is harder for people with nothing to say no to drugs." In a later discussion (personal communication, August 19, 1988), he agreed with me that the crack cocaine problem in our major cities may be much harder to cope with than past drug situations because the crack trade is becoming more and more a self-sustaining net enmeshing more and more ghetto youth. It serves as a short-term antidote to failure and despair while at the same time serving as a means of achieving upward mobility within the peer group and an enforcer of gang solidarity.

While Reinarman and Levine (1989) would not necessarily disagree with Musto's perspectives on crack, they placed even more emphasis on how the media and politicians have sensationalized its menace. While they conceded crack's dangers (especially for impoverished inner-city populations), they saw the campaign as just another in a long series of alarums and excursions dating from many generations ago, even back to the anti-Chinese agitation in California in the 1870s that focused on their opium smoking. Reinarman and Levine attributed much of the furor to the New Right elements in politics that have prospered by taking a hard line against immorality, such as in the election of Reagan as Governor of California. The New Right puts the blame on individual deviance, immorality, or weakness rather than environmental or social conditions. As they put it (1989, p. 561), "drug problems fit neatly onto this ideological agenda and allowed conservatives to engage in what might be called *sociological denial.* For the New Right, people did not abuse drugs because they were jobless or poor or depressed or alienated; they were jobless, poor, depressed, or alienated because they were weak, immoral, or foolish enough to use the wrong drugs." But even most Democratic politicians avidly pounced on drug issues to avoid the onus of being Soft on Drugs: Many candidates challenged each other to take urine tests as a sign of their commitment.

In summing up, the authors said (1989, p. 567) that "drug scares blame individual immorality and personal behavior for endemic social and structural problems, and they divert attention and resources from those larger problems. Drug scares have long linked drug use with racial minorities, the poor, or wayward youth and have blamed economic problems—and often other real and imaginary problems in society—on their use of drugs. Obscured or forgotten in all the political rhetoric on and media coverage of crack are the social and economic problems that underlie drug abuse, and that are much more widespread—especially poverty, unemployment, and the prospects of life in the permanent underclass. Dealing drugs, after all, is often quite accurately perceived by poor city kids as the highest-paying job they will ever get. . . ."

To turn to the current patterns of illicit drug use in the United States: The 1988 national household survey sponsored by NIDA and cited in an August 1989 *NIDA Capsules* press release (National Institute on Drug Abuse, 1989) found that twenty-eight million used illicit drugs at least once in the preceding year, down from thirty-seven million; current use also was down, from twenty-three million in 1985 to fourteen and a half million in 1988. Current cocaine use was cut in half from almost six million to less than three million.

Disputes on Magnitude of Drug Use

The 1988 household survey, released in August 1988, found that 862,000 used cocaine one or more times a week, compared to 647,000 three years earlier (Lewis, 1990f). However, a report prepared for the Senate Judiciary Committee chaired by Senator Joseph Biden (D-Del.), under the supervision of Mark

Kleiman (1990) of Harvard's Kennedy School of Government, contended that the number of hard-core cocaine addicts really was about 2.2 million, about two and one-half times the NIDA household survey estimate.

The Judiciary Committee report noted that it did not consider the household survey underestimation to be deliberate, but to have been occasioned by the sampling method. This method missed the homeless and those in institutions (such as prisons and drug treatment establishments), which would contain higher-than-average proportions of addicts. The Judiciary Committee report noted that drug treatment centers admit about 200,000 hard-core cocaine addicts per year, but fewer than one in ten are admitted in treatment. Also, while there may be only about 55,000 homeless addicts, their desperate straits should require attention disproportionate to their numbers. Finally, as the report pointed out, about 1.5 million hard-core cocaine addicts are arrested every year, but relatively few get treatment. (The report's estimates were based on state drug treatment admissions, FBI and National Institute of Justice information on arrests and arrestees, reports on drug abuse among the homeless from federal, state, and local officials and also the estimates of several academic, private, and government researchers.)

The report made five recommendations, based on Senator Biden's alternative National Drug Strategy (Senate bill S. 2650) proposed in the spring of 1990: (1) increase federal aid to cities hit hardest by the drug problem, (2) build treatment facilities into new prisons (the report recommended ten regional prisons and ten regional "boot camps" for addicts), (3) add 400,000 new beds to treatment centers, (4) double state and local law enforcement grants to $900 million, and (5) expand drug treatment research, especially on the development of medicines to treat addiction.

The five-part plan called for about $5.1 billion in expenditures, while the administration's drug strategy calls for about $2.7 billion for such treatment and enforcement categories. The report said, "While the Biden strategy sets ambitious targets, its cost pales in comparison to the price of inaction. For example, treating and caring for the 100,000 crack babies born each year now is costing as much as $7 billion. . . . Furthermore, hard-core addicts contract and spread AIDS, which exacts untold billions in financial and personal costs" (Committee on the Judiciary, United States Senate, 1990, p. 26).

A bill (S. 2649) related to the Biden bill was introduced at the same time by Senate Labor and Human Resources Committee Chairman Edward Kennedy (D-Mass.). It called for substantial increases in authorization for alcohol, drug abuse, and mental health services block grants to the states, additional funding for the OSAP program for pregnant and postpartum women and their infants, and for the Department of Education's Drug-Free Schools and Communities Act.

In introducing his bill, Kennedy told the Senate that the administration's drug strategy proposals were the "most recent evidence of the Administration's misplaced priorities. . . . This massive proposal is brimming with new threats to civil liberties, new criminal penalties, imposing forfeiture provisions, and novel interdiction strategies. Yet it contains no proposal for drug abuse prevention and only two treatment-related proposals" (Lewis, 1990g, pp. 1–2).

Biden added that "the Administration's legislation has focused in large part on reducing the number of casual users in the United States. This effort is critical, but the fact is that casual-drug use has been declining sharply in America in recent years. And the fact is that despite this decline, crime in America continues to rise, drug related medical emergencies are up, and the nightmare of crack babies and drug-related child abuse is soaring. This is the devastation caused by hard-core users. And this is the place where the Administration's strategy is most lacking. The only way to fight the crime menace is to fight the problem of hard-core addiction" (Lewis, 1990, p. 2).

In NIDA's opinion, crack has become the number one problem of concern. Of the eight million who used cocaine in 1988, 10.5 percent used it once a week or more, and over half of the weekly users made at least one attempt during the year to cut down (one sign of addiction). The Drug Abuse Warning Network (DAWN), which tracks medical emergencies and deaths, has found a fivefold increase since 1984 in medical emergencies because of cocaine, and cocaine-related deaths have more than doubled during that period. Emergency room episodes related to crack, or smoking freebase cocaine, have increased by a factor of 28 from 1984 to 1988. Further, as reported by Lana Harrison (1990) of the National Institute of Justice, the National Institute of Justice's Drug Use Forecasting studies, which use urinalyses to measure drug use among arrestees the last few days before arrest, shows a significant *increase* in cocaine use between 1974 and 1986.

What might explain the apparent discrepancy between the decreasing use of illicit drugs in NIDA's adult-population and youth surveys on the one hand, and the increase in cocaine-related medical emergencies and increase in cocaine use among arrestees on the other? The NIDA surveys are based on self-reports, which might be susceptible to underreporting at times of increased public disapproval of drug use; however, comparison of arrestees self-report of drug use as against the results of their urinalysis indicate a fair measure of agreement. Also, as pointed out by Harrison (1990) and in the Biden report, the NIDA High School Senior surveys do not cover school dropouts or those not in school on the day the survey is conducted. In addition, the household survey misses those institutionalized (in hospitals, jails, and so on) and the military, the homeless, and transients—and so the population surveys certainly underrepresent drug users to some extent. (One hint as to higher drug use among dropouts is the finding that among twenty- to forty-year-olds in the household surveys, 12 percent of full-time employed persons currently used illicit drugs compared to 24 percent of the unemployed.) Even so, as Harrison (1990) noted, the DAWN study also indicates that cocaine use may be causing more health consequences because of using this drug more intensely and/or the increased potency of several drugs in recent years.

While (as Harrison reported) NIDA and the National Institute of Justice are taking steps to improve their sampling methods, my own guess would be that the major part of the disparity between the survey findings and the DAWN medical reports may be because the health consequences of crack and cocaine are becoming more intense primarily due to more intensive use by the minority of more chronic users. But whatever the reason for the disparity, the DAWN findings of increased drug-related medical emergencies and deaths certainly help to bear out Senator Biden's contention that the evidence of a severely addicted subpopulation calls for much more emphasis on improving the resources for the *treatment* of such addictions, not a continuance of what he considers to be a one-sided preoccupation with punitive measures.

Changes in Drug Use

NIDA's press release said it is making progress in changing attitudes about illicit drug use: Among youth, 37 percent in 1985 had seen a "great risk" in smoking marijuana regularly; this increased slightly to 44 percent in 1988. NIDA reports a priority need for prevention efforts to reach the chronic users, children of substance abusers, the poorly educated, and the unemployed.

Findings of drug use trends among high school seniors in the 1988 NIDA-sponsored annual survey (Johnston, O'Malley, and Bachman, 1989) were partially reported in Chapter Two. These included a drop in crack use among seniors for the first time, and a continued decline in use of cocaine in any form in all three population subgroups (current seniors, those first interviewed as seniors and then later when in college, and young adult high school graduates eighteen to thirty years old). The authors (1989, p. 6) said, "We believe that the particularly intense media coverage of the hazards of crack cocaine, which took place quite early in what could have been a considerably more serious epidemic, likely had the effect of 'capping' that epidemic early by deterring many would-be users and by motivating many experimenters to desist use. (While 4.8 percent of seniors report having tried crack, only 1.6 percent report use in the past month, indicating noncontinuation by up to two-thirds of those who try it.)"

Aside from tobacco and alcohol, the leading drugs are marijuana, cocaine, and stimulants for all these youth groups in the late teens and twenties. High school seniors showed annual prevalence rates in 1988 of these three at 33 percent, 8 percent, and 11 percent, respectively. Among college students (follow-up of former high school senior samples), comparable annual prevalence rates in 1988 were 35 percent, 10 percent, and 6 percent. For all high school graduates one to twelve years out of school, they were 31 percent, 14 percent, and 7 percent.

As mentioned earlier, the encouraging finding of an apparent drop-off in crack use among high school seniors must be tempered by the realization that these school-population-based youth surveys do not cover school dropouts at all—the very group suspected of being the heaviest users of crack.

Many of the prevention efforts that were once the responsibility of NIDA and NIAAA have been turned over to OSAP since 1987. However, NIDA is still conducting extensive research with prevention implications, studying genetic or environmental factors that can make either for increased drug vulnerability or resistance to use, and identifying populations at especially high risk for drug addiction. Representative program announcements for available grants include studies of the drug abuse aspects of AIDS, research on school-based prevention intervention, behavioral and clinical research on vulnerability variables in drug abuse, and controlled clinical trials and evaluation research on effectiveness of drug abuse treatment systems. In addition, NIDA plans to establish drug abuse prevention research centers for minorities to facilitate a better understanding of the special problems and needs of Native Americans (including Alaskan Natives), Asian-Americans, African-Americans, Hispanics, and Hawaiian/Pacific Islanders.

The NIDA stance seems to be to position itself primarily as a research unit, distancing itself somewhat from the more politicized aspects of the current War on Drugs. Charles Schuster, current director of NIDA, closed his informative 1989 article (p. 26) with this long-haul perspective:

> We all know that the prevalence of drug abuse waxes and wanes. In my opinion, this vacillation occurs because activities to control drug abuse fluctuate. When prevalence rates are driven down

> by social interventions, there is a relaxation of control measures and the low-level endemic problem spreads. A parallel situation can be seen when vaccinations reduce the rate of an infectious disease. Everyone sighs with relief. Then people forget to have their children vaccinated and the disease rears its ugly head again. When our countries succeed in reducing drug use, they turn their attention to other concerns until the prevalence rates climb back up again. This fluctuation can be stopped. But it will demand a steady attention to the problem of drug use, even when it is at a low level. Only when we understand the complex biobehavioral processes responsible for addictions will we be in position to develop maximally effective prevention and treatment interventions.
>
> Our continued search for knowledge is essential for the effective control of the worldwide public health problem of drug abuse.

Because of space considerations, the two chapters in this book that deal with illicit drugs are concerned primarily with *preventive* rather than treatment programs for the three drugs of primary interest in the so-called War on Drugs—marijuana, heroin, and cocaine—with the main emphasis on cocaine, the one that is getting the most current government and media attention. For those interested in a more detailed history and inventory of neurophysiological effects of the full range of psychoactive and addictive substances, an excellent guide is Segal's *Drugs and Behavior: Cause, Effects, and Treatment* (1988).

Marijuana

Segal (1988) says that marijuana from the hemp plant has the longest history of all of the natural hallocinogens, its earliest use having been traced back to 2737 B.C. in China, where it was cited in the pharmacological literature of the day. Its desired effects can include a sense of well-being and relaxation, euphoria, and a more vivid sense of touch and perceptions. Adverse effects can include reddening of the eyes and dryness of the mouth, and occasional anxiety attacks, hallucinations, and paranoid delusions. The drug can remain in the body for up to fifty hours or longer. There is general agreement that marijuana interferes with mental functioning, driving and other psychomotor functioning, and learning.

As the University of California at Berkeley *Wellness Letter* ("Marijuana," 1990b) has pointed out, most people would agree that it is inadvisable to smoke pot and drive a truck or car or locomotive or plane, just as with alcohol. But there is still much uncertainty about its effects: Is it really a "hard drug," or is it relatively benign even in comparison to alcohol and tobacco, both of which are legal? Supporters argue that pot does not promote heart disease and lung cancer, has fewer bad social effects than alcohol or cocaine, and is not as addictive as either. But the article describes several studies suggesting that pot may do much long-term damage. The article gives pharmacological details suggesting toxicity, and notes that street pot today is thought to be about five to ten times stonger than it was in the 1960s. Since tetrahydrocannabinol (THC) content will vary and people usually smoke only sporadically, it is hard to measure its effects. However, a 1988 University of California at Los Angeles study reported that marijuana cigarettes released five times as much tar into lungs as tobacco cigarettes, and users also puff larger volumes, inhale more deeply, and hold the smoke longer. A previous study by some of the same researchers showed that three or four joints a day can do as much bronchial damage as twenty regular cigarettes.

Another study, at the Arizona College of Medicine in Tucson, found that marijuana smoking had strikingly adverse effects on lung function. Short-term adverse effects include reduction in attention span and short-term memory, inability to concentrate, apathy, lethargy, and sometimes anxiety or panic. THC can linger in the system for days or weeks, causing intoxication at inconvenient times and places, and the long-term health effects of this accumulation are unknown.

A recent news story (Witkin and Cuneo, 1990) explained how refinements in marijuana growing techniques have raised the THC content of marijuana since the 1960s to 8 percent and sometimes as high as 16 percent, compared to Colombian and Mexican THC content of only 3 to 6 percent. Sinsemilla pot prices can run as high as $300 an ounce, and the average plant yields a pound of pot. At least 25 percent of the pot consumed in the United States is now homegrown, up from 12 percent in 1984. Drug Czar Bennett's National Drug Control Strategy, released in September 1989, called for an increase in spending from $8 million to $16 million to wipe out domestic pot, with further increases probable in future years. Potraising is big business in Northern California and is also getting big in Kentucky, Florida, Michigan, and New York. Even a lot of middle-class people are growing it, for fortunes can be made in a couple of years.

Of course, pot is still illegal in all states except Alaska. Oregon, which was the leader in the decriminalization movement in the 1970s, recently hiked its maximum fine for possession of less than an ounce from $100 to $1,000, and 1989's drug bill provides for a five-year minimum mandatory prison sentence for cultivation of 100 plants or more. And Alaska voted in the November 1990 election to recriminalize pot, after years of legalization of up to four ounces of homegrown weed (Armstrong, 1990). Proponents of recriminalizing pot contended that by permitting as much as four ounces in the home, children are given the impression that this is a relatively safe and respectable substance to use.

As to marijuana's effect on youth: R. H. Schwartz (1987) reported that adolescents intoxicated from marijuana have been found to suffer considerable impairment of short-term memory and automobile driving skills, and that frequent adolescent use can impede normal maturation and contribute to an amotivational syndrome. He noted correctly that the drug is easily detected by means of immunoassay analysis of urine speciments. However, obviously parents and teachers are hardly equipped to detect marijuana use on a day-to-day basis in the same way as for alcohol use, which makes it additionally difficult to determine marijuana's degree of hazard in individuals.

A report by Petronis and Anthony (1989) of laboratory studies and anecdotal comments by users reported that heart palpitations often follow the administration of marijuana or cocaine. Epidemiologic strategies were used to detect this association, using interview data from 6,702 household residents sampled and followed prospectively for a collaborative multisite study of mental disorders in five U.S. communities. The lifetime data indicated that those who used marijuana and/or cocaine were much more likely to report an occurrence of palpitations than nonusers. These relationships remained strong after statistical adjustment for cardiovascular disease risk factors such as gender, race, and the use of sympathomimetic drugs other than cocaine. The greater risk was found among those who reported use of cocaine but not marijuana (this may reflect the sedative effects of marijuana).

Care is needed in educating the young about the dangers of marijuana. The introduction of new alcohol and cannabis education programs in Ontario schools was associated with significant increases in reported exposure to alcohol and cannabis. Significant increases were reported for both genders, all grade levels, and all geographic areas. While there were decreases in proportions of drinkers, especially among younger students, little effect was seen on heavy drinking; and the study found that increased exposure to cannabis education was not associated with reduced cannabis use (Smart, 1989).

Heroin

This drug is a narcotic analgesic obtained by treatment of morphine, which in turn is derived from opium. Heroin is a white, crystalline powder with a bitter taste, whose effect when injected is a rapid and intense high followed by contentment and often a dreamlike—but very temporary—escape from reality. Unusually high doses can result in coma and even death from respiratory failure. Most of the adverse effects from the use of heroin result not so much from its direct effects as from use of unsterile needles (which can result in hepatitis and AIDS, other infections, ulcers, and abscesses) or resultant malnutrition or other physical problems from poor living conditions (Segal, 1988).

Again, for reasons of space, the epidemiology of heroin use will not be presented here, except to say that (as reported earlier) before the recent preoccupation with crack cocaine, heroin was considered by federal authorities to be the highest priority drug menace. It is still taking a toll among many thousands of users in the form of secondary infections (including AIDS) and malnutrition. Recently a Drug Enforcement Administration officer reported that a new surge in heroin trafficking presents a law enforcement problem "ten times" worse than the one posed by Latin American cocaine cartels. The DEA spokesman explained that while cocaine is produced and exported from just one region, heroin comes to the United States from three parts of the world involving ten countries. He said that while production was off in 1989 in Pakistan and Iran and Afghanistan, it exploded in Southeast Asia, especially Burma, the largest producer. And production in Mexico and Guatemala is said to be rising. But an assistant secretary of state for international narcotics told the House Foreign Affairs drug task force that an administration strategy on heroin is still some time away ("DEA Says Heroin Poses 'Huge Problem,' " 1990).

One preventive activity among heroin addicts is "Prevention Point," a street-based AIDS prevention program in San Francisco that clandestinely distributes sterile needles within multiethnic communities with high drug use, exchanging sterile needles for used ones (Case and others, 1990). Needle exchange programs have been operating for some time in several European countries and in Canada, Australia, and several states in addition to California (Washington, Oregon, Hawaii, Colorado, New York, and Massachusetts). Prevention Point is now the largest program of this kind.

The program was mounted in some desperation, after city public health authorities found they could not authorize it politically. An estimated 57 percent of New York City's injection drug users (IDUs) is being infected with the AIDS virus, and AIDS is now believed to be the leading cause of death for women of childbearing age. A Centers for Disease Control study reports that nationwide, of all IDUs with AIDS, 49 percent are African-Americans, 20.5 percent Latino, and 30 percent white. Of the total AIDS cases assumed transmitted through heterosexual sex, an estimated 59 percent have occurred among sexual partners of IDUs.

While still against the law, the Prevention Point initiative has been so popular that police are continuing to look the other way, and pressure from public health authorities around the country is continuing to mount for legalizing such programs.

Cocaine

Segal (1988) provides a detailed summary on the nature and effects of cocaine, a strong stimulant drug similar in action to the amphetamines, which is derived from the coca plant raised in the Andes in Peru, Bolivia, and northern Chile. It may be smoked, sniffed, or injected, the latter being the most dangerous because intravenous injection of straight cocaine can result in death through overstimulation of the heart. It is most commonly available either in white powder form or as "crack," which consists of small pebbles made by mixing the powder with baking soda to yield about 75 percent cocaine in a form that can be smoked. The growing share of cocaine use in the United States is now in the form "crack," because it is convenient to handle and relatively cheaper per "high." Smoking it produces an almost instantaneous rush of euphoria, self-confidence, and heightened sensitivity.

The fascinating *National Geographic* (White, 1989) story of the history of coca and the manufacture and smuggling of cocaine from its origins in the Andes through myriad routes to its ultimate destination in the hands of street peddlers in our inner cities should be reread by everyone who thinks that this is a drug that the War on Drugs will be able to eradicate without first eradicating the American hunger for it. That hunger is now enormous. While once thought not to be as addictive as the opiates, in actuality crack cocaine is highly addictive psychologically because the brief rush is so dramatically pleasant and the inevitable letdown is so disagreeable that the user is strongly compelled to use it again and again until the supply (or the user) becomes completely exhausted.

As Segal notes, prolonged use can induce intense anxiety, agitation, and psychotic reactions that may result in violent behavior, and its long-term use may cause brain seizures or strokes, heart attacks, lung damage from inhalation of the smoke, and liver and circulatory damage. Withdrawal symptoms are psychic depression, irritability, aches and pains, disturbance of sleep, nausea, and extreme fatigue. According to Garber and Flaherty (1987), there are increasing numbers of cases of sudden death because of massive cocaine overdoses, and law enforcers have run across deaths due to "body stuffing"—the ingestion of large quantities of the drug in a panic situation to avoid arrest.

The 1988 NIDA-sponsored national survey of high school seniors, college students, and young adults through age twenty-nine (Johnston, O'Malley, and Bachman, 1989) found that crack use is now diffused through most of the nation's communities, and thus is no longer a primarily inner-city problem. As reported earlier, the leading drugs for all these youth groups are marijuana, cocaine, and stimulants (usually amphetamines). Among high school seniors, they show annual prevalence rates in 1988 of 33 percent, 8 percent, and 11 percent respectively, so only a small percentage have used cocaine (usually in crack form). However, again, these in-school high school surveys do not include dropouts, among whom much larger proportions of cocaine use may be assumed.

Among college students (follow-up of former high school senior samples), comparable annual prevalence rates were 35 percent for marijuana, 10 percent for cocaine, and 6 percent for stimulants. For the older high school graduates one to twelve years out of school, they are 32 percent, 14 percent, and 7 percent, so the use of cocaine is seen to be higher among youth after they graduate from high school.

The authors of the NIDA study considered the most important development in 1987 to be a sharp downturn in the use of cocaine among all three youth groups. Annual prevalence of use fell by about one-fifth in each group, and use within the prior thirty days fell by an even larger amount.

Regional use of crack among high school seniors was similar to that for cocaine in general: highest in the West (5.6 percent), followed by other regions at less than half that rate (2.7 percent in the South, 2.4 percent in the North Central region, and 2.3 percent in the Northeast). Crack use was highest in the large cities (3.9 percent), followed by nonmetropolitan areas (3.3 percent) and the smaller cities (2 percent). (Again, this survey does not include the estimated 15 percent of high school dropouts, who are assumed to be heavier users of crack.)

As to the psychological characteristics of cocaine addicts, Craig and Olson (1988) found that among addicts in treatment for drug abuse, the whites exhibited more psychological dependence, distress, and general maladjustment than the African-Americans. This is consistent with the more deprived environmental conditions and the heavier exposure to crack sales that might tend to draw many otherwise psychologically normal African-Americans into the crack-using net. Kandel and Raveis (1989) found, in a study of the cessation of marijuana and cocaine use in a longitudinal cohort of young adult men and women, that the factors that predicted cessation of use in adulthood paralleled those that had predicted lack of initiation in adolescence: conventionality in social role performance, social context unfavorable to the use of drugs, and good health. A most important predictor was the prior degree of involvement in any licit or illicit drugs. In multivariate analyses, friends' use was the most important predictor of continued use of cocaine. The study found that those who use drugs in response to social influences are more likely to stop using them than those who also use drugs for psychological reasons.

Aside from the relationship of cocaine to its involvement in environments of violence and other crime and getting caught up in the criminal justice system, one of the currently more widely publicized side effects of cocaine is its role in damage to newborn children and the spread of venereal disease. A recent study by the Senate Finance Committee suggests that this spread will soon increase greatly. According to an internal memo from Senate Finance Committee Chairman Lloyd Bentsen to his staff, it will cost $15 billion a year to care for 375,000 babies born annually who are addicted to drugs, since about 400,000 pregnant women currently have serious drug problems. Senator Bentsen is campaigning for better health care for pregnant women who have no health insurance and giving a top priority to combat drug abuse among young women in order to save their children (Anderson, 1989).

Similar opinions were voiced during a recent press interview (Halstuk, 1990) with Dr. Rick Fulroth, the chief of newborn services at Highland Hospital in Oakland, California. Fulroth dwelt on the twin epidemics of crack cocaine use and syphilis that are causing a surge in the death rate of African-American babies across the nation, reversing gains won in the battle against infant mortality during the past decade. Also cited was the National Commission to Prevent Infant Mortality's finding that the United States has dropped to twentieth place among developed nations in infant mortality. (Japan is in first place, recording only half the U.S. rate of 10.1 deaths per 1,000 live births.) In addition, the commission said the "mortality gap" between African-American and white babies in the United States is the widest since the nation began keeping records fifty years ago. Fulroth noted that crack accounts for much syphilis as well as addiction among newborn babies. Treatment costs between $50,000 and $200,000, all at public expense. He says (in Halstuck, 1990, p. A2) that "if society doesn't have concern for its children, it should at least have a concern for the bottom line."

A review by Chasnoff, Lewis, Griffith, and Willey (1989) found that the rate of cocaine use by pregnant women in the United States is much higher than previously realized, and an increasing number of infants are being born to cocaine-using mothers. In their study of seventy infants born to cocaine-using women, these infants were matched to a drug-free comparison group selected from the population of the same hospital: children of pregnant women of a similar racial and socioeconomic distribution, but with no history or evidence of licit or illicit drug use during pregnancy. Cocaine-exposed infants had lower birth weight, shorter gestation, and a smaller head circumference than control infants. Cocaine-exposed infants also had neurobehavioral abnormalities at initial evaluation and a higher rate of perinatal complications. Similar results were found in a study of cocaine effects on newborn children reported by Neerhof, MacGregor, Retzky, and Sullivan (1989).

The Deadly Drug Traffic

Another deadly by-product of the drug traffic is the high death rate among inner-city young African-American men. McAllister (1990) cites horrendous recent increases in death rates in this group in Washington, Boston, Baltimore, and Los Angeles. Homicide is a leading cause of death among urban African-American men, with a one in ten chance of being killed compared to one in eighty for white men. For African-American males age fifteen to twenty-four, homicide is the leading cause of death. The Urban League estimates that African-Americans are unemployed at a rate 2.2 times greater than for whites. The number of African-American children under eighteen living in poverty reached 45.6 percent in 1987. African-Americans have higher death rates from cancer, heart disease, and AIDS. While African-Americans account for only 12 percent of the U.S. population, they account for 46 percent of the nation's prisoners. Wade Nobles, an African-American researcher, said in an interview reported in McAllister (1990, p. 7), "Look, if you don't do something quickly to save black boys, there ain't going to be another generation."

Inner-city drug-related gang violence is spreading to a growing number of elementary and high schools. Addressing a Boston conference on addiction and violence, Anthony Borbon of Turning Point Family Services in Garden Grove, California, told how teenage drug gangs were prominent in an increase in 1988–89 of 32 percent in weapons on California school campuses and nearly 193,000 incidents of crime and violence. He said that newspaper accounts of gang violence only swell the pride of these gangs, adding, "We observe and condone violence all the time in this country. In the United States, we love sending people to incarceration. But what about when they get out? We've sentenced them to gladiator's school and they've gotten their PhD's in extortion and stealing on the 'inside' " (O'Connell, 1990).

Drug offenders are overcrowding federal prisons. The U.S. General Accounting Office reports that in 1988 about 44 percent of all federal prisoners were in for drug offenses. A congressional watchdog agency estimated that 60 percent of all federal prisoners serving time for drug violations had no prior prison records. The U.S. Sentencing Commission of the judicial branch of the federal government reported that the state and District of Columbia prisons were holding about 577,000 prisoners—23 percent over capacity. Representative Charles Rangel (D-N.Y.), in introducing legislation requiring constructive alternatives to incarceration for nonviolent offenders, said, "Such an approach should include vocational training and education to held reduce prison overcrowding and make better individuals instead of producing hardened criminals" (Culhane, 1990b, p. 6).

Official law enforcement and juridicial concern over the overcrowding of jails and prisons with drug offenders is growing. A recent *New York Times* article (Reinhold, 1989) cites police chiefs in major cities as saying that overfilled prisons are no answer. Homicides in Washington have tripled in four years, and more than half are considered drug-related. Many drug slayings are also reported for Los Angeles County, Kansas City, and even Columbus, Ohio. In many cities, police are going into elementary schools to teach children how to be more assertive, how to manage stress, and how to avoid drugs. The Drug Abuse Resistance Education (DARE) program set up by the Los Angeles Police Department and Los Angeles Unified School District has uniformed police providing lessons to help children learn how to resist drugs. Police say such programs are cheaper than incarceration of offenders. The district attorney's office in Los Angeles County sees truancy as an early indicator of delinquency, and truant children and their parents are now meeting with lawyers and hearing officers in trying to steer them away from gang involvement. The assistant director of the bureau of special operations that deals with gang crimes says that "we decided it was time to look at the beginning of the pipeline instead of concentrating all our resources on the other end, when it's too late" (Reinhold, 1989, p. A13). But many police officials lament that the schools themselves are not doing an effective job in cooperating in drug prevention.

A police strategy fairly common in large cities is being followed in San Francisco, which is disbanding its plainclothes drug unit and reassigning uniformed officers to public housing sites. While police authorities contend that this will help to make the crack problem more manageable and that officers should be more visible and that unnecessary and dangerous duplication of effort by uniformed and plainclothes officers is to be avoided, public housing residents say that dealers have merely moved their business elsewhere (DelVecchio, 1990a). DelVecchio wrote a follow-up article reporting how social workers in San Francisco have been working with teachers to identify those with poor grades who might be susceptible to gang membership and have been providing tutoring, organizing recreational programs, and trying to direct the allegiances of these students away from gangs. But the police have tended to be skeptical of the project, saying that more sweeping remedies will be needed before the environmental conditions that promote the attractiveness of gang membership can be overcome.

Among the most unfortunate victims of the cocaine drug trade have been the government and people of Colombia. At the end of 1989, President Baco Vargas's war against his country's top drug dealers had led to 497 arrests, nine suspects extradited to the United States, and the seizure of $200 million in property, weapons, and drugs. The cocaine cartels have retaliated by killing 187 officials and civilians and perpetrating 265 bombings, causing more than $500 million in property damage as of late 1989 (Moody, 1989), and many more since. Moody's *Time* article (1989, p. 34) ends with the tale of Interior Minister Carlos Lemos Simmonds: " 'I go from an armored car to a guarded office. My feet have not touched the street for weeks. My family lives in terror.' An understandable lament, but Lemos and his family—as well as the rest of the country—will continue to live in terror as long as the U.S. demand for cocaine remains keen and Colombia's drug masters insist on being the main suppliers."

Because of the enormous profits to be made in trafficking in cocaine, astute drug wholesalers can afford to cover their tracks carefully. "The Cocaine Trail" (Williams, 1990) tells the story of one shrewd Colombian drug wholesaler educated in Miami who has moved millions of dollars of cocaine to the Oakland ghetto. The story shows a map of the trail of cocaine from Bogota and Medellin to New York City, Haiti, and New Mexico, to Los Angeles, where he operated a safe house. His files show sales of millions of dollars of cocaine. But he was only one of a number of big-time operators. The DEA Operation Pisces exposed a ring of wealthy, powerful, and violent drug dealers from Medellin beginning in 1985 that was thought to control 80 percent of the cocaine being sold in the United States, with retail sales of $20 billion. Drugs entered through private jets and yachts, trucks from Mexico, and hidden consignments in everything from furniture to fruit pulp. Operation Pisces, in targeting the cartel's wealth, discovered several tiers: the drug lords, then money launderers, then brokers who moved large quantities of dope and made payments and collected and moved money to laundries, and of course the little dealers. Thus far, relatively few of the top people have been caught and convicted.

Decriminalization?

In frustration over the mounting toll in lives and costs to the public in terms of robberies and thefts occasioned by the illicit drug trade, and the costs of the War on Drugs for law enforcement and the incarceration of growing thousands of offenders, the last several years have seen a minority movement toward decriminalization of the sale of all drugs. Its adherents have included some prominent people, including former Secretary of State George Schultz and conservative essayist and public debater William F. Buckley.

One of the earliest voices in favor of drug legalization has been Princeton professor Ethan Nadelmann. In an interview, he suggested that we legalize marijuana first: not like tobacco, but like alcohol, where purchasers have to show proof of legal age, and with THC content and health warnings on the label (Yoffe, 1990). He recommended that after legalization of marijuana, the country should legalize not crack but 15 percent cocaine (it now runs higher than 60 percent). He admits there would be some black marketing of stronger cocaine, but the government would add a suggested 70 percent tax and people would know better how to regulate their dosage because they would know what they were getting. As to PCP (penclycidine), methamphetamine, and heroin, Nadelmann would introduce them, in government-regulated outlets, only in areas where there already is a lot of use.

Nadelmann contended that a great hypocrisy in our politics is that drug treatment often turns out to have a lower recidivism rate than throwing people in prison, and it costs $15,000 a year at Phoenix House compared to $52,000 at Riker's Island. "The problem is, treatment sounds like a 'liberal' solution. Politicians want to sound like they're tough on drugs" (quoted in Yoffe, 1990, p. 18). Nadelmann (in Yoffe, 1990, p. 19) argued that "legalization would help eliminate the worst effects of drugs on the community—the rising violence, rising crime, little kids growing up with drug dealers as role models . . . Almost every society that we know of in human history has found some form of chemical substance to alter one's state of consciousness. Some societies have been very successful in integrating this into their culture and using it in almost totally non-destructive ways."

Sentiments receptive to decriminalization have been voiced by a number of judges and law enforcement figures, largely because of the frustrations they have been experiencing in trying to enforce what they see as unenforceable antidrug laws. For example, Representative George Crockett (D-Mich.) and U.S. District Court Judge Robert W. Sweet of New York have suggested that decriminalization is the only solution, since the court systems are swamped by drug cases. A Crockett staff member reported getting more than fifty calls from around the country, most supporting his position (Crockett is from drug-ravaged Detroit and is a former judge). Crockett would handle drugs like alcohol—tax them and make sales to minors illegal. Sweet says decriminalization would eliminate the profit motive and activities of criminal gangs. While former Drug Czar William Bennett has complained that America's liberal intellectuals "are on the editorial and op-ed pages . . . telling us with an ignorant sneer that our drug policy won't work," Ethan Nadelmann of Princeton has countered by saying, "The problem is that it's not all liberal intellectuals. His allies in the conservative movement are turning against it (the drug war). I think Bennett is running a little scared" (quoted in Culhane, 1990a, p. 2).

A highly negative reaction to decriminalization was voiced by Robert L. DuPont (former director of NIDA) and Ronald L. Goldfarb (former Justice Department prosecutor) in a byline article in the *Washington Post National Weekly Edition* (1990). They said (1990, p. 29) that "the world's most reasonable-sounding but dumb idea is the one that advocates solving the country's drug problem by legalizing drugs." They went on to make the point that the costs of drugs in terms of lost lives and potential would be much higher than costs of enforcement: "Fourteen million Americans now pay $100 billion a year for illicit drugs. How many more Americans would consume how much more if drug prices were cut by 90 percent or more as the legalization advocates propose?" They contended that crack was the only drug problem that is getting worse, but that legalizing marijuana or giving intravenous drug users sterile needles will not dent the crack problem, and that physicians should not be put in the position of prescribing such drugs.

They pointed out that during Prohibition, consumption of alcohol declined drastically and alcohol-related arrests dropped by half . . . . The most recent NIDA survey of Americans over twelve showed that in 1988 there were 106 million alcohol users, 57 million cigarette smokers, but only 12 million users of marijuana and 3 million users of cocaine; use of all four of these drugs was down from 1985. They contended that it is not easy to conclude from these figures that prohibition of illegal drugs is not working: "The best way to cut the drug market is to decrease society's tolerance for illicit drug use. That means creating painful consequences for illicit drug use to help the nonuser stay clean.

There need to be more and better programs to help drug users get clean." But they don't believe law enforcement aimed at the supply is more than a small part of the solution: "We agree with the Harlem barbershop owner who said the idea that jails stop drugs is 'like saying cemeteries stop death' . . . Why now, when only a few months ago the Federal government showed statistics that showed a 37 percent decline in the regular use of illicit drugs in America, a fall that included every region in the nation, all races, both sexes and all social classes? With that sort of progress in the war on drugs, this is a particularly odd time to give up a battle" (1990, p. 29).

William Bennett, former National Drug Control Policy Director, made an angry rejoinder to the advocates of legalization in a Harvard speech, accusing American intellectuals of advocating a "scandalous" surrender in the national War on Drugs. While a common theme is that legalization would put an end to drug trafficking and the violent crime it spawns, he contended that consumption of drugs would still be very high. He argued that criminal sanctions are a "vital incentive to stay away from a life of crime"; under legalization addicts would still continue to rob and steal and street traffickers would still sell to minors or try to undercut the legalized price ("Drug Czar Assails 'The Legalizers,' " p. A13).

Shortly thereafter, another strong voice against decriminalization of drugs was heard from syndicated columnist James Kilpatrick (1989, A18), who opened by saying that Representative Charles Rangel (D-N.Y.) was right in saying that proposals to legalize the sale of drugs are no more than "a lot of cocktail party kind of talk."

Kilpatrick noted that it was interesting that decriminalization proponents included such conservatives as Milton Friedman and William F. Buckley, Jr., along with Ramsey Clark (former attorney general under President Carter) and Ira Glasser of the American Civil Liberties Union, with the chief spokesperson being Ethan Nadelmann of Princeton. Kilpatrick went on to question Nadelmann's claims that repeal of drug prohibition would reduce government expenditures and provide new tax revenues of at least $10 billion a year to support drug treatment programs and educational and job-training programs. He also doubted that the quality of urban life would rise, the rate of homicide and other crimes would decline, and U.S. foreign policy would be freed to pursue more realistic goals. Nadelmann would prohibit sale to minors and outlaw drug advertising of newly legalized products, and would limit the time and place of sale: Libertarians like him do not think marijuana and heroin do much harm, and they resent enforcers in our bedrooms. Kilpatrick pointed out that when Prohibition was repealed in 1933, the demand for booze soared out of sight, and that state options on legalization would cause confusing jurisdictions. He ended by saying (1989, p. A18), "Questions of right and wrong seem never to flower in academic groves. Suppose we face the issue squarely: Is it morally right to make such dangerous drugs freely available to the public? The prospect strikes me as dead wrong. In this instance, libertarian theory be damned."

Morton Kondracke (1989) of the *New Republic* echoes most of the antilegalization arguments listed previously and adds that even if legalization were to save $30 billion in enforcement costs, a likely doubling of use might raise the costs of drug damage to as much as $210 billion—which would hardly be a bargain for the American people.

To venture a personal opinion about legalization of all drugs: As a public health professional, I would have to be opposed to it under the principle of the Hippocratic oath, "First, do no harm." Enough harm is being done already under the present War on Drugs—harm that should be mitigated by fairer application of law enforcement for rich and poor alike. As I have said elsewhere, considering our unfortunate experiences with slack controls over the advertising and marketing of alcohol and tobacco, legalization of the sale of now-illicit drugs would lead to heavy commercial pressure on the part of the drug industry to move such goods through retail channels (Cahalan, 1989). The "American free enterprise system" is so efficient, and the potential profits and tax revenues so enormous, that we would be bound to wind up with even greater numbers of addicts than we have now. And in any case, a move toward legalization would be giving our young people the wrong message: that doing drugs is really okay.

The "National Drug Control Strategy"

The Office of National Drug Control Policy monograph titled *National Drug Control Strategy,* the second volume of which was issued in January 1990, is a remarkable document in its candid, nonjargonish statements about federal drug policies and the plans for carrying them out.

Congress and the administration vied with each other in 1987 to pass hastily written laws to prove that they were going to do something drastic about drug problems, particularly the growing cocaine trade. In September 1988, President Bush pronounced a control strategy that would carry $9.5 billion in federal funding to carry it out, and the administration proposed to expand the funding to more than $10.6 billion for fiscal 1991. For that year, $492 million was requested to supplement the state and local criminal systems, the Drug Enforcement Administration (DEA) will have its funding augmented by $151 million to hire more agents and support personnel for foreign and domestic operations, and the Bureau of Alcohol, Tobacco, and Firearms (which claims that about 50 percent of its enforcement work is drug-related, such as its seizure of nearly 3,000 firearms from drug traffickers) will get more funding. Funding for domestic marijuana eradication will almost double to $35 million. The Federal Bureau of Prisons plans to build seven new detention centers, and the Prison Transportation and Detention program will be expanded by $11.6 million to help in managing the estimated 85,000 drug-related prisoners in federal prisons alone. It is anticipated that U.S. attorneys will be handling 23,000 drug-related cases in fiscal 1991, and so additional attorneys and staffs are being expanded considerably, as are the rolls of federal judges. Considerable additional money is also to go into money laundering investigations, about a half billion dollars in assistance will go to state and local law enforcement activities, and creation of a drug testing information clearinghouse to promote drug testing within the criminal justice system is planned.

Federal drug treatment efforts are discussed in more detail in the next chapter. Briefly, though, they are being stepped up by an additional $1.5 billion in funding for fiscal 1991 (70 percent of federal drug budgets are being spent on criminal justice activities, including much hardware for use of DEA and other agents in trying to stem the flow of drugs from Latin and South America and Asia). Fiscal 1990 state block grants for treatment amount to $477 million, which the administration is proposing to raise by $100 million for fiscal 1991. An Office for Treatment Improvement (OTI) has been created within ADAMHA to provide leadership and to administer the block grant program and provide technical assistance to the states. OTI will work with NIDA to provide treatment outcome information and guidelines. The administration is requesting an additional $6 million in 1991 for the Office of Human Development Services for partial funding of demonstration grants in treating the estimated 100,000 "cocaine babies" born every year.

As discussed in Chapter Two, the new Office for Substance Abuse Prevention (OSAP) within ADAMHA has been granted very substantial funding to support demonstration programs in prevention, education, and early intervention. NIDA also is getting additional funding for research and development of outreach programs and treatment services for pregnant addicts and their children, as well as funding to expand and supplement its basic Household and High School Senior drug use surveys and the National Drug and Alcohol Treatment Unit Survey (NDATUS), which provides nationwide information on numbers in treatment, costs, and financing.

About $1 billion is proposed for fiscal 1991 for funding prevention programs through the Departments of Education and Health and Human Services, Justice Department, Housing and Urban Development, and other federal agencies. Most federally sponsored prevention programs are intended to follow the general guidelines in the OSAP strategy manuals discussed in Chapter Two: to concentrate on reaching youth with constructive supports for avoiding starting to use tobacco or alcohol as well as illicit drugs.

The administration is also attempting to encourage drug testing within private industry to facilitate a "drug-free workplace," with the requirement that federal contractors and grantees provide assurances that they maintain drug-free workplace programs. Drug testing is to be implemented among federal employees on a random basis. Special priority on drug testing is to be exerted within the transportation industry, to ward against accidents caused by operators whose control is impaired by alcohol or other drugs. As noted later, many controversies may be expected over the likelihood of overzealous mass random urine testing of employees as such "drug-free workplace" initiatives continue to be implemented.

One of the most controversial areas of antidrug activity is in the application of federal international initiatives. These include increased economic, military, and law enforcement assistance to Colombia, Peru, and Bolivia; similar activities concerning Mexico; and support for law enforcement programs in other Latin American producer and transit countries, including Ecuador, Venezuela, Paraguay, Argentina, Chile, and Central American and Caribbean nations. Other priorities include increased attempts to interdict supplies of opium, heroin, and hashish from Asia, and expanded efforts to reduce the manufacture and shipment of chemicals used in illicit drug production.

In support of such interdiction of drugs, the federal strategy calls for an enhanced and expanded role for the Department of Defense in the detection and monitoring of drug trafficking, improved coordination of air, land, and maritime interdiction efforts, increased focus on stopping drug smuggling across the Southwest Border, a tightening of U.S. Customs drug interdiction resources, and an integration of antidrug Command, Control, Communications, and Intelligence systems with the Department of Defense Joint Task Forces. A total or $2.4 billion is proposed for interdiction efforts.

This plan fits in with the military's fear of personnel cutbacks occasioned by the end of the Cold War. As Jehl and Healy (1989, p. A19) put it, "Less than a year after struggling mightily to avoid a principal role in the nation's war on drugs, the armed forces have abruptly reversed course and begun scrambling to win a share, seeing it as a lucrative haven at a time when their traditional mission is shrinking." The story goes on to say that ten top Pentagon field commanders have outlined a host of new antidrug missions, ranging from launching satellites that spy on cocaine traffickers to seizing heroin shipments at sea as they are smuggled out of Southeast Asia. "With peace breaking out all over," said one (unnamed) two-star general, "it might give us something to do."

Another interesting cocaine-eradicating scheme is the U.S. Department of Agriculture's research program, allegedly initiated at the urging of former Drug Czar William Bennett, to quadruple to $6.5 million the budget for "a secretive Agriculture Department research program to develop chemical and biological agents for the destruction of drug crops" (Isikoff, 1990, p. A1,A10). The principal focus of the effort is the malumbia, a white moth that, in its caterpillar stage, eats Andean coca leaves that otherwise might be harvested to make cocaine. The moth is a pest that Peruvians already are trying to eradicate from their food crops with insecticides, but some USDA thinking is that *spreading* these moths—of course with the consent of the local countries—would help wipe out the coca-leaf crop. But as Isikoff (1990) stated, hundreds of thousands of peasants in Peru and Bolivia earn their livelihoods through growing coca plants, and until some alternative support is found, no such eradication programs will be acceptable to their governments.

William Bennett, while director of the ONDCP, designated five areas as high-intensity drug trafficking localities singled out for special enforcement efforts: New York City and surrounding areas, Los Angeles and Orange County, Miami and environs, Houston and neighboring municipalities, and the Southwest Border and adjacent areas. Congress appropriated $25 million for fiscal 1990 for extra law enforcement resources in these areas, and the administration sought to double this amount for fiscal 1991. In addition, the administration asked for more than $1.3 billion for drug enforcement, treatment, and prevention activities for these five areas.

Bennett also designated Washington, D.C., for augmented federal surveillance and assistance, the first year of which was not an outstanding success. Bennett admitted, one year after he pledged to make the District of Columbia a "test case" in the nation's Drug War, that the results of federal efforts were "mixed, spotty, incomplete." The plan for Washington was estimated to cost $80 million, calling for the creation of a multiagency law enforcement task force, construction of a new federal prison and a 500-bed detention facility, more prosecutors, eviction of drug dealers from public housing projects, and new model drug treatment clinics. The prison never got off the ground because of local opposition, and there have been other delays ("D.C. Drug War a Year Later," 1990, p. A6).

There has been a continual verbal war over the War on Drugs in the halls of Congress and from the ranks of law enforcement officers and judges, primarily over the lopsided amount of money to be spent on *supply reduction* (conceded by the administration as being about 71 percent of total federal drug funding), in contrast to *demand reduction* (about 29 percent). Some of the adverse arguments are presented in the following paragraphs.

President Bush planned to increase by 50 percent the 1991 military's budget for halting international drug smugglers ("Bush, Biden Unveil," January 25, 1990). But Bush's total increase for the War on Drugs of $1.2 billion is less than the $5 billion increase sought by Senator Joseph Biden, chairman of the Senate Judiciary Committee.

Biden criticized the plan to have the military use nearly one-third of Bush's extra money to help Colombia, Peru, and Bolivia combat drugs; New York, Miami, Los Angeles, and Houston have been targeted for extra funds; drug treatment in prisons would be intensified; and the death penalty would be sought for drug kingpins even when their crimes do not result directly in deaths. Biden's plan would greatly expand treatment facilities, guaranteeing treatment for all addicts within the next three years (the administration had proposed only limited expansion and mandating ten new regional federal prisons that states could use for drug-addicted offenders; Bush would leave new prisons up to states). Biden would also toughen federal gun controls on semiautomatic weapons (Bush repeatedly has rejected this) and proposes a debt relief in Andean nations in exchange for crop substitution and development. Because of the current high federal deficit, Bush has left most of the costs of drug control to state and local governments; but Biden would greatly expand the federal share of the cost, adding 1,000 new DEA agents, 900 new prosecutors, and hundreds of new FBI agents as well as picking up the costs of prison construction. Biden's plan would concentrate on hard-core users and would favor the major urban centers, where drugs have created a tremendous strain on resources.

A month later, Senator Biden ("Bennett Rejects," Feb. 3, 1990) criticized Bennett for continuing to emphasize law enforcement to attack the drug problem rather than focusing on treatment and education programs: Biden said that only 40 percent of schoolchildren will be exposed to antidrug education programs each year. Bennett responded that drug education programs are sometimes laughed at unless coupled with strong punitive sanctions, and that he thinks we are beyond the turning point in the war against drugs.

In 1989, Bennett prodded the Bush administration to ban imports of assault rifles, but later adamantly rejected any further gun curbs (he knew that Bush is a member of the National Rifle Association and is opposed to most gun controls). Senator Kennedy pressed Bennett on why he has changed his tune, and Bennett said only that "I don't know a damn thing about guns!"

Another news story (Rosenthal, 1990) reported that the final document issued at a Barranquilla summit attended by Bush and the presidents of Colombia, Bolivia, and Peru included few specific economic, military, or law enforcement agreements. Bush did not increase the $2.2 billion, five-year aid program he had previously sent to Congress, which is already under attack (Senator Biden urged shifting Bush's emphasis on military and law enforcement to economic aid). But at the conference, at least the United States agreed to provide increased equipment and training for law enforcement and the military, with each country to be respnsible for policing its own national territory.

The participants also agreed to call a world conference on illegal drug trafficking in 1991 and to hold a follow-up session within six months. In addition, the United States agreed to help train Andean farmers on how to switch to legal crops and intended to request an aid package from Congress for this purpose.

A representative of the American Public Health Association had these sharp criticisms of the current status of the War on Drugs

> In 1988, APHA approved the policy, "A Public Healh Response to the War on Drugs: Reducing Alcohol, Tobacco, and Other Drug Problems Among the Nation's Youth." In the subsequent 15 months, the tough talk and bellicose action from the Reagan Administration purportedly aimed at the U.S. Drug problem have included invasion of a foreign country, threats to blockade other countries, attacks on civil rights of American citizens, and a massive increase of spending on military and police activity: all because of a supposed worsening grip of drug barons on young people and huge costs of illicit drug use.
>
> Nothing could be further from the truth. And if the Adminstration intended to thwart the advice of the nation's public health experts, it could hardly have done better than the Bennett blueprint for a War on Drugs [Schade, 1990, p. 20].

Schade went on to say that APHA policy called for high priority to tobacco and alcohol problems, but there is not a single mention of them in the Bennett priorities, "and only grudging admission to the document that the educational programs which work are the broad based ones focusing on averting all substance abuse." APHA has urged attention to environmental factors as well as individuals, and insists that punitive measures should be used with caution. The Bennett plan calls for more funds for street-level law enforcement and vigorous prosecution and increased fines for misdemeanors. "Meanwhile, the Administration continues to underfund essential social, environmental and mental health services for poor people, among whom the major drug-abusing populations can be found." APHA has urged attention to prevention, treatment and recovery, dealing foremost with alcohol and tobacco use (because these are responsible for many more deaths than are illicit drugs), with massive increases in treatment funding, restriction of advertising of alcohol and tobacco, comprehensive workplace and school education and prevention programs, and increased taxes on alcohol and tobacco. "Money spent for treatment, although slated for a nearly one-third growth in fiscal year 1990, will still amount to only two-thirds of the new funds for corrections alone, i.e., to locking people up."

The author noted that the General Accounting Office recently reported that law enforcement gets 70 percent of antidrug expenditures and prevention and treatment only 30 percent. All treatment combined got less money in the 1989 budget than one single law enforcement effort: the Coast Guard's interdiction program. Schade (1990, p. 20) noted that "The 'epidemic' of illicit drug use among high school students, if it ever existed, has long since abated. . . . Meanwhile, the War on Drugs, by putting total emphasis on illicit drugs, may be sending the very dangerous message that cigarettes and alcohol are not nearly as hazardous."

One of the most stinging indictment of the stewardship of the War on Drugs came from Lewis Lapham, longtime essayist for *Harper's Magazine* (1989). He asserted that the government's own figures show that addiction to illegal drugs troubles a relatively few Americans and that the current generation of American youth is the strongest and healthiest in the nation's history. He then took President Bush to task for going on television to demonstrate a bag of crack that had been bought in the park across from the White House—concealing the fact that police had enticed the dealer into traveling some distance to get into the park to make the sale.

Lapham said that the War on Drugs is a political war, waged not by scientists and doctors but by police officers and politicians, whereas it should be a public health issue. He pointed out that the American Medical Association regards addiction as a disease, not a crime or a moral defect. He noted that in 1988, American hospitals counted 3,308 deaths attributed to cocaine, as opposed to 390,00 deaths attributable to tobacco and 100,000 deaths directly related to excessive use of alcohol. He observed that the root causes of use of cocaine among the poor are poverty, homelessness, lack of education, and general hopelessness and called politicians cynical: Bush asked for $7.9 billion to wage his "assault on every front" of the drug war, but the Pentagon allots almost as much ($5 billion a year) to a single weapon, the B-2 bomber. He excoriated (1989, p. 47) Bush's then commander-in-chief of the drug war, William Bennett, as never missing a "chance to demand more police, more jails, more judges, more arrests, more punishments, more people serving more millenia of 'serious time.'" He closed by saying (1989, p. 48), "As a consequence of President Bush's war on drugs, society gains nothing except immediate access to an unlimited fund of resentment and unspecific rage. In return for so poor a victory, and in the interests of the kind of people who would build prisons instead of schools, Bush offers the nation the chance to deny its best principles, to corrupt its magistrates and enrich its most vicious and efficient criminals, to repudiate its civil liberties and repent of the habits of freedom. The deal is as shabby as President Bush's trick with the bag of cocaine. For the sake of a vindictive policeman's dream of a quiet and orderly heaven, the country risks losing its constitutional rights to its soul."

Another bitter criticism of the War on Drugs was voiced in an editorial in *Newsweek* (King, 1990), by a Washington lawyer who has served on several congressional investigations and has written much on drug law reform. He said that we have been fighting this drug war unsuccessfully for seventy years, and cited a NIDA report that the official 1988 toll in drug-caused deaths in twenty-seven cities was 3,308 for cocaine products, 2,480 for heroin and morphine, and zero for marijuana. In comparison, smoking killed 390,000 last year and alcohol at least 100,000, the latter being responsible for more fetal damage than crack and being *the* leading menace on our highways. The last Reagan budget was $3.4 billion; Bush's first was nearly $6 billion, which he raised to $7.9 in September 1989, calling for 75 percent interdiction and enforcement, 15 percent for education and prevention, and 10 percent for treatment. "Could anyone be serious about interdicting drug supplies when the plants that produce drugs grow almost anywhere?" (King, 1990, p. 4).

A growing number of critics have contended that the War on Drugs has really turned out to be a War on African-Americans. Harris (1990, p. A12) noted that while whites sell most of the nation's cocaine and account for 80 percent of its consumers, it is African-Americans who continue to fill up the country's courts and jails "because in a political climate that demands that something be done, they are the easiest people to arrest." Harris cited a Washington, D.C., study that found that one in four African-American men in their twenties is either in prison or on parole or probation, as contrasted to only 6 percent of white men in their twenties. He also quoted a University of Chicago law professor as saying, "The whole law-and-order movement that we've heard so much about is, in operation, anti-black and anti-underclass. Not in plan, not in design, but in operation."

The U.S. military's growing involvement in the War on Drugs needs to be emphasized. In the spring of 1990, Secretary of Defense Richard Cheney unveiled initiatives in which the White House assigned the Pentagon the lead responsibility to provide surveillance and to serve as an intelligence and communications hub linking the antidrug efforts of all U.S. agencies. The U.S. Pacific Command will step up drug-hunting patrols off Southeast Asia. (It is said that drug production in the "Golden Triangle" of Southeast Asia is sharply on the rise.) Naval forces out of California, Japan, the Philippines, and Hawaii will ply the narrow channels of the South China and Philippine Straits. Shore patrols off Florida will be increased, with new "eye-in-the-sky" stationary surveillance balloons along our southern coast ("Military's New Drug War Role," 1990).

The Defense Department is now soft-pedaling its earlier talk about operating a flotilla of ships off the coast of Columbia, much resented when its announcement came just after the invasion of Panama. However, with the cutbacks in military defense forces in Europe as a result of a winding down of the

Cold War, there is considerable Pentagon temptation to find other ways to keep our armed forces busy. In the past, the United States wisely has used its military only on missions of war and military defense, but there is continuing risk of getting our military embroiled in civil wars in Latin America through its roles in antidrug missions. In an incident in Peru, about 200 armed Sendero Luminoso guerrillas attacked an antidrug base in Peru's main cocaine-producing region while many U.S. Drug Enforcement Agency representatives and contract pilots were assisting Peruvian police forces in breaking up cocaine-producing plants in the jungle. Although no Americans were shot, the incident raises questions as to whether the United States would be able to protect Americans sent to a base near the center of a fierce guerrilla war ("U.S. Agents Help Peru Repel Guerrillas," 1990). The administration has earmarked millions to continue this activity, which is drawing us more and more into what is really a civil war.

A growing number of analysts are saying that attempts to cut off the supply of addictive drugs from outside the country are doomed to failure unless we can do more to reduce the *demand* for drugs. One argument in this regard is that if foreign drug supplies are cut off, "designer drugs" such as "ice" (smokable methamphetamine) will readily become available to fill the demand. In early 1990, detectives in Sacramento, California, seized what they said was the first "ice" laboratory in the continental U.S. and arrested five people ("5 Jailed in Seizure of first 'Ice Lab,'" 1990). "Ice" is described in the *National Drug Control Strategy* monograph (Office of National Drug Control Policy, 1990) as having originated in Asian laboratories and then entering the United States through Hawaii, where it rapidly is becoming the illegal drug of choice. The rather pessimistic account in the monograph continues:

> Like crack, ice is convenient to use and relatively inexpensive. Its main difference from crack is the length of the high. A crack high lasts about 20 minutes, while the effects of ice can persist for up to 8 hours. Another difference is that ice users are

> more likely to become highly agitated, violent, and prone to paranoia and schizophrenia-like symptoms. As with cocaine, chronic use of ice can lead to permanent neurological damage, severe weight loss, and life-threatening heart and lung disorders.
>
> Ice may be where crack was five years ago. If so, we have an opportunity and an obligation to head off a destructive threat before it begins, through intensive, targeted prevention and law enforcement efforts. We need to identify the areas of the country most likely to be affected and seek to pinpoint the groups that may be most susceptible. [1990, p. 45].

Another pessimistic note about trying to control drug use through interdicting the supply was voiced by columnist Jean Kirkpatrick (1990), once one of the court favorites of the Reagan administration. She reminded us (1990, z-6, p. 5) that the State Department's March 1990 *International Narcotics Control Strategy Report* conceded that the 1989 drug control record was mostly bad, since "worldwide narcotics production reached new levels, corruption undermined enforcement efforts. . . . Worldwide abuse of illegal drugs is rising." This includes a dramatic rise in the production of opium, and the countries of the Andes planting, harvesting, processing, and shipping more coca than ever before, and the cultivation of opium expanding in Mexico and Guatemala.

Kirkpatrick (1990, z-6, p. 5) reported that no matter how much effort and money the U.S. government expends in assisting other countries in controlling drugs and in trying to interdict them, it is not working because "cocaine provides income, jobs, and hard currency in areas where all are rare." She concluded that "the solution—if there is a solution—will be found not in the Golden Triangle nor in the Andes, but in the streets of the United States, where demand attracts supply. And most Americans know it. . . . Obviously, the U.S. government can hardly hold others responsible for a failure to control problems that we cannot control in our own nation's capital."

The War on Drugs has had another adverse side effect in addition to contributing to tensions between the United States and its Latin American neighbors over our interventionist approaches in trying to stamp out production of illicit drugs at their sources. This side effect is the encroachment on civil liberties occasioned by government-induced random testing of employees for drugs. The federal administration's policies of encouraging testing among government employees has been criticized fairly frequently, as in an editorial in the *Washington Post Weekly Edition* (1990) expressing disappointment over the Supreme Court's refusal to review two decisions authorizing random drug testing among Justice Department professionals (lawyers and economists) with top secret security clearances and Army civilian drug counselors. The editorial (1990, p. 26) said that "an ominous message is being sent: A significant number of justices are content to let the government expand random drug-testing. Dozens of cases involving different kinds of government employees have yet to reach the high court. These cases involve no probable cause, no accidents, and no threat to public safety. There is no encouragement here for public employees hoping to be rescued from an intrusive and humiliating testing program by a Supreme Court alert to civil liberties."

At the present state of the art, drug testing is done by subjecting the testee to the embarrassment of having to urinate in a bottle or pan, under the surveillance of a monitor so that someone else's urine is not substituted. The process is at risk of escalating into a power struggle between bosses and subordinates not too unlike the loyalty oaths required during the McCarthy era. But a recent Gallup poll found that the majority of employees themselves supported some kind of drug testing: One in three believed illegal drugs are sold at work and one-fourth either had seen or heard of illegal drug use during work hours. Sixty-eight percent supported drug testing of employees suspected of drug use, while 53 percent supported random testing of employees. Several Washington-area companies that have instituted workplace drug testing have fired a goodly number who have tested positive. However, some unions and civil-liberties advocates challenge the reach of some drug testing programs, especially the reliability of tests and the random testing of employees. One union official said, "The majority of employees and our members aren't on drugs. They resent it when they see someone doing drugs and want it stopped. But they don't like [it] when they are forced to use the bottle" (Skrzycki, 1990a, p. 38).

Some employees are fighting back. A recent California Court of Appeal decision upheld a $485,042 award to a computer programmer who was fired from the Southern Pacific Transportation Company after she refused to submit to a random urine sample for drugs. Her attorney said the ruling applies to every employer, public or private, in California. "The employer must have an overriding interest in the safety of that employee and the public before they can require testing." Another of her attorneys said it is important to note that this decision applies only to those in jobs that are not considered "safety sensitive" (Stroock, 1990, p. A4).

Additional juridicial reinforcement for civil liberty concerns about overzealous drug testing is provided by the ruling of U.S. District Judge Lowell Jensen that the Navy, with 300,000 civilian employees throughout the world, has a legitimate interest in randomly testing top security personnel, firefighters, motor vehicle operators, train and flight engineers, aircraft pilots, and boat operators. But he blocked random testing of the military's public health and safety personnel as well as other general categories. He also banned the Navy from testing workers after an accident unless there is reasonable grounds to suspect alcohol or drug involvement.

The Navy was among scores of federal agencies that were complying with President Reagan's 1986 executive order calling for testing of all federal employees in "safety sensitive positions." Many of such programs have been blocked in court: In the Navy case, several labor unions joined in the lawsuit, claiming that the rules violated the workers' right to privacy and their constitutional protection against unreasonable searches. However, Judge Jensen said that those with top secret clearances "have a greatly reduced expectation of privacy" because they are subject to periodic background checks (Chiang, 1990, p. C13).

It is expected that a great deal more litigation will arise over random drug testing—particularly since at present the test itself is so embarrassing and unesthetic to the person tested. Such incursions against civil liberties are sometimes defended by the old axiom (Stalin's?), "You can't make an omelet without breaking eggs." But the jury is still out on whether the current War on Drugs is the right kind of omelet for our government to be cooking.

A recent critical review of the outlook on the War on Drugs from a legal and public policy standpoint questions Bennett's strategy of singling out the casual drug users as the root of the drug problem because their behavior is likely to be more contagious than the habits of the heavy drug users (Skolnick, 1990). Skolnick, a Berkeley law professor and sociologist, argues that heavy drug users are the root of the problem because they consume 63 percent of the cocaine in the United States even though they constitute only 6.9 percent of the drug-using population. He contends that rehabilitation of these addicts presents a formidable challenge because most are hard-core urban poor who lack the societal supports needed for rehabilitation. And he does not think a get-tough-on-drug-criminals approach in itself can be successful, citing a study he conducted recently in Alameda County, California, where special state funding was provided for expanding for three years the prosecution and incarceration of drug criminals, with no apparent improvement in stemming the drug trade. He concludes that unless this country acknowledges the social roots of addiction, it has little chance of winning its war on drugs.

To sum up whether we are winning the War on Drugs: We will not win it if we persist on calling it a "war," which implies justification to resort to draconian paramilitary measures. Instead we should deal with drug use as a very major public health problem, to be mitigated in the long run by firm, consistent programs to prevent addiction from developing, and by programs to treat the addicted through strict but humane regimens that break the cycle of hopelessness, chronic unemployment, and drug-using networks. No doubt our governmental agencies still should maintain such programs to interdict drugs from abroad as are of proven effectiveness and that do not intrude on other countries' sovereign rights. Certainly drug-related crimes of violence should be dealt with swiftly and decisively. And (as discussed earlier) certainly the most addictive illicit drugs should not be decriminalized if we do not want to risk encouraging the setting up of free-enterprise drug markets that would swell the ranks of the addicted even further. But what is really needed is better balance: less blustering punitiveness, and more patient but firm national and local programs to shrink the demand for drugs to a manageable minimum.

CHAPTER EIGHT

Key Problems in Treating Drug Addiction

Since this book concentrates on prevention rather than treatment, this chapter will be relatively brief. However, much drug treatment is really tertiary prevention—attempting to stop the process of readdiction. Therefore it deserves discussion here even if about all one can do is to point to the relatively underdeveloped and unsuccessful status at present of drug treatment as prevention (some authorities say that more than 90 percent of heroin and cocaine addicts resume use after treatment).

Jay Lewis reports the following numbers under treatment (not including those currently in prisons or jails), as derived from a 1987 National Drug and Alcohol Treatment Unit Survey (NDATUS), sponsored by ADAMHA and NIAAA, from information compiled by individual states:

There were 5,158 drug treatment facilities reported, of which 1,075 treated only drug addicts and 4,083 also treated alcoholism. The number of drug clients reported rose 51 percent from 1982 to 263,510 (in contrast to 350,613 alcoholics in treatment), a 20 percent rise. The total expended on treatment by all reporting units in 1987 was just over $3 billion, with about

$1.7 billion for alcoholism treatment and $1.3 billion for drug treatment.

The biggest share of drug abuse treatment funding was from state governments totaling $355,402,000, private third-party payments (Blue Cross/Blue shield, HMOs, and other insurance carriers) $346,963,000, fees from clients $157,185,000, and public third-party mechanisms (Medicare, Medicaid, and CHAMPUS) 139,224,000. Of the 263,510 drug abuse clients in treatment on October 30, 1987, only 4.1 percent were in a hospital/inpatient environment, 10.4 percent in a residential setting, and 86.5 percent in an outpatient environment. Females accounted for 32.8 percent of drug abuse clients; Whites for 57.5 percent, Blacks 24.8 percent (or double their proportion in the total population), and Hispanics 15.9 percent. Drug abuse clients under 18 totaled 15.4 percent, or more than double the percentage of alcohol clients in that age group.

The NDATUS survey reported unduplicated counts of drug and alcohol clients treated during 12 months as totaling 834,077 for drug abuse clients treated in 4,880 facilities, and 1,430,034 alcoholism clients treated at 5,582 units. New York State and California together accounted for nearly one-third of all clients in treatment for alcohol and drug abuse (Lewis, 1989a).

The *National Drug Control Strategy* monograph of January 1990 (Office of National Drug Control Policy, p. 36) estimates that the nation spends at least $2 billion and possibly as much as $3 billion a year on treatment of drug addiction. According to the same NDATUS report mentioned earlier, treatment was funded that year by state and local governments (33 percent), the federal government (23 percent), third-party insurers (27 percent), and private individuals or charities (17 percent).

Those interested in a detailed account of the evolution and present status of drug treatment in the United States should consult Segal (1988, pp. 341–364). He relates how opium dependency in the United States arose primarily from Civil War soldiers' addiction to morphine for relief of pain, with their being treated primarily by private physicians to help them through withdrawal with sedatives or undertaking morphine maintenance in controlled doses.The 1914 Harrison Act subsequently led to banning of use of opiates to treat dependency and to driving opiate use underground. Establishment of morphine maintenance clinics in a few large cities did provide some short-term care, but could not deal with long-term resumption of opiate use, and so these clinics were discontinued by 1925. By that time addiction was most prevalent not among the middle-aged, but among young, male users who preferred heroin to morphine.

In 1929 Congress established two narcotic treatment hospitals, in Lexington, Kentucky, and Fort Worth, Texas, to treat primarily adults, both addicted prisoners and voluntary commitments. Primary treatment was detoxification in prolonged isolation from the addictive environment, but the recidivism rate for readdiction after discharge was estimated as being as high as 97 percent. Similar high rates for return to narcotics occurred among youths covered in a New York State hospital program in the 1950s. Segal attributes the high recidivism rates to relying only on attempts to induce abstinence rather than basic behavioral and personality changes, to the lack of resources to forestall the patients' return to the same drug-infested environments, and to the "self-fulfilling prophecy" in the attitudes of most of those addicts that heroin addiction is incurable.

As Segal reports, the explosion of illicit drug use during the 1960s led to the federal government's turning the treatment of addicts primarily over to the states, providing some funds to help establish treatment programs. The policy was instituted of diverting heroin users from the criminal justice system through the program called Treatment Alternatives to Street Crime (TASC), which facilitated the development of more community-based treatment programs. These included therapeutic communities, medical treatment, psychotherapeutic treatment, behavioral approaches, drug-free outpatient treatment, and multimodality treatment.

Therapeutic communities, which includes such organizations as Synanon and Phoenix House, claim a high success rate, which may be attributable in part to the largely highly motivated clientele willing to subject themselves to a very challenging and often harsh environment.

While the medical complications of addiction to heroin and cocaine are usually not life-threatening in themselves (except for the risk of AIDS from nonsterile needles), at the present state of the art about all that the medical profession can do to help the heroin addict is to administer sedatives during withdrawal. The addict is then put on an orally administered methadone maintenance program to block the "high" of heroin—but that leaves the client with a methadone addiction. Narcotic antagonists such as Naltrexone can block the effects of opiates, and thus are useful adjuncts to long-term rehabilitation programs. Acupuncture also is used increasingly in relieving withdrawal symptoms.

As in the treatment of alcoholism, behavioral techniques to offset drug addiction include aversive conditioning, covert sensitization, electrical aversion therapy, and systematic desensitization. These techniques are showing some promise of being useful in improving the efficacy of medical treatment.

Long-term psychotherapeutic approaches have not been very successful with drug addicts, although "reality therapy" (dealing with immediate problems) has produced some good results, particularly with adolescents.

A vast variety of drug-free outpatient programs are also practiced in the United States, including crisis intervention (for example, help provided by free clinics during "bad trips"), counseling centers, and self-help groups such as Narcotics Anonymous, built on the Alcoholics Anonymous model.

Segal cautions us that for cocaine addiction, there is not as yet anything available to provide even the temporary palliative effect of methadone for opiate addiction.

In closing his chapter on treatment of drug addiction, Segal says that our society needs to apply a realistic standard with respect to *what* types of addiction should get the highest priority, should define reasonable treatment *goals,* and should develop *specific standards* for what constitutes "success" in treatment.

According to the *National Drug Control Strategy* monograph (Office of National Drug Control Policy, 1990), the federal administration has proposed an increase in funding for drug treatment of $1.5 billion for fiscal 1991. Most such federal funds are allocated in the form of block grants to the states, administered through the Office of Treatment Improvement (OTI) within ADAMHA. Fiscal 1991 block grant funding is nearly $577 million, including a $100 million increase, which should provide for an additional 11,000 treatment slots. Current block grants already support the equivalent of 71,000 treatment slots able to serve about 178,000 patients per year. (As noted earlier, there were 263,510 drug abuse clients in treatment on October 20, 1987, exclusive of those in jails or prisons.)

The *Strategy* monograph recognizes the necessity to develop programs that not only help users to get off drugs, but to *stay off.* Users often need many kinds of help in addition to getting rid of their addiction, including medical attention for mothers and children who are HIV positive, treatment of addiction in the estimated 100,000 "crack babies" born each year to addicted mothers, psychiatric care, and vocational training to help to get them a new start in life. Since the recidivism rate is so high, preventive aftercare and counseling should get a high priority in the future. The administration would like to see the development of more systematic statewide treatment action plans for better coordination of needed treatment services.

According to Schuster (1989), intravenous (IV) drug users make up about 25 percent of all AIDS cases in the United States. These abusers can spread that deadly infection to other IV users through sharing contaminated needles, and to their sexual partners and their unborn children. Approximately 65 percent of all U.S.-born AIDS cases attributed to heterosexual contact report having had sex with an IV drug abuser. About 70 percent of all the children with AIDS are born to IV drug-using women or those who are the sexual partners of IV drug abusers. Currently, the number of IV drug abusers with AIDS is doubling every fourteen to sixteen months. NIDA is expediting research to develop AIDS risk-reduction strategies and is running demonstration programs to target those at high risk of AIDS to help in getting more of them into earlier treatment.

The new drug initiative has meant substantial additional funding to NIDA so that it can expand and supplement its Household and High School Senior drug surveys on an annual basis, for evaluation of treatment methods, and for in-service training for professionals.

As for the criminal justice system, an estimated half of federal prison inmates and nearly 80 percent of state prison inmates have used drugs, but most convicts finish their terms without having been treated, and consequently many return to a life of drugs and crime soon after release. The federal moneys allocated for in-prison treatment for fiscal 1991 ($8 million for federal prisons plus $28 million through the U.S. Probation Office for those released under court order for further treatment) sound small. The *Strategy* monograph admits the need to devote more money and attention to the addicts in state prisons and jails to provide better enforced legal sanctions against parolees who return to drugs, and also more counseling and treatment services to help released prisoners remain drug-free.

The U.S. Department of Justice maintains a Drugs and Crime Data Center and Clearinghouse, which provides useful drug-related crime statistics on a toll-free number (see the resource). The following statistics makes it clear that while very large proportions of either state or federal prisoners have been users of illicit drugs, a very small proportion are incarcerated just for simple possession of drugs:

From *Drugs and Crime Facts, 1989* (Office of Justice Programs, 1990): Between 1974 and 1986, the proportion of *state prisoners* under the influence of an illegal drug at the time of the offense for which they were imprisoned rose from 25 to 35 percent (cocaine use grew from 1 to 10.7 percent; heroin use fell from 16.2 to 7 percent). Of all those *referred to federal* prosecutors in fiscal 1987, 24.9 percent were *suspected* of drug law violations. *Among* those, almost 87 percent were alleged to have distributed or illegally manufactured drugs, 9 percent were suspected of importing drugs, and 4 percent were suspected of simple possession. The number of persons *convicted* of violating federal drug laws rose to 13,423 in 1987 from 5,135 in 1980.

From *Profile of State Prison Inmates, 1986* (Office of Justice Programs, 1988): Only 2.9 percent of state prison inmates were incarcerated for drug possession and 5.4 percent for drug trafficking. (Contrast this with 54.6 percent incarcerated for violent crimes and 31.9 percent for property offenses.)

Improving Treatments for Addiction

AIDS and the continuing high usage of heroin make the development of more effective treatment approaches a vital concern to

NIDA (Schuster, 1989). Buprenorphene, a long-lasting opiate antagonist with apparently low physical-dependence properties, is being tested in heroin addicts. Tricyclic antidepressants, which appear to lessen craving, are also being given scientific trials with cocaine addicts. In addition, NIDA is accelerating its neuroscience research to study how environmental factors interact with brain chemistry to affect vulnerability to addiction, particularly in regard to the role of opioid receptors in the brain. Studies of the neurotoxic effects of drugs are continuing on such matters as the role of amphetamines in killing nerve cell terminals of neurons containing dopamine (the neurotransmitter lost in Parkinson's disease) and marijuana's damaging effects on brain memory centers.

As noted earlier, Senator Biden, chairman of the Senate Judiciary Committee, has recommended a $1 billion, ten-year federal effort to conduct research on promising drug treatment medicines. He recognizes that NIDA already has a medications development program, and is seeking to make the program permanent and increase its funding. The research program would set top priorities on research on medications for pregnant women and their fetuses and would address the problem of simultaneous use of heroin and cocaine (Culhane, 1990c, pp. 1, 16).

In the 1980s, cocaine was considered incapable of producing dependence because clinical consensus then held that cocaine did not produce a withdrawal syndrome (Gawin and Kleber, 1988). However, recent clinical investigations demonstrate that cocaine produces unique abuse and withdrawal patterns that differ from other major abused drugs. Evolving preclinical research over the past two decades now suggests that chronic cocaine abuse produces neurophysiological alterations in specific areas of the central nervous system that regulate the capacity to experience pleasure. As suggested previously by Schuster, this type of research appears to be leading to applications of promising experimental pharmacological treatments for cocaine abuse.

A. M. Washton, long-term analyst of addiction processes, insists that an effective treatment program for cocaine addiction must incorporate education and counseling. The abstract of one of his recent articles runs as follows:

> Education is a key element in preventing relapse; patients must be taught to understand the subtle cues by which they are affected, the multiple factors that drive their cocaine use, and the need for complete abstinence from all mood-altering substances, including alcohol and marijuana. Although abstinence is essential to relapse prevention, it is not the only issue. Recovery can be achieved only when patients change their attitudes and behaviors that led to and/or were associated with drug use. Patients must learn: (1) that relapse begins long before drug use occurs, (2) to anticipate high-risk situations, and (3) to develop alternative coping skills to manage the stress and frustration of daily life. Moreover, if relapse does occur, it must be viewed as a learning event rather than as a negative, guilt-provoking disaster in order to avoid recurrences. Analytically oriented psychotherapy is contraindicated early in therapy; counseling and self-help groups must provide support that is reality-based [Washton, 1988, p. 34].

It is important for clinicians to be alert to the likelihood of multiple dependence on alcohol, cocaine, and other drugs in their patients (Miller, Millman, and Keskinen, 1989). The use of alcohol by cocaine addicts is a common cause for relapse to cocaine. The treatment of cocaine addiction is simplified if alcohol dependence is also present because the same methods can be used for both. In Miller, Millman, and Keskinen's study, 94 percent of patients who qualified for the diagnosis of cocaine dependence were also diagnosed as having alcohol and other drug dependence.

Youthful cocaine users are very hard to get into treatment. Brown, Rose, Weddington, and Jaffe (1989) were able to recruit 12 cocaine-using clients twenty-one or younger over a period of nine months, while recruiting 122 adult cocaine clients during a comparable time frame. An examination of admissions data for the city, state, and nation indicated that their experience is typical. However, data from the most recent national household survey indicate that, to the extent need for treatment is determined by frequency of cocaine use, the authors would anticipate a much greater proportion of admissions to treatment to come from persons twenty-one years of age and younger in the near future. "Yet, there appears to be an under-recruitment of youth into treatment, particularly evidenced by low rates of self-referral for juvenile as compared to older treatment admissions. Younger cocaine users may be less severely impaired and/or dependent, or may be more reluctant to use the treatment resources available. Whatever the barriers are to getting help, it becomes the special task of agencies and individuals in the community to help assure that younger cocaine users will obtain the assistance they need. Four community resources are seen as particularly relevant: family, schools, the medical community, and public agencies in the areas of health, social services, and criminal justice" (Brown, Rose, Weddington, and Jaffe, 1989, p. 8).

Therapeutic communities are growing in influence within the drug treatment field. While the number of clients who can be accommodated within any single total-immersion, tough-love mutual support therapeutic community is obviously relatively small, it may well be that these communities are the most cost-effective mode of treatment in view of the fact that most other treatments have such high recidivism rates.

One prototype for this sort of community is the Delancey Street movement in San Francisco. This work/rehabilitation program, a success for many years, has a high percentage of deprived minorities of low education, but 70 percent complete the basic two-year course consisting of useful tasks and technical training, cooperative living, general education, rap sessions, and self-evaluation. Some stay four years, learning crafts and trades as well as work in construction, retail, and wholesale businesses. Delancey Street runs a lot of small businesses and services, including moving and trucking, Christmas tree sales, and handicrafts. While it has enjoyed some support from foundations, it is largely self-supported by the revenues of its client residents, and it even has accumulated enough capital to buy an imposing amount of real estate for living quarters and shops! ("Ex-Users Get a Fresh Start," 1989). The organization, headed for years by Mimi Silbert (who has doctorates in criminology and psychology), brings in $6 million a year through its homegrown services. Their new $14 million headquarters will be home to 350 one-time addicts, felons, prostitutes, and derelicts, who carried out most of the construction work themselves. Silbert claims a success rate in reforming addicts of close to 90 percent (Stein, 1990).

As discussed in the preceding chapter, Senator Biden and others have been highly critical of what they see as Drug Czar Bennett's apparent emphasis on punitiveness rather than treatment in dealing with drug addicts. Bennett's (1990) rejoinders appear in a thirty-one-page "White Paper," *Understanding Drug Treatment.* In the press briefing accompanying the release of the White Paper, Bennett defended his position by saying that he recently had visited twenty drug treatment programs all around the country, and that he was a firm believer in the necessity for treatment. However, he defended (1990, p. 10) what some have called his punitive attitude in his comments in rejecting the concept of treatment "on demand": "The call for such a system obscures the far more pressing and practical needs of drug treatment. Addressing those needs requires us to come to grips with the fact that while the need for treatment is high, the actual demand for it is relatively low. The overwhelming majority of addicts must be 'jolted' into drug treatment and induced to stay there by some external force: the criminal justice system, employers who have discovered drug use, spouses who threaten to leave, or the death of a fellow addict." Although he cautioned that relatively few addicts kicked the habit without relapses, he spoke favorably of the results achieved by long-term treatment in therapeutic communities that maintain strict control over the addict's environment and behavior. But this White Paper did not indicate that Bennett had any intention of reallocating any substantial funding from criminal justice and drug interdiction programs to the treatment of drug addicts.

Although some of the measures utilized to deal with drug addiction that have been described in this chapter have been relatively successful, the more effective ones tend to be very expensive and time consuming because they are dealing with a very powerful addictive process that is continually reinforced by cultural and socioeconomic influences. For humanitarian reasons as well as to keep a relatively bad situation from becoming worse, we are obligated to continue to treat addicts as best we can. However, in the long run the solution to a substantial reduction in drug problems in America is to be found through application of *better primary prevention* efforts. Some of the newer thinking about improving prevention is presented in the final two chapters of the book.

PART FOUR

Building a Stronger Climate of Prevention

CHAPTER NINE

Organizing Effective Prevention Programs

Sir Edmund Burke, in his notable speech before the British Parliament, emphasized that if democracy is to be effective, the "four estates" of executive and legislative power, organized religion, the people, and the media must all pull together. This chapter presents some ideas on how at least these four estates can do a better job in reducing the prevalence of destructive use of tobacco, alcohol, and illicit drugs.

Certainly we need more leadership in Congress to bring about better control of tobacco, alcohol, and other drug problems. Because of heavy campaign contributions and organized pressures from the constituents of alcohol and tobacco companies, most members of Congress are still in a position that they will catch more flak than support if they back legislation that runs counter to alcohol and tobacco companies' interests. Fortunately there are growing signs that some progress may be made soon in reducing the influence of campaign contributions on congressional decisions. But there is also much need for the general public to provide more support for the underfunded nonprofit organizations that are attempting to provide research findings and moral support to bolster congressional actions to bring about more effective control of alcohol and other drug problems.

While many of the current prevention programs in the United States are worthwhile, growing numbers of those who have studied the problem for a long time have come to the conclusion that the situation will not get very much better until we do more to eliminate some of the *basic causes* of addiction and the desire to find surcease from misery through use of drugs. As Representative Charles Rangel, chairman of the Congressional Select Committee on Narcotics Abuse and Control, put it in a letter to the editor of the *New York Times* (1989, p. A18),

> Unless we attack the root causes of drug abuse, we are likely to see continued record prison overcrowding—and record hospital emergency room cases, record economic loss to society through lost productivity and lost tax revenues—no matter how many prisons we build or how much we threaten punishment.
>
> We need to focus on the problems that bring people to the desire for illicit drugs—homelessness, unemployment, lack of education, lack of health care, lack of family, and above all, poverty. There is a major gap in the President's antidrug strategy in not examining the causes of drug abuse and possible solutions. . . .
>
> We need coordinated community-based efforts to address the many social and economic conditions that are at the root of serious drug addiction and drug crime. We must look at these root causes and how to plug the gaps in our national drug strategy that make our cities especially vulnerable to drug abuse and to drug crime.

An even sharper polemic on the need for change in our ways of achieving our national goals was voiced by Anthony Lewis (1990). He had just returned from South Africa, where he found many winds of change; he observed (1990, p. A 27) that "in South Africa, the most profound assumptions of the society are changing. In the United States, the political system is frozen." He said that the U.S. government and public seems "determined to close its eyes to the realities that menace its future." He listed as our serious problems the decline on savings and investment capital and our crumbling infrastructure of roads and bridges and other public facilities. Ours is an ill-educated society in a world in which education is essential, and thirty-one million of our people have no medical insurance. "A vast underclass mocks America's reputation as a just society. Homeless men and women huddle on the fanciest streets of our cities."

He said that President Bush's economic "remedy" is to cut the capital gains tax, "irrelevant at best," and that "he is unwilling to challenge the prevailing public mood of antipathy to government. It takes leadership for a country to face the need for change. This country has no leadership: not in the White House and not in the opposition party."

Yet even before the collapse of the Cold War in Europe, the American public voiced a desire to reduce military spending but not social programs to pay for antidrug programs. A Harris poll of August 27, 1989 (Harris, 1989a) found that by margins of 4 to 1 or better, sizable majorities of the American people simply were not prepared to cut federal health and education programs, nor assistance to the elderly or the homeless in order to pay for the new Bush administration's antidrug program. Of the eight areas of major federal spending tested, the only case where people were willing to make spending cuts to finance the antidrug campaign was in defense spending.

Another Harris poll reported on October 1, 1989 (Harris, 1989b) found an 82 to 18 percent majority of parents felt that in contrast to when they were growing up, problems relating to children have "gotten worse." The number of parents who felt "very satisfied" with the reliability of child care had gone down from 54 to 28 percent just in 1989. "The child care problem is made far worse due to the fact that over 6 in 10 mothers of children 6 or under are working and on the average have over three different kinds of care they utilize in a given week for their children. This uncertainty has led 7 in 10 to want Federal and governmental help to develop a child care infrastructure that can adequately serve their needs."

Still another Harris poll—on October 29, 1989, (Harris, 1989c)—found that the number of "alienated" in the United States had risen from 54 to 58 percent in just one year. This was below the all-time high of 62 percent in 1983, but was double the 29 percent level back in 1966. (The Harris Alienation Index is made up of five basic questions: "The rich get richer and the poor get poorer," "Most people with power try to take advantage of people like yourself," "What you think doesn't count very much anymore," "The people running the country don't really care what happens to you," and "You are left out of things going on around you.") Most alienated: people earning $7,500 or less, 72 percent; African-Americans, 68 percent; Hispanics, 63 percent; women, 61 percent; and those over age sixty-five, 59 percent.

And still another Harris poll, on November 5, 1989 (Harris, 1989d), found that "the number of Americans who favor the Federal government using 'its powers more vigorously to promote the well-being of all segments of the people' has increased from 30 percent back in 1982 to a current high of 51 percent today. By the same token, the number who feel the 'Federal government has too much power' has dropped over the same period to 29 percent." When people were asked where the federal government might be more active, the following findings emerged:

Strictly enforcing environmental cleanup, 92 percent
Helping people who are homeless, 89 percent
Building and staffing more drug treatment centers, 87 percent
Finding ways for people to find affordable housing, 85 percent
Sending more aid to victims of earthquakes and hurricanes, 80 percent
Building more prisons to control crime, 78 percent
Being more active in moving toward ending discrimination against minorities, such as African-Americans and Hispanics, 73 percent (Harris, 1989d)

Our children are especially the victims of long-term inadequacy in our social programs. A recent report by the Select Committee on Children, Youth, and Families of our House of Representatives has found that one in five American children lives in poverty—a tie with Australia for the highest poverty rates among the dozen developed countries compared ("Troubled Children," 1990). Eighteen countries, including Singapore, Spain, and Ireland, have lower infant mortality rates than the United States. American teenage females had a higher birth rate than any other developed country surveyed except Hungary, and ten times the teenage birth rate for Japanese females. The United States also leads in the proportion of all the deaths of young people caused by accidents, suicide, homicide, or other violence (78 percent). Young U.S. males are more than five times as likely to be murdered as those in other developed countries. The United States ranks nineteenth in teacher-pupil ratios, behind such countries as Libya, East Germany, and Cuba; twelfth in eighth-grade mathematical achievement among eighteen nations studied; and fourteenth among sixteen countries in expenditures on elementary and secondary education as a percentage of gross national product.

Census Bureau data for 1988 show that one in five children live in households below the poverty line. As recently as 1960, 91 percent of white children and 67 percent of African-American children lived with two parents, but in 1988 the white figure had dropped to 79 percent and the African-American figure to 39 percent. Now more than seventeen million children are living with fewer than two parents, and are thus more at risk of neglect (Rich, 1989).

Even in the face of such embarrassing statistics on how poorly our children are doing in comparison with those in other developed countries, the one outstandingly successful twenty-five-year-old program to build a foundation of self-esteem, social skills, and basic lessons for poor preschool children, Head Start, still has to limp along with grossly inadequate funding. Child advocates and business leaders repeatedly have called for enough funding to enroll all of the estimated 2.5 million children age three to five who are eligible (only 20 percent of these are currently enrolled). The current budget is $1.4 billion. Congressional leaders say that more than $6 billion is needed, but the administration says it would approve only about $1 billion (Cooper, 1990).

For years, demographers have been warning employers about the fact that soon there will be even fewer young, entry-level workers, and many will lack the skills for their jobs. However, a recent study of 4,000 employers found that while nearly 85 percent of the companies surveyed said they were aware of existing or impending shortages of entry-level workers, only one-third of those expressing concern have formulated plans to find and keep employees (Skrzycki, 1990b).

Fortunately, even some of the more business-minded leaders in our country are getting more and more uneasy about the low level of education and training provided in our schools. Former Labor Secretary Elizabeth Dole said in a Chicago speech that "the United States is one of the few industrialized nations without a formalized school-to-work transition. With our workforce growing at its slowest rate in 40 years, we can't afford this any longer . . . Mechanics who once tightened bolts on assembly lines now have to operate computers which control millions of dollars' worth of complex machinery. Soon over half the jobs in our workplace will require education beyond high school, and almost every job will demand workers who possess a solid basic skills foundation" (in Greene, 1990, p. A5).

As Labor Secretary, Dole appointed a commission of business, education, and labor leaders to develop national guidelines for work readiness. Her commission was headed by William Brock, former Labor Secretary, and members included at least two former state governors and heads of corporations. It outlined criteria that employers require for certain jobs, for use by schools and training programs. One of Dole's proposals was the "two-plus-two" program, under which students spend four years in intensive work-study programs, two years in high school, and two years in community college if they are still unsure about their place in the workforce. Employers would serve as partners by hiring students during the learning process, which would begin during the last two years of high school.

This Commission on the Skills of the American Workforce came out with a report in the summer of 1990 that called for a multibillion-dollar program, to be financed by both government and industry, to accomplish at least the following primary goals:

- Require every U.S. student to meet by age sixteen educational standards as high as those of any other country.
- Ensure that virtually every student achieve this level by creating and paying for alternative learning environments as necessary. Dropouts would be discouraged by prohibiting children under eighteen from working unless enrolled in a program to meet the educational performance requirement.
- Provide extensive technical and professional training for the 70 percent of the population that does not go to college.
- Require every employer to spend at least 1 percent of its payroll to educate, train, and improve the skills of its workers. (Currently, few U.S. companies come close to spending the recommended 1 percent of the payroll on training, but German firms already are required to spend 3.5 percent, and 2.5 percent is required in Sweden.)

The report suggests that these proposals could increase federal and state spending by $36.2 billion per year, and the panel chairman said corporate spending on training would jump by almost $25 billion to meet the 1 percent requirement (Eckhouse, 1990). Of course, at a time of massive federal deficits and urgent needs to repair America's roads and other public facilities and to try to improve the health of a sick public educational system, it will be surprising if very much will be done to meet these commendable worker training goals very soon.

Our leaders still have to learn that it costs far less in the long run to *prevent* disability, drug abuse, slum conditions, and unemployability than it does to try to treat them after they have become endemic. There is an urgent need to change our attitude toward public education and training from considering it an onerous but necessary civic obligation—like welfare—to thnking of our investment in education as our seed money for our country's future. We cannot hope to be competitive in the world markets of tomorrow unless we have a well-educated citizenry working in an atmosphere of mutual trust that everyone is being treated fairly.

"But where will the money come from?" has been the stock response from the White House for a generation. Yet all through the Reagan years, taxes rose and rose again—on the one hand being wasted on excessive esoteric military equipment instead of being invested in our people, and taken out of the hides of states and cities in the way of higher property taxes, sales taxes, garbage disposal fees, and state income taxes.

As Henry Aaron, senior fellow at the Brookings Institution, has said, "We are an extremely rich country. The question is whether we are raising enough to cover the public expenditures that bipartisan majorities insist the nation requires. And we aren't" (Uchitelle, 1990). In many respects, we have seen our country sliding back toward being a confederacy of states instead of acting like a national union, when we consider how the states and cities hardest hit by unemployment and crime, like New York and Detroit, are being left largely to their own devices in raising the money to cope with their pressing problems—and with little if any national moral support or leadership to help them.

It is barely possible that the political paralysis of both the federal administration and Congress over fear of losing votes by raising taxes may give way under public pressure to do something to patch up our sickly schools, slums, highways and public transportation, huge fiscal deficits, and slump in competitiveness in international trade. A modest biting of the bullet by increasing taxes would hurt the U.S. citizenry very little in the long run compared to the damage that would result from our continuing to drift deeper in debt to the point where we would be even less able to cope with our gradually worsening set of social problems.

But we need more than mere money in coping with such social illnesses as alcohol and other drug problems. Community pride and mutual supportiveness need to be reawakened in an era in which we have such a heavily transient population and so many latchkey young people who are not getting proper attention from family members. One remedial program that bears promise is in Berkeley, California, whose mayor, Loni Hancock, says,

> People don't understand the relationship between tax cuts and homelessness, or between deinstitutionalization and mental health problems. And often they don't understand that doing poorly in school, growing up in a low-income house, getting into trouble with the law and teenage pregnancy are all related.
>
> That's why reinvesting in young people has to start in the community. In November, we started funding a high-risk youth program that involves a consortium of agencies. There are 130 young people in the program, and each one has access to family counseling, tutoring, recreation and role models who can serve as mentors. We had more than 400 applications for 130 spots. I think this is the kind of involvement, and concentration of resources, that it will take to make a real difference [MacNamara, 1990, p. 12].

OSAP's Community Relations Program

This rather modest Berkeley project is just one illustration of what individual communities and neighborhoods can do to deal with drug and alcohol problems as well as providing more positive guidance and inspiration to young people. OSAP's community relations programs include a growing number of pump-priming grants to neighborhood organizations around the country that couple both funding for meeting places and access to plans and guides on how to go about more effective community action. This action can involve improving zoning on liquor stores, getting rid of crack-dealing outlets, dealing with youth gangs and truancy problems, and encouraging more wholesome recreational facilities for young people.

The publication *Prevention Plus II: Tools for Creating and Sustaining Drug-Free Communities* (Office for Substance Abuse Prevention, 1989), readily obtainable without charge from NCADI (see the resource), is a helpful 541-page guide for community organizations on general and specific strategies for prevention of problems with tobacco, alcohol, and other drugs. The book provides readily understandable descriptions of the dynamics of addiction and of strategies focused on the individual, peer group, parents, school-based, mass media, and regulatory and legal action. It is replete with specific plans and efforts. While a few of the earlier specific community prevention programs smack too much of the now-questioned, shallow "Just say no!" approaches of the Reagan years, this monograph is recommended as an important document for community leaders to have on hand.

The OSAP management appears pretty well aware of the many potential risks and benefits involved in launching such an ambitious number of community prevention demonstration grants. The risks include the pressures toward hasty funding inherent in a program in which many members of Congress will be intent on getting additional moneys for communities within their constituencies. While the OSAP guidelines emphasize that community demonstration grants are only to be pilot projects for the purpose of developing innovative ways of coping with local alcohol and drug problems, many communities will hope to get continued funding. Thus there is an inherent risk that communities that get demonstration grants will exert extra pressure to get more permanent funding, with loss of community morale if not achieved, as well as additional pressure put on the generally poorly funded state alcohol and drug agencies to fill the funding gap. Further, while OSAP guidelines emphasize the need for the application of careful scientific methods in evaluating the effectiveness of programs initiated under each grant, few communities have adequate access to such skills. Also, although each OSAP community demonstration grant carries along with it explicit standards for fiscal accountability, management of several hundred grants always entails some risk of misuse of funds. It is hoped that such grants' added stimulus to community interest in prevention programs, and the useful lessons that can be learned about which kinds of projects are the most successful, will be more than enough reward to offset the risks entailed.

OSAP has just published another monograph that explores many other problems (and opportunities) to be encountered in conducting community action research programs in various settings (for example, schools, workplaces, and drinking establishments). An international collaborative effort between OSAP, the Addiction Research Foundation of Toronto, and Health and Welfare Canada, this OSAP Monograph 4 (Giesbrecht and others, 1990) contains thirty-two separate papers by authors from eleven countries. Of practical interest to research methodologists and community program administrators alike, some of the more noteworthy articles are those of Robin Room (who spells out why community prevention programs have an inherently different dynamic than those of national programs, with more community emphasis on alcohol-related traffic casualties, crime and family violence, and alcohol-related public disorders), Harold Holder and Norman Giesbrecht (perspectives on the community in action research), and Robert Reynolds (his California experiences in the perils and rewards of specific community prevention programs).

Those experienced in the field of community organization warn that helping a community to organize itself requires special skills in the way of sensitivity to the community's primary needs. Charles Minor Huff and Robin Wechsler, of the Marin Institute in Northern California, warn that good community programs are planned from the bottom up rather than from the top down.

As Huff says, "The organizer trusts people who live in a given community to have the best understanding of the problems they face and to have the best guess at what the solution might be. . . . If you come into a community and claim to be an expert, you'll wind up doing all the work and in essence no one will learn from the process" (University of California at San Diego, Summer 1990e). Wechsler tells how she started working within one community by joining a local gospel choir, where members spent the first hour of choir practice talking about problems in their personal lives and in the community. Thus she learned what problems were most important to local residents and to gain the confidence and trust of people in the community by showing an informed, personal concern about local problems.

Another encouraging sign that more effective primary prevention of alcohol and other drug problems is well underway is that both national and local agencies are now progressing in getting their act together. Only a few years ago, nonprofit organizations (in the field of alcohol problems especially) were often at loggerheads, competing for official attention over whether treatment *or* primary prevention should have the highest priority. Now more of the agencies listed in the coalitions described in Chapter One are pulling together in agreeing that *both* treatment and prevention are important, but that it is often more cost-effective if prevention can lessen the need for treatment.

One recent illustration of cooperative activity on the party of federal, state, community, and private agencies is the current drive to marshal support for the Sensible Alcohol Family Education Act (SAFE) sponsored by Senator Albert Gore and Repesentative Joseph Kennedy, which would require that five different health and safety messages be rotated for both broadcast and print advertising. The print messages would be coupled with a federally funded telephone number to offer individuals access to more information about alcohol use. The National Association of State Alcohol and Drug Abuse Directors (NASADAD) sent out a broadside to all their member agencies, requesting that they publicize the merits of the Gore-Kennedy bills and urge people to write or call their senators and representatives to support the bills (Heldman, 1990). Attached was a long list of supportive nonprofit health and educational organizations entitled the "Coalition on Alcohol Advertising and Family Education." Two leading advocacy agencies, the Washington-based Center for Science in the Public Interest and the National Council on Alcoholism and Drug Dependence (NCADD), appended an Action Plan that recommended not only writing to legislators in support of the bills, but also asking local media to stop airing alcohol advertisements that appeal to youth, protesting the sponsorship of local events (such as sports contests) by alcohol producers, and working with the media to educate the community about the role of alcohol in health problems.

Jean Kilbourne (1990), speaking on behalf of the NCADD before a congressional committee, emphasized the vulnerability of youth to alcohol advertising by pointing out that many youngsters below legal drinking age actually are heavy drinkers. She cited the 1989 National Institute on Drug Abuse survey of high school seniors in which one-third reported they had consumed five or more drinks on at least one occasion within the previous two weeks. She pointed out that the eighteen- to thirty-four age group, which makes up about 40 percent of the population, drinks about 50 percent of all beer consumed, and that wine coolers, targeted to youth, have become almost a $2 billion industry.

My book *Understanding America's Drinking Problem: How to Combat the Hazards of Alcohol* (1987) made a number of recommendations for reorganizations within federal agencies to bring about more effective application of preventive measures. Since that time, as discussed earlier, the vastly increased funding through the War on Drugs initiatives has made it possible to carry out many promising preventive activities on a state and community level—although (again) fully 70 percent of the money is being spent on trying to stop the flow of drugs into our country, with a relatively small proportion being devoted to programs to reduce consumer demand for illicit drugs. A better balance in funding is sadly needed.

Another move should be to streamline and clarify the somewhat overlapping responsibilities of the series of agencies within the Department of Health and Human Services that were so hastily patched together in the setting up of the War on Drugs. Thrown together under the ADAMHA umbrella agency were the NIAAA, NIDA, OSAP, and other auxiliary units, with all these having had a somewhat ambiguous responsibility to the White House agency under William Bennett. While many dedicated people in these agencies are trying hard to work together effectively, some battles over turf were inevitable when certain prevention responsibilities were taken away from NIAAA and NIDA and turned over to OSAP; and continuing leadership will be needed from the office of the Secretary of Health and Human Services to mediate occasional conflicts over responsibilities and funding.

Bennett was not entirely helpful in this process, since (for example) he denied that the War on Drugs initiative had any authority concerning alcohol—yet at the same time OSAP has been trying to carry out a prevention program designed to reduce consumption among the young for alcohol as well as for tobacco and illicit drugs.

Bennett's adversarial style, exhibited in frequent clashes with congressional committee members, made him temperamentally unsuited to be "Drug Czar," a position with rather limited authority but with urgent responsibility to persuade local, state, and federal agencies to pull together in drug prevention, treatment, and law enforcement. On the day of Bennett's resignation, right after the 1990 election, Gerald Kaplan, a law professor at George Washington University and a member of the American Bar Association committee on drugs, did give him some credit for improving the coherence of drug efforts at the federal and state levels. However, Kaplan said, "But I also think he manipulated the issue politically and proclaimed success prematurely. He should have said straight out this is going to be a very long struggle and the costs would be high" (Savage, November 9, 1990, p. A18). It is hoped that his successor will be more adept at patient fence-mending with administrative agencies and Congress; but successful future federal drug programs will depend primarily upon much better cooperation of the President and Congress in agreeing upon a realistic set of priorities (and budgets) for dealing with national drug problems over the long haul.

One chronic jurisdictional problem still exists: the continued assignment of responsibility for monitoring advertising and marketing of tobacco and alcohol to the Bureau of Alcohol, Tobacco, and Firearms (BATF) in the Department of Treasury. As I pointed out in Chapter Three of my 1987 book, this long-term assignment to the BATF has caused a chronic conflict of interest. This is because the Treasury-based BATF sees its role primarily as maintaining an orderly (and profitable!) market in tobacco and alcohol so as to bring in steady taxes for its boss, and the BATF long has had a much-too-cosy relationship to the tobacco and alcohol industries. While more than half the 145,000 injury deaths per year in the United States in 1985 were directly associated with alcohol, tobacco, or firearms (McLoughlin and Wang, 1989), the BATF has consistently shirked its responsibility for policing tobacco and alcohol advertising. As noted in earlier chapters, only recently has the BATF grudgingly yielded, under extreme congressional pressure, to require labeling of health hazards on alcohol containers and some improvement in the visibility of similar warnings on tobacco advertising. In my 1987 book, I recommended that marketing and advertising of tobacco and alcohol be reassigned to the Food and Drug Administration, but thus far Treasury has resisted any change despite widespread dissatisfaction with the stewardship of the BATF.

Further suggestions on improving the stewardship of prevention programs within the federal government can easily be made. Regarding the control of *tobacco,* again the government should eliminate the subsidies now given to tobacco growers, eliminate tax deductions for tobacco advertising, spend more money on antismoking campaigns, and encourage private businesses in their control of smoking in enclosed spaces frequented by the general public or in rooms occupied by nonsmokers. Also, funding for smoking-cessation research should be maintained at an adequate level, for it should pay for itself in reduction of medical costs for treatment of emphysema, lung cancer, and heart disease.

Regarding NIDA's role in dealing with *illicit drugs,* it is different from tobacco and alcohol because the latter are legal products that require marketing controls and enforcement of manufacturing standards in addition to attempts to try to minimize the damage they cause. For its own continued survival in such a controversial field, NIDA probably will be wise to continue to carry out its relatively low-profile primarily research and educational missions rather than expanding into any policing functions—at least until more dust settles over former Drug Czar Bennett's War on Drugs. As mentioned earlier, NIDA has a number of promising long-term monitoring projects (such as its national surveys of illicit drug use) and laboratory research on drug effects, and is now trying to accelerate its progress in the development of drug antagonists to neutralize the effects of cocaine in the treatment of addicts. Currently, NIDA is attempting to develop or refine measures for testing individuals for alcohol or other drug use that are reliable and that are less intrusive than urine tests. One such promising test, for the use of cocaine, is conducted through spectrographic analysis of human hair, which could have the advantage not only of being less embarrassing than urine testing, but also of providing a time profile of use over past weeks or months. However, NIDA officials say that it may take five years before this particular type of test could be validated sufficiently to stand up in court cases.

Concerning *alcohol,* it appears that a great many more remedial administrative measures are possible and necessary for the legal and still widely consumed alcoholic beverages than is the case for tobacco and illicit drugs. I recommended in Chapter Eleven of my 1987 book that NIAAA be given the authority and funds to carry out more of the same comprehensive set of responsibilities as the alcohol control agencies in the Scandinavian countries, which would include:

1. Coordinating more of the alcohol-relevant activities of a host of other federal agencies (for example, Treasury, Agriculture, Commerce, Transportation, and so on) to make sure the public interest is being served.
2. Cooperating with the Food and Drug Administration to set standards for purity and adequacy of labeling of alcoholic beverages.
3. Establishing constraints against misleading alcohol advertising or advertising and marketing practices that contribute to alcohol abuse (for example, promotion of sales or service to below-age minors).
4. Strengthening liaison with state agencies that administer laws or regulations over alcohol. While ever since repeal the states have had much control over alcohol within their

own boundaries, uniform laws should be encouraged to minimize differences in enforcement practices in adjoining states.

5. Continuing development of model regulations for coverage of alcoholism as a condition treatable under health insurance, dramshop (service of alcohol) liability laws, and zoning standards for alcohol outlets.
6. Expanding data gathering operations on state laws and regulations regarding alcohol and on treatment and prevention activities within all states.
7. Continuing to put a high priority on comparative studies of alcohol control policies and practices throughout the world, so as to be able to exchange ideas on alcohol control policies with other countries and to cooperate with the World Health Organization on programs to minimize alcohol problems.

As noted in Chapter One, Christine Lubinski (1988), in congressional committee testimony, recommended that controls over alcohol like those listed previously should be taken over by the Food and Drug Administration. This might be more to the liking of the NIAAA management itself, considering its present evident desire to concentrate on scientific research, which usually entails less risk of becoming embroiled in political controversy than is true in the arena of alcohol control.

Several other responsibilities proposed for the NIAAA in my 1987 book are already under way, including the extensive pilot studies of patient-matching treatment programs described in Chapter Six of this book, more demonstration projects to promote primary prevention on the community level (now taken over largely by OSAP), and strengthening the information retrieval programs that had been skeletonized by lack of funding (also taken over under OSAP in its National Clearinghouse for Alcohol and Drug Information [NCADI], with somewhat increased funding).

Dealing with Media Problems

One of the prevention issues on which there has been concerted effort on the part of many organizations is the pressure toward better control of tobacco and alcohol marketing and advertising. Through dogged persistence and concerted campaigns to get the attention of Congress, these coalitions finally have managed to bring about regulations to put health warnings on both tobacco and alcohol labels and all tobacco advertising, and an increasing number of states are imposing increased cigarette and alcohol taxes with provision for spending part of the money on prevention and treatment. Early passage of similar federal taxes now looks very likely.

As noted in Chapter One, the National Council on Alcohol and Drug Dependence has come out with an appeal for curbs on utilizing "current or traditional heroes of the young or active or retired, amateur or professional athletes or athletic events" in alcohol advertising or promotions. It has also recommended requiring broadcasters to give equal time for health and safety messages to promote accurate information about drinking, especially directed toward those under twenty-one; eliminating alcohol advertising and promotion and sponsorships of events on college campuses and eliminating billboards on alcohol advertising from mass transit systems and sports stadiums; not allowing billboard alcohol advertising any closer than 500 feet from residences, schools, parks, churches, community centers, or other places youth might gather; and eliminating the deductibility of alcohol advertising expenditures. If the media wish to avoid a protracted confrontation with influential prevention advocacy groups like the NCADD that have active chapters in communities throughout the country, they will be well advised to cooperate in any acceleration of the process of voluntary controls over offensive alcohol and tobacco advertising.

The medium with the greatest power to influence public attitudes on life-styles and acceptable behavior is *television*. Audience measurements have shown that the average household set is in use seven hours a day, and many children watch it avidly for long hours under conditions of passive acceptance of the behavior on the screen as acceptable social norms and aspirations. Studies have measured the enormous amount of violence on television (Rowland, 1983). They have also shown that use of alcohol and drugs is commonplace in many of the programs children watch (Wallack, 1984b), and that beer ads on television emphasize a go-for-the-gusto gulp-it-down scene full of sportive young people (Jacobson, Atkins, and Hacker, 1983). Yet the television industry and the advertising industry in general have stonewalled the question about alcohol advertising with the stock alibi that after all, it has not been *proven* that alcohol advertising is a bad influence—that all such advertising does is try to influence brand preferences. As noted earlier, Wallack's reasonable rejoinder is that it is also the case that it cannot be proven that advertising does *not* lead to increased consumption. He suggests that in a society so steeped in television that it is impossible to do a controlled before-and-after study on the adverse effects of the showing of unhealthy life-styles as being an acceptable social norm, at least the television industry ought to agree to be more responsible about the role models it shows on the screen.

In an article on the role of mass communication, Wallack (1990a) stresses the usefulness of "social marketing" as a framework in which to integrate marketing principles and social-psychological theories to accomplish behavior-change goals. However, he says social marketing too often has failed to try to counteract the pervasive anti-health education messages in advertising and television programming. He says that a campaign emphasizing the culpability of alcohol companies that promote deadly products to teenagers can help to shift attention away from defining alcohol problems as solely the property of individuals, and to highlight the role of those who shape the environment. He tells how the tobacco industry has presented itself as the champion of civil rights and protectors of free speech and characterizes antismoking groups as zealots, health nuts, and health fascists, but that antismoking people lately have helped to reframe the issues by casting tobacco producers as "merchants of death" and exploiters of women, youth, and minority groups.

Actually, the general public can have considerable power in bringing about deletion of television marketing of harmful products, through organized boycotts of such products and letter-writing campaigns directed to the companies sponsoring the advertising, requesting them to cancel or modify the misleading or offensive programs. Any growth in the modern-day "good health" movement is likely to lead to more such applications of consumer power in the near future.

Prevention Goals for the Health Care Professions

Both financial and ethical incentives for those in the health care professions (physicians, nurses, psychologists, and social workers) need a thoroughgoing overhaul if any real progress in prevention of tobacco, alcohol, and other drug problems is to be attained. Because of the traditional American fee-for-service culture, at present almost all financial rewards are based on treating or confining the sufferer *after* he or she has become addicted. This situation has worsened in recent years because of the escalation of the Medicare and Medicaid and private insurance programs' emphasis on expensive tertiary treatment or detention instead of primary prevention. Present American values have called for the dominance of the medical profession in the health care field, and this expectation has carried over to a considerable extent into the area of dealing with the prevention of addictions. However, the present training, traditions, and financial incentives of the medical profession are focused primarily around a fee-for-service treatment of the individual patient rather than upon primary prevention. While Health Maintenance Organizations (HMOs) serve clients on a per capita basis and thus have considerable fiscal incentives to *keep* their clients from becoming ill, the HMOs in general still have much to learn in organizing to play a really effective role in primary prevention. One might predict that HMOs will be motivated to accelerate their outreach prevention programs once there have been conclusive demonstrations that such programs can be very cost-effective, but such proofs may be years in coming.

The recent change in medical reimbursement for Medicare toward increasing the incentives for the physician to spend more time with the individual patient could be utilized to encourage the physicians to pay more attention to the patient's overuse of tobacco, alcohol, and other drugs. However, physicians traditionally are reluctant to alienate patients by being inquisitive about their smoking, drinking,and drug use. Medical schools and the medical and other health care associations will need to put more emphasis on primary prevention, and health care clients will need to become more accustomed to frequent (but confidential) questioning about their health-relevant habits, before any satisfactory program of primary and secondary prevention can be achieved.

On the other hand, the health care professions need to be sensitive to avoiding a backlash among its clients against overzealousness in their questioning about their habits. One way to forestall this is for the professional always to adopt the perspective of former Surgeon General Koop, who often opened his frank talks about AIDS and other sexually or needle-transmitted diseases by saying that he was responsible for the nation's health, not its morals.

One positive force for the encouraging of effective primary prevention on the community level is the new OSAP-sponsored program of grants to communities to encourage prevention initiatives to cope with such problems as drug dealing and the need for better zoning and control over alcohol service establishments. Health care professionals usually will find they can have a very positive impact on the community's health by endorsing and joining in on such community prevention activities, and such participation can serve to enhance the professionals' standing among their clients.

To sum up the need for more effective prevention progams to lessen the damage done by tobacco, alcohol, and other drugs: Organization leaders need to be watchful lest they demand unwarranted constraints on the use of these substances that go beyond reasonable health and safety considerations. This problem particularly could arise in communities if agencies become overzealous in vying with each other over turf or funds to the point of pushing substance control measures beyond the limits of public tolerance.

Too, all politicians and public agencies need to be watched constantly. They may be ducking the more unpleasant issues concerning public health and safety by blaming outside scapegoats or by hasty adoption of short-term palliative measures instead of long-term reforms. This is particularly the case with prevention issues involving tobacco, alcohol, and illicit drugs. The prime reason for the damage caused by these addictive substances is simply that the American public uses them excessively, yet legislators are slow to adopt controls over tobacco and alcohol because those industries are powerful lobbyists and campaign contributors and provide a lot of jobs for voters throughout the country. As for the market in illicit drugs, thus far the federal administration has put the blame more heavily on foreign suppliers than upon our own people's demand for those dangerous substances. But it is clearly impossible to bring about much reduction in illicit drug use by expensive and risky paramilitary strikes against the foreign suppliers, because unless we diminish the demand for drugs, the foreign drugs will merely be supplanted by such domestically produced synthetic drugs as methamphetamine "ice."

America is indeed a nation of individualists, and we are greatly concerned about preserving our freedom of choice. But like the fish who are little aware of the water around them, we are not sufficiently aware of how much our life-styles and choices within our culture are influenced by marketers and politicians who have a stake in selling us substances and ideas that may not be good for our long-term health and prosperity. "Eternal vigilance is the price of victory" is really the watchword of a new book by Phyllis Langton of George Washington University, *Drug Use and the Alcohol Dilemma* (1991), which is recommended as a systematic, fact-oriented summary on how much political and marketing institutions can shape our lives if we let them.

With all the media emphasis on our "me" generation, it might look as though we have an inherently selfish middle-class and wealthy population who are simply determined to turn their backs on the problems of poverty, homelessness, and race prejudice that constitute much of the root causes of our current alcohol and other drug problems. However, in the past the American people have responded magnificently to *sudden* huge crises, such as World Wars I and II and massive earthquakes and hurricanes either at home or abroad. It may well be that part of the apparent current indecision about giving the problems of poverty and prejudice a higher priority is that we often respond decisively to try to solve serious social problems only in the face of an obvious immediate crisis. It will take more determination on the part of the national administration and Congress to face up to doing much more about the problems of poverty and prejudice, if we are to stave off the prospect of even worse crises in the near future stemming from our current drift into a society deeply divided between the affluent and the desperately poor. Fortunately, there are many signs from recent public opinion surveys that the American public would be willing to tighten belts to provide the resources to provide us with better education and training, housing, and health care—*if* our political leadership really faces up to the urgency of our country's most urgent human needs.

CHAPTER TEN

Rebuilding a Prevention-Oriented Society

An increasing number of observers of our American culture are concluding that while much lip service is being paid by leading politicians to our becoming a kinder, gentler nation by bringing up our housing, educational, and health standards to at least the level of other leading industrialized countries, we are courting disaster by our moving too slowly in that direction. Robert Reich (1984) points out that our taking better care of the poor and unfortunate can more than pay for itself in the long run.

Reich notes that every time unemployment in the United States rises 1 percent, deaths from all causes rise by 1.9 percent. When a person is unemployed, he or she is likely to have more gastrointestinal problems, more infections, and higher blood pressure. Ironically, when most workers lose their jobs, they also lose their health insurance.

Two out of every five African-American teenagers are now out of school and out of a job. Social programs not only are inadequate, but have been the first targets of campaigns to reduce expenditures, because of the assumption that all they do is prepare economic laggards for traditional employment or save people from destitution. They are seen as analogous to charity—affordable only when resources can be spared from more pressing matters.

Reich points out (pp. 206–207) that because education, job training, health, housing, and nutrition are considered by many to be social luxuries and consequently are poorly planned and inadequately funded, the national work force is now inadequate; American workers lack the training to shift into flexible-system production. They do not get the necessary training because public schools, colleges, and job-training programs are so inadequate; and they can't move to locations where they can get adequate on-the-job training because they lack the housing, health care, and financial backing to make this possible.

Reich adds that U.S. social politics are not properly connected to the country's economic development, because social programs tend to follow the same organizational pattern as the no longer adequate high-volume, standardized production of material goods. For example, education is too often evaluated in terms of such standardized commodities as years of education rather than adequacy of preparation for roles in real life. He notes (p. 218) that because educational and many other social programs are evaluated on the basis of the number of "units" delivered rather than their effects in improving competency and sound health and economic improvements, those who pay taxes tend to resent social programs as "charity" because they are unaware of the programs' real contributions to our nation's assets. In turn, those who are permitted to participate in social programs tend not to receive full benefit from their participation because they are made to feel the stigma that is attached to their status as dependents.

Reich reminds us that social security and unemployment insurance are more generous in continental Europe and Japan than in America. Japan, Sweden, and West Germany all have substantial national health programs. Infant mortality is much lower in Sweden, Japan, and West Germany than in the United States, and life expectancy is longer in all of these three countries, which spend a larger portion of their gross national product on all forms of social services than does America. While our school system is more egalitarian and more than 75 percent of American pupils graduate from high school and more than half enter college, in most other industrialized countries less than 30 percent graduate from high school and many go on to technical and vocational schools rather than college. Thus they may be making a better living than if they had not acquired any specialized skills.

Reich (1984, p. 239) says that America could facilitate better training and employability by "merely alternating the mix of tax incentives and subsidies flowing to American business, which now encourage paper entrepreneurialism and historic preservation and discourage investments in human capital." He says we could establish government-subsidized vouchers to pay for part of on-the-job training, retrain older workers for new jobs, and provide more tax incentives for productive investment and fewer for corporate takeovers and other speculations. He also recommends replacing personal income tax with a progressive tax on consumption, to encourage savings.

Paul Kennedy (1987) sounds similar warnings: He sees America riding for a fall if we do not shape up in our social programs as well as our technological efforts. We are slipping in productivity relative to Japan and China, and West Germany and France are now ahead of us in gross national product per capita and Japan is gaining fast. Japan spends much more per capita on research and development and the Japanese save much more because of the difference in tax systems. The European Economic Community has the potential in size, wealth, and productive capacity to be a truly formidable trade competitor, since its twelve-member population totals around 320 million—50 million more than the Soviet Union and almost half as large as the U.S. population. It is a highly trained population, with hundreds of colleges and universities and millions of scientists and engineers, and yet as noted earlier, several of these European countries also manage to maintain higher standards of health care and social safety-net programs than we do.

Turning now to the plight of our young people: American children are much more likely to be murdered, to live in poverty, or come from broken homes, than children in many of the world's other developed nations (McLeod, 1990). In a study produced for Congress by the U.S. Census Bureau's Center for International Research (1988) and reported by Representative George Miller (D-Calif.) of the Select Committee on Children, Youth, and Families, twelve countries were compared: the United States, Australia, Canada, France, West Germany, Hungary, Italy, Japan, Norway, Sweden, the Soviet Union, and the United Kingdom. The United States matched Australia in having the highest child poverty rates (17 percent), the United States had the highest percentage of children affected by divorce (23 percent), the U.S. infant mortality rate was twice that of Japan's, and male youths in the United States were more than five times as likely to be murdered as those in other developed countries. U.S. girls aged fifteen to nineteen gave birth (mostly outside of marriage) at more than ten times the rate for Japanese girls.

The arrival of the 1990s has stimulated increased soul searching by social commentators on the deterioration of the quality of life in America within the last generation. As Reeves says,

> If "we"—I mean the people of the United States and Canada, Western Europe and Japan—will be seen by history to have been steadfast and triumphant over most of the world during the past 40 years, we have paid a high price at home, particularly we Americans. We have lost control of our own destiny.
>
> The wreckage at home seems appalling as we begin a decade where events will certainly speed up even more. Our ambition for our children became greed for ourselves, and some of the worst of us accumulated the vast fortunes at the expense of the weaker. The accumulation or just the survival of families took so much energy and time, requiring the work of mothers and children, too, that we were too busy to notice that some of those children never learned to read and others never learned anything—and are lying on our streets or lurking in doorways willing to kill for the price of a handful of drugs [1989b, p. A25].

A White House Conference on Food, Nutrition, and Health resolved in 1969 "to put an end to hunger in America for all time." Yet twenty years later, the United States still falls far short: Nearly 10 percent of the population is malnourished. Nearly half the population is living in poverty, at risk of stunted growth and mental retardation because they do not get enough to eat. Half of all poor families who rent a house or apartment put at least 70 percent of their income into rent and utilities, leaving little money to pay for food (Squires, 1989).

MacNamara (1989), one of many recent writers who have emphasized the importance of dealing with poverty as a means of combating crime and alcohol and other drug problems, reminds us that we now have 250,000 to 3 million homeless people across the country, and a vastly greater number of "working poor" who are right on the edge of abject poverty. He cites a growing belief that poverty is a rubric for a host of spreading social ills: inadequate public education, the high rate of teenage pregnancies and high school dropouts, drugs, gangs, and the fact that 40 percent of the poor people in this country are children. Further, if half the workers of the next generation are poor and without skills, we will not have the gross national product necessary to produce the taxes to pay for the baby boomers' retirement.

The one long-term poverty prevention strategy that everyone agrees on is *education,* particularly at the elementary school level. Lisbeth Schorr (1989) says that this is a terribly important time to mend our ways: that if we do not make the needed changes, polarization in our society will become even more severe, and eventually we will have to wall ourselves off from the unfortunates in our society.

Fortunately Louis Sullivan, Secretary of Health and Human Services, continues to speak out on the importance of primary prevention. In a speech before the American Public Health Association, he said that each American must accept personal responsibility for better health practices, and he urged public health officials to mention prevention in every appropriate context, making it a major theme of every speech and presentation and working with poor and minority citizens to inform them. He noted that recent figures show life expectancy for

African-Americans has declined in the last several years, that African-Americans have death rates one and one-half times those of whites, and that infant death rates are twice as great among African-Americans as among whites. He is especially concerned about improving prenatal care and medical and nutritional support for mothers and children in poor families (American Public Health Association, December 1989a).

Again, I am convinced that we cannot begin to bring about effective prevention programs to solve our alcohol and other drug problems until we get the "four estates" of the legislative and executive bodies, the courts, the media, and our adult population to work together to build a more wholesome cultural climate that deemphasizes alcohol and drugs. We must also change most drastically the ways in which we relate to our own young people.

We have to begin to realize that our children can be either among our nation's greatest assets or its greatest liabilities, depending on how we nurture and educate them. This fact becomes more and more self-evident when we see how several European countries and Japan are forging ahead of us in their quality of life, largely because their younger people are provided with better training and other resources and incentives to become productive members of society. Particularly in the United States, what we do to help our children in the future is becoming increasingly urgent because the proportion of children of non-English-speaking, undereducated parents is growing very rapidly, taxing the resources of our schools and other community agencies.

At present, most of us expect both too little and too much of our youth. We make it too easy for them to gratify their immediate whims, and too many of us convey to them an attitude of "Don't do as I do, do as I say" when they know we may be drinking a considerable amount but they are not supposed to touch the stuff. Many of us are so taken up with making a living that we do not spend enough time with our children to make sure they are developing the right attitudes and skills to cope with the world of tomorrow and that they do not run around with those who will set them a bad example.

And what about the households where there is only a single parent? The present level of child care resources is abysmal. Even in France, which we might not think of as a particularly affluent country, they do a much better job of seeing that youngsters get proper care and supervision. Recently a delegation of prominent Americans spent two weeks studying child care in France and concluded that "France is a country at a level of economic development similar to that of the United States but far ahead of us in ensuring that its young children are well and safely cared for." Even parochial child care centers are heavily subsidized by the state. A member of the delegation said, "We have seen the future, and we're behind" (Reeves, 1989a).

Some might think that governmental provision for adequate daytime child care facilities is a socialist or mollycoddling idea, but a great many parents would be able and willing to pay for daytime child care and nursery schools if only they were readily available. Even for those who cannot afford to pay for such daytime care, the lack of such resources means that the taxpayers simply have to shell out a great deal more money to pay for the jails and emergency medical care for the neglected children who turn to lives of petty crime and drug dealing out of sheer desperation or lack of proper supervision.

If grandparents or guardians are taking care of a child, it should be possible for them to get government assistance in fulfilling this important role. And it should not be necessary to build up a vast bureaucracy of government-run child care centers or supervisory agencies. It can actually be made relatively easy to provide reimbursements for child care costs through tax deductions or direct remittances for those who cannot afford to pay, or through employers in the same fashion as for much health coverage. (Again, as with so many cost-effective prevention programs, it costs the taxpayers a great deal more in the long run for prisons and hospitals and disability and unemployment costs to incarcerate or to patch up those who fall by the wayside because of preventable alcohol and drug use.)

American adults tend to be too inconsistent in their attitudes toward children. Little toddlers are almost always so adorable, with their trusting, upturned smiling faces. But when they become teenagers, when many of them turn away from us with scowls and when we cross inner-city streets fearfully to avoid meeting with a gang of them, they are regarded (and treated) by many of us as evil people to be avoided or punished. Such attitudes on our part are reciprocated, in turn, by bitterness and alienation among the young.

Ideally, every child should have or be assigned one or more adults who will be responsible for his or her welfare and behavior. Parents and guardians should be kept aware of their very real responsibility for their children's development as good citizens. Substantial financial incentives and educational programs should be provided where necessary to make such commitments have a fair chance of succeeding. Being an effective guardian or parent must often be learned; it does not necessarily come about through sheer instinct. Therefore, there should be much readier access to learning how to be a good parent or guardian—through convenient parenting discussions and classes in which parents and guardians learn more about how others have solved the kinds of problems they are having in raising their own children.

Too often we set our children up to be losers by giving them either too much or too little attention at crucial times. Children who grow up with a realistic sense of self-worth are better prepared than others to cope with an often unfriendly and overcompetitive adult world. The California Task Force to Promote Self-Esteem and Personal and Social Responsibility, directed by Assemblyman John Vasconcellos and chaired by Andrew Mecca of the California Health Research Foundation, has produced a 144-page book entitled *Toward a State of Esteem* (California State Department of Education, 1990). The book fulfills the first stage of 1986 legislation authored by Vasconcellos. It found correlations between low self-esteem and deviant behavior, showing that feelings of poor self-worth are both a cause and a result of social problems emerging from institutions that deprive and warp the development of young people. While the report could not offer much in the way of remedial legislative action, and although the very concept of the task force was ridiculed by cartoonist Garry Trudeau in *Doonesbury,* at least it drew attention to the importance of providing attainable goals for youngsters and encouraging the development of their self-esteem when they are at a very insecure age.

Finally, turning again to the War Against Drugs, we have to be careful to guard against its developing into a War against Young African-Americans as we try to cope with the crack cocaine trade. It is true that in the past America has often cried wolf over so-called drug "epidemics," only to find them gradually subsiding. But today, the truth is that for the first time in our nation's history, here is a highly pleasurable, addictive substance that is relatively inexpensive for each "high" it produces, is much in demand, and is compact enough for several hundred dollars' worth to be concealed in a youngster's pockets. Crack cocaine thus provides a ready-made "solution" for neglected, dropout youths in inner cities. It allows them to temporarily forget their miseries and artificially boost their self-esteem and at the same time be able through their hustling to bring in enough money to feed their own habit and maybe bring a little money home—if they have a home.

Bootlegging during Prohibition was not attractive enough to sustain many youthful entrepreneur street merchants in the inner cities, because the profit margins were slim and the product too bulky to be carried around in one's pockets. In any case, the market was dominated by Caucasian ethnic groups that later became upwardly mobile and lived to see their grandchildren become lawyers, judges, and physicians. But crack appears to have all the advantages of a self-perpetuating career for inner-city minority youth. The pity of it all is that as more and more minority youth drop out of school and join up with drug gangs, the more their communities deteriorate and the less the local authorities can cope with the problem. And over time, the outside world takes an increasingly punitive attitude toward those caught up in the system and demands severe punishment for even minor drug dealers—who then in turn ultimately are back on the streets again after their postgraduate prison course in crime.

To sum up: We all can join together to build a kinder, gentler nation—if we try. To expand our present ounce of prevention so that it is worth more than a pound of cure for our addictions to tobacco, alcohol, and other drugs, we have to develop the hardihood to do more to solve the root causes of those addictions—poverty, homelessness, lack of education and job training, and racism. It is not a question of whether we can *afford* to solve those basic problems of our nation, because such problems while unsolved will cost us far more in the long run. And considering the far worse problems in the way of wars and depressions that we have surmounted during the last 200 years, certainly we can bring about a better life for all our people, if we just roll up our sleeves and get to it.

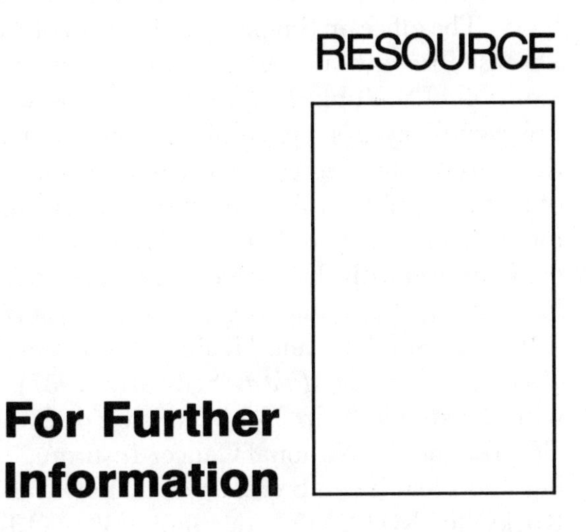

For Further Information

Information on the use of alcohol, tobacco, and illicit drugs and preventive and treatment programs concerning such substances is expanding at an exponential rate. (There were only six alcohol or other drug journals when NIAAA was founded in 1971; there are now at least thirty.) Below are listed some key sources of such information from federal government agencies or nonprofit prevention advocacy groups. Much information is provided free of charge, although some publications are procurable at nominal cost.

The most comprehensive single source is the National Clearinghouse for Alcohol and Drug Information (NCADI) within the Office for Substance Abuse Prevention. It can provide researchers or the general public with abstracts on new findings concerning alcohol, tobacco, and other drugs and kits on the availability of prevention information. Each month NCADI answers more than 12,000 telephone and mail inquiries. The NCADI is also an excellent source for the serial or occasional publications of NIAAA (for example, *Alcohol Alert*) and NIDA (for instance, *NIDA Notes*). For information or to get a free materials catalog, contact the NCADI via P.O. Box 2345, Rockville, MD 20852, or telephone 301-468-2600, or call the toll-free number, 1-800-SAYNOTO.

The office on Smoking and Health of the Center for Chronic Disease Prevention and Health Promotion, Centers for Disease Control, U.S. Public Health Service, aids in preparing the annual Surgeon General's reports on the epidemiology and health consequences of nicotine use (see Chapter Three), as well as a host of popular public information pamphlets and selected technical monographs, such as *A Decision Maker's Guide to Reducing Smoking at the Worksite* (with the Office of Disease Prevention and Health Promotion, 1985), *The Health Consequences of Using Smokeless Tobacco* (Office on Smoking and Health, 1986), and *Review and Evaluation of Smoking Cessation Methods* (Schwartz, 1987), which was prepared with the sponsorship of the Division of Cancer Prevention and Control and the National Cancer Institute. The Office on Smoking and Health can be reached at: Park Building, Room 1–16, Rockville, MD 20857, telephone 301–443–1690.

The Institute of Medicine (IOM), a nonprofit arm of the National Academy of Sciences operating under congressional charter, has completed five landmark NIAAA-sponsored studies since 1980. *Prevention and Treatment of Alcohol Problems: Research Opportunities* (1989; see Chapter Five) received partial financial support from the Pew Foundation and the National Research Council Fund. This report completed the second stage of the Institute of Medicine's mission to study alcohol research progress and needs. The first stage was completed with publication of the IOM report on the causes and consequences of the misuse of alcohol (Institute of Medicine, 1987). The other IOM book-length reports, all published through National Academy Press, include *Alcoholism, Alcohol Abuse and Related Problems: Opportunities for Research (1980); Alcohol and Public Policy: Beyond the Shadow of Prohibition* (Moore and Gerstein, 1981), the 1987 study on the causes and consequences of alcohol problems just mentioned, and *Broadening the Base of Treatment for Alcohol Problems* (1990). Information as to costs can be obtained from National Academy Press, 2101 Constitution Avenue, NW, Washington, DC 20418. To order any of these books by telephone using a credit card, use the IOM's toll-free number: 800-624-6242.

The National Council on Alcoholism and Drug Dependence (NCADD) (see Chapter One) publishes occasional Fact Sheets covering topics on alcohol and drug effects such as those especially relevant to women, on birth defects, and involving children and youth. Some of their Fact Sheets are printed in Spanish. For information, write or call the NCADD Public Information Officer, 12 W. 21st St., New York, NY 10010, telephone 212-206-6770.

One of the best-known publications of the Center for Science in the Public Interest (CSPI) (see Chapter One) is *The Booze Merchants: The Inebriating of America* (Jacobson, Atkins, and Hacker, 1983). Recent publications include a *Citizen's Action Handbook on Alcohol and Tobacco Billboard Advertising* (McMahon and Taylor, 1990); a brief monograph on *State Alcohol Taxes* (1990); *Alcohol Warning Signs: How to Get Legislation Passed in Your City* (Schechter, 1986); *Impact of Alcohol Tax Increases on Federal Revenues, Alcohol Consumption, and Alcohol Problems* (by the National Alcohol Tax Coalition, 1989); two books on minority populations, *Marketing Disease to Hispanics* (Maxwell and Jacobson, 1989) and *Marketing Booze to Blacks* (Hacker, Collins, and Jacobson, 1989); and *What You Can Do to Support Health Messages in Alcohol Ads* (Coalition on Alcohol Advertising and Family Education, 1990). CSPI also gets out prevention-oriented press releases and newsletters, including *Booze News,* a semimonthly newsletter covering current issues concerning alcohol prevention policies. New address for the CSPI: 1875 Connecticut Avenue, NW, Suite 300, Washington, DC 20009-5728; telephone 202-332-9110.

The *Advocacy Institute's* advisory newsletters to prevention advocacy groups on how to advance their causes generally follow a specific who-what-when-where pattern: succinct advice on where to direct advocacy efforts, brief slogans and "media bits" to convey messages, useful quotations from authorities, and suggested specific actions. Address to get on the Institute's mailing list for their information or Action Alerts, and for further information on the Institute's activities: 1730 Rhode Island Avenue, NW, Suite 600, Washington, DC 20036-3118; telephone 202-659-8475; FAX (202) 659-8484.

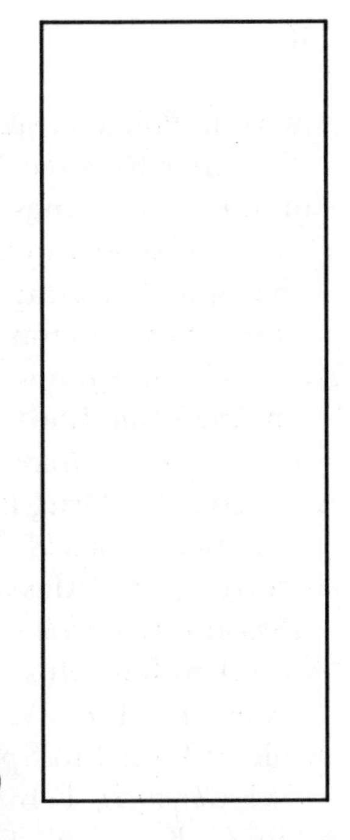

References

"Alcohol, Heart Disease, and Mortality." *Harvard Medical School Health Letter,* May 1989, pp. 1–2.

American Cancer Society, American Heart Association, and American Lung Association. *A Decision Maker's Guide to Reducing Smoking at the Worksite.* Report to the Office of Disease Prevention and Health Promotion and Office on Smoking and Health. Washington, D.C.: U.S. Government Printing Office, 1985.

American Psychiatric Association. *Diagnostic and Statistical Manual of Mental Disorders.* (3rd ed.) Washington, D.C.: American Psychiatric Association, 1987.

American Public Health Association. "HHS Head Sullivan Tells APHA: Make Prevention an Obsession." *Nation's Health,* Dec. 1989a, p. 8.

American Public Health Association. "Policy Statement 8817, 'A Public Health Response to the War on Drugs: Reducing Alcohol, Tobacco and Other Drug Problems Among the Nation's Youth.'" *American Journal of Public Health,* 1989b, *79* (3), 360–364.

American Public Health Association. "Kennedy Introduces Anti-Smoking Package." *Nation's Health,* Jan. 1990, p. 1.

Ames, G., and Janes, C. R. "Prevention of Alcohol Problems Among American Blue Collar Families." Paper presented at the annual meeting of the American Anthropological Association, Washington, D.C., Dec. 1985.

Ames, G., and Janes, C. R. "Heavy and Problem Drinking in an American Blue Collar Population: Implications for Prevention." *Social Science and Medicine,* 1987, *25* (8), 949–960.

Anderson, J. "'Drug Babies' May Be a Fiscal Time Bomb." *San Francisco Chronicle,* Nov. 29, 1989, p. A27.

Armstrong, S. "Alaska's Version of a Drug Crackdown." *San Francisco Chronicle,* Apr. 11, 1990, p. A10.

"Amtrak to Ban Most Smoking, Lawmakers Say." *San Francisco Chronicle,* Mar. 22, 1990, p. A3.

"Athletes Urged to Spurn Tobacco 'Blood Money.'" *San Francisco Chronicle,* Feb. 24, 1990, p. A1.

Atkin, C. K. "Alcoholic-Beverage Advertising: Its Content and Impact." In. H. Holder (ed.), *Control Issues in Alcohol Abuse Prevention: Strategies for States and Communities. Advances in Substance Abuse.* Suppl. 1. Greenwich, Conn.: JAI Press, 1987, 267-287.

Austin, G. A. *Perspectives on the History of Psychoactive Substance Use.* Rockville, Md.: National Institute on Drug Abuse, 1978.

Austin, G. A. *Alcohol in Western Society from Antiquity to 1800.* Santa Barbara, Calif.: ABC–Clio International Services, 1985.

Barabak, M. Z. "Van de Camp's New Target." *San Francisco Chronicle,* Apr. 19, 1990, p. A13.

Beckett, J. "Stop-Smoking Product Sales Heating Up." *San Francisco Chronicle,* Apr. 18, 1990, p. 1.

Bell, R. M., Gareleck, C., and Ellickson, P. L. *Baseline Nonresponse in Project ALERT: Does It Matter?* Publication N-2933-CHF. Santa Monica, Calif.: The Rand Corporation, Apr. 1990.

"Bennett Rejects Further Curbs on Guns." *San Francisco Chronicle,* Feb. 3, 1990, p. A10.

Bennett, W. *Understanding Drug Treatment: An Office of National Drug Control Policy White Paper.* Washington, D.C.: Office of National Drug Control Policy, June 1990.

Bezilla, R., and Gallup, G., Jr. "How Drugs Became the Public's Most Important Problem Facing the Country." Paper presented at the 45th annual conference of the American Association for Public Opinion Research, Lancaster, Pa., May 1990.

Blum, K., and others. "Allelic Association of Human Dopamine D2 Receptor Gene in Alcoholism." *Journal of the American Medical Association,* 1990, *263* (15), 2055–2060.

Bohman, M., Sigvardsson, S., and Cloninger, C. R. "Maternal Inheritance of Alcohol Abuse: Cross-Fostering Analysis of Adopted Women." *Archives of Genetic Psychiatry,* 1981, *38,* 965–969.

Bolos, A. M., and others. "Population and Pedigree Studies Reveal a Lack of Association Between the Dopamine D2 Receptor Gene and Alcoholism." *Journal of the American Medical Association,* 1990, *264* (24), 3156-3160.

Boyd G. M., and Glover, E. D. "Smokeless Tobacco Use by Youth in the U.S." *Journal of School Health,* 1989, *59* (5), 189–194.

Brandon, T. H., Tiffany, S. T., Obremski, K. M., and Baker, T. B. "Postcessation Cigarette Use: the Process of Relapse." *Addictive Behaviors,* 1990, *15,* 105–114.

Braverman, M. T., D'Onofrio, C. N., and Moskowitz, J. M. *Marketing Smokeless Tobacco in California Communities: Implications for Health Education.* NCI Monographs, no. 8. Washington, D.C.: U.S. Government Printing Office, 1989, 79–85.

Brecher, E. M., and the editors of *Consumer Reports. Licit and Illicit Drugs.* Boston: Little, Brown, 1972.

Brown, B. S., Rose, M. R., Weddington, W. W., Jr., and Jaffe, J. H. "Kids and Cocaine—a Treatment Dilemma." *Journal of Substance Abuse Treatment,* 1989, *6* (1), 3–8.

Bruun, K., and others. *Alcohol Control Policies in Public Health Perspective.* Helsinki: Finnish Foundation for Alcohol Studies, 1975.

Buchanan, D., with Lev, J. *Beer and Fast Cars: How Brewers Target Blue-Collar Youth Through Motor Sport Sponsorships.* Washington, D.C.: AAA Foundation for Traffic Safety, 1990.

"Bush, Biden Unveil Rival Plans for Fighting the War on Drugs." *San Francisco Chronicle,* Jan. 25, 1990, p. A8.

Butynski, W. *Resource Directory of National Alcohol-Related Associations, Agencies, and Organizations.* Washington, D.C.: National Association of State Alcohol and Drug Abuse Directors, 1985.

Cahalan, D. *Problem Drinkers: A National Survey.* San Francisco: Jossey-Bass, 1970.

Cahalan, D. "Quantifying Alcohol Consumption: Patterns and Problems." *Circulation,* 1981, *64* (suppl. 3), 7–14.

Cahalan, D. *Understanding America's Drinking Problem: How to Combat the Hazards of Alcohol.* San Francisco: Jossey-Bass, 1987.

Cahalan, D. "Public Policy on Alcohol and Illicit Drugs." *Drugs and Society, 3* (3/4), 1989, 169–186.

Cahalan, D., Cisin, I., and Crossley, H. *American Drinking Practices.* New Brunswick, N.J.: Center of Alcohol Studies, Rutgers University, 1969.

Cahalan, D., and Room, R. *Problem Drinking Among American Men.* New Brunswick, N.J.: Center of Alcohol Studies, Rutgers University, 1974.

California State Department of Education. *Toward a State of Esteem.* Sacramento, Calif.: Bureau of Publications, 1990.

Campbell, J. "'Nickel a Drink' Tax Initative Boosted." *Davis* [Calif.] *Enterprise,* Feb. 16, 1990, p. 4.

Case, P., and others. "Needle Exchange: From Civil Disobedience to Public Policy." *MIRA Quarterly Newsletter* [Bayview-Hunter's Point Foundation, San Francisco], 1990, *4* (4), p. 1.

Castro, J. "Volunteer Vice Squad." *Time,* Apr. 23, 1990, p. 61.

Center for International Research, U.S. Bureau of the Census. *Children's Well-Being: an International Comparison: a Report of the Select Committee on Children, Youth and Families, One Hundred First Congress.* Washington, D.C.: U.S. Government Printing Office, 1988.

Center for Science in the Public Interest. "Industry Moves: Producers Battle to Redefine Alcohol." *Booze News,* Nov. 1989, p. 1.

Center for Science in the Public Interest. "Hiking State Excise Taxes Makes Sense/Cents." *Booze News,* Mar. 1990, p. 1.

Chasnoff, I. J., Lewis, D. E., Griffith, D. R., and Willey, S. "Cocaine and Pregnancy: Clinical and Toxicological Implications for the Neonate." *Clinical Chemistry,* July 1989, *35* (7), 1276–1278.

Chiang, H. "Judge OKs Drug Testing for High-Risk Navy Jobs." *San Francisco Chronicle,* Mar. 17, 1990, p. C13.

"Cigarette Ads for Blacks Dropped." *San Francisco Chronicle,* Jan. 20, 1990, p. A2.

Clark, W., and Midanik, L. "Alcohol Use and Alcohol Problems Among U.S. Adults: Results of the 1979 National Survey." In National Institute on Alcohol Abuse and Alcoholism (ed.), *Alcohol Consumption and Related Problems.* Rockville, Md.: National Institute on Alcohol Abuse and Alcoholism, 1982, 3–52.

Cloninger, C. R., Bohman, M., and Sigvarsson, S. "Inheritance of Alcohol Abuse." *Archives of Genetic Psychiatry,* 1981, *38,* 861–868.

Coalition on Alcohol Advertising and Family Education. *What You Can Do to Support Health Messages in Alcohol Ads.* Washington, D.C.: Center for Science in the Public Interest, Feb. 1990.

Coate, D., and Grossman, M. "Effects of Alcoholic Beverage Prices and Legal Drinking Ages on Youth Alcohol Use." *Journal of Law and Economics,* 1988, *31,* 145-171.

Cohen, R. "More Work for Dr. Sullivan." *Washington Post National Weekly Edition,* Feb. 5–11, 1990, p. 28.

Cohen, S. J., and others. "Encouraging Primary Care Physicians to Help Smokers Quit. A Randomized, Controlled Trial." *Annals of Internal Medicine,* 1989, *110* (8), 648–652.

Committee on the Judiciary, United States Senate. *Hard-Core Cocaine Addicts: Measuring–and Fighting–the Epidemic.* Washington, D.C.: U.S. Government Printing Office, May 10, 1990.

"Consumption of Liquor Hits 30-Year Low." *San Francisco Chronicle,* Nov. 25, 1989, p. A4.

Cooper, K. H. "25 Years of Giving Kids a Head Start." *Washington Post National Weekly Edition,* Apr. 20–May 6, 1990, p. 9.

Coulehan, J. L., and others. "Recognition of Alcoholism and Substance Abuse in Primary Care Patients." *Archives of Internal Medicine,* 1987, *147,* 349–352.

Craig, R. J., and Olson, R. E. "Differences in Psychological Need Hierarchies Between Black and White Drug Addicts." *Journal of Clinical Psychology,* 1988, *44* (1), 82–86.

Cranshaw, A. B. "The New Pay-As-You-Smoke Medical Plans." *Washington Post National Weekly Edition,* Mar. 19–25, 1990, p. 19.

Culhane, C. " Controversy Continues over Drug Legalization." *U.S. Journal of Drug and Alcohol Dependence,* 1990a, *14* (2), 2.

Culhane, C. "Drug Offenders Crowd Federal Prison Cells." *U.S. Journal of Drug and Alcohol Dependence,* 1990b, *14* (2), 6.

Culhane, C. "Biden Seeks Research on Addictions." *U.S. Journal of Drug and Alcohol Dependence,* 1990c, *14* (2), 1, 16.

Cullen, J. W. "The National Cancer Institute's Intervention Trials." *Cancer,* 1988, *62* (8 suppl.), 1851–1864.

Cummings, K. M., Giovino, G., and Mendicino, A. J. "Cigarette Advertising and Black-White Differences in Brand Preference." *Public Health Reports,* Nov.-Dec. 1987, *102* (6): 698–701.

Cummings, S. R., Rubin, S. M., and Oster, G. "The Cost-Effectiveness of Counseling Smokers to Quit." *Journal of the American Medical Association,* 1989, *61* (1), 75–79.

Davis, R. M. "Current Trends in Cigarette Advertising and Marketing." *New England Journal of Medicine,* 1987, *316* (12), 725–732.

Davis, R. M., and Kendrick, J. S. "The Surgeon General's Warnings in Outdoor Cigarette Advertising: Are They Readable?" *Journal of the American Medical Association,* 1989, *261* (1), 90–94.

"D.C. Drug War a Year Later." *San Francisco Chronicle,* Apr. 14, 1990, p. A6.

"DEA Says Heroin Poses 'Huge Problem.'" *San Francisco Chronicle,* Mar. 14, 1990, p. A11.

Dean, P. "Citizen Koop." *Los Angeles Times,* Nov. 19, 1989, pp. E1, E8.

Debussmann, B. "A Nation of Drug Users." *San Francisco Chronicle,* Nov. 25, 1989, p. 1.

DelVecchio, R. "New Strategy in S.F. Cops' War on Crack Cocaine." *San Francisco Chronicle,* Jan. 8, 1990a, p. A1.

DelVecchio, R. "An Army of S.F. Social Workers Offers Alternatives to Gangs." *San Francisco Chronicle,* Apr. 10, 1990b, p. A6.

Denniston, R. W. "Comments of the Chairperson, Alcohol and Drugs Section, American Public Health Association." *1990 Section Newsletter,* Spring 1990, 2–3.

Doria, J. J. "Matching Patients to Treatment." *ADAMHA News Supplement,* 1990, *16* (1), 4–5.

"Drug Czar Assails 'The Legalizers.'" *San Francisco Chronicle,* Dec. 12, 1989, p. A13.

"Drugs: Still Testing." *Washington Post National Weekly Edition,* Feb. 5–11, 1990, p. 26.

DuPont, R. "Youth at High Risk of Chemical Dependence: Identification and Intervention Opportunities for the Psychiatrist." *Directions for Psychiatry,* 1988: Lesson 8, June 1988.

DuPont, R. (ed.) *Stopping Alcohol and Other Drug Use Before It Starts: The Future of Prevention.* Office for Substance Abuse Prevention Monograph 1. U.S. Department of Health and Human Services, Publication No. (ADU) 89-1645. Washington, D.C.: U.S. Government Printing Office, 1989.

DuPont, R., and Goldfarb, R. "Drug Legalization: Asking for Trouble." *Washington Post National Weekly Edition,* Feb. 5–11, 1990, p. 29.

Eckhouse, J. "U.S. Worker Training Criticized." *San Francisco Chronicle,* June 19, 1990, p. 1.

Edell, D. "Smoking Drug Won't help You Quit." *San Francisco Chronicle,* Apr. 18, 1990, pp. Z-6, Z-8.

Ellickson, P. L., and Bell, R. M. *Prospects for Preventing Drug Use Among Young Adolescents.* Santa Monica, Calif.: Rand Corporation, Publication R-3896-CIF, 1990.

Elliott, D. S., Huizinga, D., and Ageton, S. S. *Explaining Delinquency and Drug Use.* Newbury Park, Calif.: Sage, 1985.

Ernster, V. L. "Advertising and Promotion of Smokeless Tobacco Products." *NCI Monographs,* no. 8. Washington, D.C.: U.S. Government Printing Office, 1989, 87–94.

"Ex-Users Get a Fresh Start." *San Francisco Chronicle,* Dec. 28, 1989, p. A5.

Farhi, P. "A Drug by Any Other Name." Washington, D.C.: *Washington Post National Weekly Edition,* Jan. 8–14, 1990, pp. 31–32.

Farquhar, J., Maccoby, N., and Wood, P. "Education and Communication Strategies." In W. Holland, R. Detels, and G. Knox (eds.), *Oxford Textbook of Public Health.* Vol. 3. London: Oxford University Press, 1985, 207-221.

"Fascinating Facts." *Wellness Letter,* University of California, Berkeley, Dec. 1989, p. 1.

Fillmore, K. "The 1980s Dominant Theory of Alcohol Problems—Genetic Predisposition to Alcoholism—Where Is It Leading Us?" *Drugs and Society,* 1988, *2* (3/4), 69–87.

Fillmore, K., Johnstone, B. M., Leino, E. V., and Ager, C. R. "A Cross-Study Contextual Analysis of Effects from Individual-Level Drinking and Group-Level Drinking Factors." Paper presented at the 16th annual Alcohol Epidemiology Symposium, Budapest, Hungary, June 1990.

Fingarette, H. *Heavy Drinking: The Myth of Alcoholism as a Disease.* Berkeley: University of California Press, 1988.

"5 Jailed in Seizure of First 'Ice' Lab in Continental U.S." *San Francisco Chronicle,* Jan. 20, 1990, p. A4.

"Flap over U.S. Archives' Deal with Philip Morris." *New York Times,* Nov. 10, 1989, p. A13.

Flay, B. R., and Sobel, J. L. "The Role of Mass Media in Preventing Adolescent Substance Abuse." In T. Glenn and C. Lukevald (eds.), *Preventing Adolescent Drug Abuse: Intervention Strategies.* Washington, D.C.: U.S. Government Printing Office, 1983, 5–35.

Flay, B. R., and others. "One Year Follow-Up of the Chicago Televised Smoking Cessation Program." *American Journal of Public Health,* 1989, *79* (10), 1377–1380.

Freedman, A. M. "Rebelling Against Alcohol, Tobacco Ads." *Wall Street Journal,* Nov. 19, 1989, p. B1.

Gallagher, J. E. "Under Fire from All Sides." *Time,* Mar. 5, 1990, p. 41.

Garber, M. W., and Flaherty, D. "Cocaine and Sudden Death." *American Family Physician,* 1987, *36* (4), 227–230.

Gawin, F. H., and Kleber, H. D. "Evolving Conceptualizations of Cocaine Dependence." *Yale Journal of Biology and Medicine,* 1988, *61* (2), 123–136.

Giesbrecht, N., and others. *Research, Action, and the Community: Experiences in the Prevention of Alcohol and Other Drug Programs.* Office for Substance Abuse Prevention Monograph 4. Department of Health and Human Services, publication no. (ADU) 89-1651. Washington, D.C.: U.S. Government Printing Office, 1990.

Glantz, S. A., and Parmley, W. W. "Passive Smoking and Heart Disease: Epidemiology, Physiology, and Biochemistry." *Circulation,* 1991, *83,* (1), 1–12.

Glaser, G. "Billboards: Blight or Boon? Groups Target Ads for Liquor, Tobacco Aimed at Minorities." *San Francisco Examiner,* Nov. 5, 1989, p. 3.

Gordis, E. "National Institute on Alcohol Abuse and Alcoholism." *British Journal of Addiction,* 1988, *83,* 483–493.

Gordis, E. "Science Aid to Policy Dilemmas: Implications of Alcohol Research to Policy Formulation in U.S.A." *Drug and Alcohol Dependence, 25,* 1990, 183–186.

Gordis, E., Tabakoff, B., Goldman, D. and Berg, K. "Finding the Gene(s) for Alcoholism." *Journal of the American Medical Association,* 1990, *263* (15), 2094–2095.

Greene, L. "Teenage Grads Lack Skills, Mrs. Dole Says." *San Francisco Chronicle,* April 6, 1990, p. A5.

Greenfield, T., Huff, C., Jones, R., and Wechsler, R. "Community Organizing to Reduce Alcohol and Other Drug Problems in Marin County, California." Summary of paper presented at conference on Evaluating Community Prevention Strategies: Alcohol and Other Drugs, sponsored by UCSD Extension, Alcohol and Other Drug Studies, University of California, San Diego, Jan. 1990.

Grossman, M., Coate, D., and Arluck, G. M. "Price Sensitivity of Alcoholic Beverages in the United States: Youth Alcohol Consumption." In H. Holder (ed.), *Control Issues in Alcohol Abuse Prevention: Strategies for States and Communities.* Greenwich, Conn.: JAI Press, 1987, 169–198.

Hacker, G., Collins, R., and Jacobson, M. *Marketing Booze to Blacks.* Washington, D.C.: Center for Science in the Public Interest, Mar. 1989.

Halstuk, M. "Syphilis and Crack Taking Big Toll of Black Babies." *San Francisco Chronicle,* Mar. 26, 1990, p. A2.

Hamm, A. "Community Intervention Trial (COMMIT) for Smoking Cessation." Bethesda, Md.: *Update* newsletter of the Office of Cancer Communications, National Cancer Institute, June 1988.

Harris, L. "Public Willing to Cut Defense Spending But Not Social Programs to Pay for New Anti-Drug Program." New York: Harris Poll, Aug. 27, 1989a.

Harris, L. "Parental Worries About Adequate Child Care Mount Sharply." New York: Harris Poll, Oct. 1, 1989b.

Harris, L. "Number of Alienated in Nation Rises from 54 to 58 Percent Since 1988." New York: Harris Poll, Oct. 29, 1989c.

Harris, L. "In Turnabout, Public Favors Big Increase in Federal Role." New York: Harris Poll, Nov. 5, 1989d.

Harris, R. "Experts Say the War on Drugs Has Turned into a War on Blacks." *San Francisco Chronicle,* Apr. 24, 1990, p. A12.

Harrison, L. D. "Nature and Extent of the Drug Use Problem: What We Know from Survey Research." Paper presented at the 45th annual conference of the American Association for Public Opinion Research, Lancaster, Pa., May 1990.

Harwood, H. J., and others. *Economic Costs to Society of Alcohol and Drug Abuse and Mental Illness: 1980.* Research Triangle Park, N.C.: Research Triangle Institute, 1984.

Heath, D. "The New Temperance Movement: Through the Looking-Glass." *Drugs and Society,* 1989, *3* (3/4), 143–168.

Heather, N., and Robertson, I. *Problem Drinking.* (2nd rev. ed.) New York: Oxford University Press, 1990.

Heldman, C. "Re: Alcohol Advertising." Memorandum of fourteen pages to State Alcohol and Drug Abuse and NPN Coordinators. Washington: National Association of State Alcohol and Drug Abuse Directors, Apr. 26, 1990.

Hilton, M. "Drinking Patterns and Drinking Problems in 1984: Results from a General Population Survey." *Alcoholism: Clinical and Experimental Research,* 1987, *11,* 157–175.

Holder, H. D. "A Review of Research Opportunities and Issues in the Regulation of Alcohol Availability." *Contemporary Drug Problems,* Spring 1988, pp. 47–66.

Holder, H. D. "Prevention of Alcohol-Related Problems." *Alcohol Health and Research World,* 1989, *13* (4), 339–342.

Holder, H. D., and Blose, J. O. "The Reduction of Community Alcohol Problems: Computer Simulation Experiments in Three Counties." *Journal of Studies on Alcohol,* 1987, *48* (2), 123–135.

Holder, H. D., and Stoil, M. J. "Beyond Prohibition: the Public Health Approach to Prevention." *Alcohol Health and Research World,* 1988, *12* (4), 292–297.

Howard, J. "Prevention Research at NIAAA: Confronting the Challenge of Uncertainty." In K. H. Rey, C. L. Faegre, and P. Lowery (eds.), Office for Substance Abuse Prevention

Monograph 3. *Prevention Research Findings: 1988.* U.S. Department of Health and Human Services, publication no. (ADU) 89-1615. Washington, D.C.: U.S. Government Printing Office, 1990, 243-252.

Institute of Medicine. *Alcoholism, Alcohol Abuse, and Related Problems: Opportunities for Research.* Washington, D.C.: National Academy Press, 1980.

Institute of Medicine. *Causes and Consequences of Alcohol Problems: An Agenda for Research.* Washington, D.C.: National Academy Press, 1987.

Institute of Medicine. *Prevention and Treatment of Alcohol Problems: Research Opportunities.* Report of a study by a committee of the Division of Mental Health and Behavioral Medicine. Washington, D.C.: National Academy Press, 1989.

Institute of Medicine. *Broadening the Base of Treatment for Alcohol Problems.* Washington, D.C.: National Academy Press, 1990.

Isikoff, M. "U.S. May Enlist Caterpillars in Cocaine War." *San Francisco Chronicle,* Feb. 20, 1990, pp. A1, A10.

Jacobson, M. "Prevention Priorities: Taxes, Advertising Top the List." *Prevention File: Community Responses to Alcohol Problems.* San Diego: Extension Department, University of California, Spring 1990, 11-12.

Jacobson, M., Atkins, R., and Hacker, G. *The Booze Merchants: The Inebriating of America.* Washington, D.C.: Center for Science in the Public Interest, 1983.

Jason, L., and others. "Incentives and in a Worksite Smoking Cessation Intervention." *American Journal of Public Health,* 1990, *80* (2), 205-206.

Jehl, D., and Healy, M. "Armed Forces Want to Be Drug Warriors," *San Francisco Chronicle,* Dec. 15, 1989, p. A19.

Jernigan, D., Mosher, J., and Reed, D. "Alcohol-Related Problems and Public Hospitals: Defining a New Role in Prevention." *Journal of Public Health Policy,* 1989, *10* (3), 324-352.

Jessor, R., Close, J. A., and Donovan, J. E. "Psychological Correlates of Marijuana Use and Problem Drinking in a National Sample of Adolescents." *American Journal of Public Health,* 1980, *70,* 604-613.

Jessor, R., and Jessor, S. L. "Theory Testing in Longitudinal Research on Marijuana Use." In D. Kandel (ed.), *Longitudinal*

Research in Drug Use: Empirical Findings and Methodological Issues. Washington, D.C.: Hemisphere Press, 1978.

Johnston, L., O'Malley, P., and Bachman, J. *Drug Use, Drinking, and Smoking: National Survey Results from High School, College, and Young Adults Populations.* Rockville, Md.: National Institute on Drug Abuse, 1989.

Kandel, D. B. "Convergences in Prospective Longitudinal Surveys of Drug Use in Normal Populations." In D. B. Kandel (ed.), *Longitudinal Research in Drug Use: Empirical Findings and Methodological Issues.* Washington, D.C.: Hemisphere Press, 1978.

Kandel, D. B. "On Processes of Peer Influence in Adolescent Drug Use: a Developmental Perspective." *Alcohol and Substance Abuse in Adolescence, 4,* 1985, 139–163.

Kandel, D. B., and Raveis, V. H. "Cessation of Illicit Drug Use in Young Adulthood." *Archives of General Psychiatry,* 1989, *46* (2), 109–116.

Kennedy, P. *The Rise and Fall of the Great Powers.* New York: Vintage Books, 1987.

Kenney, R. D., and others. "Smoking Cessation Counseling by Resident Physicians in Internal Medicine, Family Practice, and Pediatrics." *Archives of Internal Medicine,* 1988, *148* (11), 2469–2473.

Kerr, P. "Rich vs. Poor: Drug Patterns Are Diverging." *New York Times,* Aug. 30, 1987, pp. 1, 17.

Kilbourne, J. "Statement on Behalf of the National Council on Alcoholism and Drug Dependence Before the [Congressional] Committee on Energy and Commerce Subcommittee on Transportation and Hazardous Materials on HR 4493." Washington, D.C.: National Council on Alcoholism and Drug Dependence, July 18, 1990.

Kilpatrick, J. "Legalize Drugs? It's a Bad Idea." *San Francisco Chronicle,* Dec. 18, 1989, p. A18.

King, R. "A Worthless Crusade." *Newsweek,* Jan. 1, 1990, pp. 4–5.

Kirkpatrick, J. "Don't Blame Andes Countries for America's Drug Problems." *San Francisco Chronicle,* Mar. 21, 1990, (Z-6), p. 5.

Kleiman, M. *Hard-Core Cocaine Addicts: Measuring—and Fighting—*

the Epidemic. Staff report prepared for the Committee on the Judiciary, U.S. Senate, May 10, 1990. Washington, D.C.: U.S. Government Printing Office.

Kondracke, M. M. "Don't Legalize Drugs." *Drugs and Society, 3* (3/4), 1989, 209–215.

Koop, C. *Reducing the Health Consequences of Smoking: 25 Years of Progress.* Washington, D.C.: U.S. Department of Health and Human Services, 1989.

Kozlowski, L. T., and others. "Comparing Tobacco Cigarette Dependence with Other Drug Dependencies." *Journal of the American Medical Association,* 1989, *261* (6), 898–901.

Kumpfer, K. L. "Prevention of Alcohol and Drug Abuse: A Critical Review of Risk Factors and Prevention Strategies." In D. Schaffer and others (eds.), *Prevention of Mental Disorders, Alcohol and Other Drug Use in Children and Adolescents.* Office for Substance Abuse Prevention Monograph 2. Washington, D.C.: U.S. Department of Health and Human Services, Publication no. (ADM) 89-1646. U.S. Government Printing Office, 1989.

Langton, P. *Drug Use and the Alcohol Dilemma.* Needham Heights, Mass.: Allyn & Bacon, 1991.

Lapham, L. "A Political Opiate: The War on Drugs Is a Folly and a Menace." *Harper's Magazine,* Dec. 1989, 41–48.

"Lawmakers Want Liquor Ads to Carry Health Warnings." *San Francisco Chronicle,* Apr. 5, 1990, p. 13.

Ledermann, S. *Alcohol, alcoholisme, alcoolisation, donnée scientifiques de charactère physiologique, economique, et social.* Institut National d'Etudes Démographiques, Cahier no. 29. Paris: Presses universitaire de France, 1956.

Lester, D. "The Hereditability of Alcoholism: Science and Social Policy." *Drugs and Society,* 1989, *3* (3/4), 29–68.

Lewin, K. *A Dynamic Theory of Personality.* New York: McGraw-Hill, 1936.

Lewis, A. "It's Time for Change in America." *San Francisco Chronicle,* Apr. 16, 1990, p. A27.

Lewis, J. "President Reagan Called for a Major Drive Against Drug Abuse . . ." *Alcoholism Report,* 1982, *X* (17) 1.

Lewis, J. "Reagan Administration Reveals Drug Initiative Details: Includes Widespread Testing." *Alcoholism Report,* 1986a, *14* (22), 1–5.

Lewis, J. "ADAMHA Rapidly Implements New Prevention Agency." *Alcoholism Report,* 1986b, *15,* (4), 1.

Lewis, J. "NDATUS Survey Shows Decline in Alcohol-Only Units." *Alcoholism Report,* 1989a, *17* (7), 3.

Lewis, J. "NCA Urges Bolder Warning Labels." *Alcoholism Report,* 1989b, *17* (8), 4.

Lewis, J. "Gordis Optimistic About HHS Secretary's Support." *Alcoholism Report,* 1989c, *17* (9), 3.

Lewis, J. "Study Finds Anheuser-Busch Largest Alcohol Supplier." *Alcoholism Report,* 1989d, *17* (10), 4.

Lewis, J. "Nat'l Wine Coalition Formed." *Alcoholism Report,* 1989e, *17* (10), 7.

Lewis, J. "Alcohol Programs Not in Drug Czar's Purview." *Alcoholism Report,* 1989f, *17* (10), 10.

Lewis, J. "Koop Urges Congress to Raise Taxes, Curb Advertising." *Alcoholism Report,* 1989g, *17,* (11), 1.

Lewis, J. "BATF Stonewalls Glenn Committee Hearings." *Alcoholism Report,* 1989h, *17* (12), 1.

Lewis, J. "New Wine Organization to Push Research and Education." *Alcoholism Report,* 1989i, *18* (1), 7.

Lewis, J. "Coalition Charges Malt Liquor Pitched to Blacks/Hispanics." *Alcoholism Report,* 1989j, *18* (2), 5.

Lewis, J. "Coalition Seeks to Include Drunk Driving, Other Alcohol Problems in War on Drugs." *Alcoholism Report,* 1989k, *18* (5), 2.

Lewis, J. "NCA Protests National Archives/Philip Morris 'Bill of Rights' Blurbs." *Alcoholism Report,* 1989l, *18* (5), 6.

Lewis, J. "NCA Officially Becomes NCADD." *Alcoholism Report,* 1990a, *18* (6), 9.

Lewis, J. "Drug Strategy." *Alcoholism Report,* 1990b, *18* (7), 1–2.

Lewis, J. "Coalition Forms to Promote Surgeon General's Workshop Recommendations." *Alcoholism Report,* 1990c, *18* (7), 2.

Lewis, J. "Treasury Department, in Final Rule, Strengthens Alcohol Label Requirements." *Alcoholism Report,* 1990d, *18* (7), 5.

Lewis, J. "CDC Reports Alcohol-Related Deaths Top 105,000." *Alcoholism and Drug Abuse Week,* 1990e, *2* (13), 7–8.

Lewis, J. "Senate Staff Report Says 2.2 Million Cocaine Addicts in U.S." *Alcoholism and Drug Abuse Week,* 1990f, *2* (19), 3–4.

Lewis, J. "Senators Introduce Expansive Drug Bills, Surpass President's Plan." *Alcoholism and Drug Abuse Week,* 1990g, *2* (20), 1-2.

Lubinski, C. "An Overview of Federal Alcohol Policy." Statement on behalf of the National Council on Alcoholism, Inc., before the Senate Committee on Governmental Affairs, U.S. Senate, May 25, 1988.

Lucas, G. "Deukmejian Cool Toward Anti-Smoking Blitz." *San Francisco Chronicle,* Apr. 11, 1990, p. A1.

McAllister, B. "The Plight of Young Black Men in America." *Washington Post National Weekly Edition,* Feb. 12-18, 1990, pp. 6-7.

McLeod, R. G. "U.S. Low in Child Welfare." *San Francisco Chronicle,* Mar. 14, 1990, p. 1.

McLoughlin, E., and Wang, C. "Alcohol, Tobacco, and Firearms: Filling or Spilling the National Treasury?" In D. Gann (ed.), *Problems in General Surgery,* 1989, *3* (2), 306-320.

McMahon, E. T., and Taylor, P. A. *Citizens' Action Handbook on Alcohol and Tobacco Billboard Advertising.* Washington, D.C.: Center for Science in the Public Interest, 1990.

MacNamara, M. "Fight Against Poverty Now Stresses Prevention." *San Francisco Chronicle,* Nov. 23, 1989, p. A1.

MacNamara, M. "Where We're Going." *This World,* Mar. 4, 1990, p. 12.

McNicholas, R. "Northern California Vintners to Fight Tax Increase." *San Francisco Chronicle,* July 28, 1990, p. B1.

Makela, K., and Viikari, M. "Notes on Alcohol and the State." *Acta Sociologica,* 1977, *20* (2), 155-178.

Mangan, G. L., and Golding, J. F. *The Psychopharmacology of Smoking.* Cambridge, England: Cambridge University Press, 1984.

Marcus, A. C., Crane, L. A., Shopland, D. R., and Lynn, W. R. "Use of Smokeless Tobacco in the United States: Recent Estimates from the Current Population Survey." *NCI Monographs,* no. 8. Washington, D.C.: U.S. Government Printing Office, 1989, 17-23.

"Marijuana: What We Know." *Wellness Letter,* University of California, Berkeley, Mar. 1990, pp. 3-4.

Marlatt, G. A. "Cognitive Features in the Relapse Process." In G. A. Marlatt and J. R. Gordon (eds.), *Relapse Prevention: Maintenance Strategies in Addictive Behavior Change.* New York: Guilford Press, 1985.

Maxwell, B., and Jacobson, M. *Marketing Disease to Hispanics: The Selling of Alcohol, Tobacco, and Junk Foods.* Washington, D.C.: Center for Science in the Public Interest, 1989.

"Military's New Drug War Role." *San Francisco Chronicle,* Mar. 9, 1990, p. A17.

Miller, N. S., Millman, R. B.,and Keskinen, S. "The Diagnosis of Alcohol, Cocaine, and Other Drug Dependence in an Inpatient Treatment Population." *Journal of Substance Abuse Treatment,* 1989, *6* (1), 37–40.

Miller, W. R. "Motivation and Treatment Goals." *Drugs and Society,* 1987, *1* (2/3), 133–151.

Miller, W. R. "Matching Individuals with Interventions." In R. K. Hester and W. R. Miller (eds.), *Handbook of Alcoholism Treatment Approaches: Effective Alternatives.* Elmsford, N. Y.: Pergamon Press, 1989.

Miller, W. R., and Baca, L. M. "Two-Year Follow-Up of Bibliotherapy and Therapist-Controlled Drinking Training for Problem Drinkers." *Behavior Therapy,* 1983, *14,* 441–448.

Miller, W. R., Gribskov, C. J.,and Mortell, R. L. "Effectiveness of a Self-Control Manual for Problem Drinkers With and Without Therapist Contact." *International Journal of Addiction,* 1981, *16,* 827–837.

Miller, W. R., and Hester, R. "The Effectiveness of Alcoholism Treatment: What Research Reveals." In R. Miller and N. Heather (eds.), *Treating Addictive Behaviors.* New York: Plenum, 1986.

Miller, W. R., and Taylor, C. A. "Relative Effectiveness of Bibliotherapy Individual and Group Self-Control Training in the Treatment of Problem Drinkers." *Addictive Behavior,* 1980, *5,* 13–24.

Miller, W. R., Taylor, C. A., and West, J. C. "Focused Versus Broad-Spectrum Therapy for Problem Drinkers." *Journal of Consulting Clinical Psychology,* 1980, *48,* 590–601.

Moody, J. "Noble Battle, Terrible Toll." *Time,* Dec. 18, 1989, 33–34.

Moore, M. H., and Gerstein, D. R. (eds.). *Alcohol and Public Policy: Beyond the Shadow of Prohibition.* Washington, D.C.: National Academy Press, 1981.

Morgan, P. "Examining United States Alcohol Policy: Alcohol Control and the Interests of the State." Paper presented at the Ninth World Congress of Sociology, Uppsala, Sweden, Aug. 1978.

Morgan, P., Wallack, L., and Buchanan, P. "Waging Drug Wars: Prevention Strategy or Politics as Usual." *Drugs and Society, 3* (1/2), 99–124, 1988.

Mosher, J. F. "Alcohol Tax Policy Reform." *American Journal of Public Health,* 1987, *77* (1), 106–111.

Mosher, J. F., and Colman, V. *Alcoholic Beverage Control in a Public Health Perspective: A Handbook for Action.* Center for Injury Prevention, Trauma Foundation, San Francisco General Hospital, and Marin Institute for the Prevention of Alcohol and Other Drug Problems, Mar. 1989.

Mosher, J. F., Delewski, C., Saltz, R., and Hennessy, M. *Monterey–Santa Cruz Responsible Beverage Service Project.* San Rafael, Calif.: Marin Institute for the Prevention of Alcohol and Other Drug Problems, Oct. 1989.

Mosher, J. F., and Jernigan, D. "New Directions in Alcohol Policy." *Annual Review of Public Health,* 1989, *10,* 245–279.

Mosher, J. F., and Mottl, J. "The Role of Nonalcoholic Agencies in Federal Regulation of Drinking Behavior and Consequences." In M. Moore and D. Gerstein (eds.), *Alcohol and Public Policy: Beyond the Shadow of Prohibition.* Washington, D.C.: National Academy Press, 1981.

Moskowitz, J. "The Primary Prevention of Alcohol Problems: A Critical Review of the Research Literature." *Journal of Studies on Alcohol,* 1989, *50* (1), 54–88.

Murphy, G. E. "Suicide and Substance Abuse." *Archives of General Psychiatry,* 1988, *45,* 593–594.

Murray, R. H., Clifford, C. A., and Gurling, H. M. D. "Twin and Adoption Studies: How Good Is the Evidence for a Genetic Role?" In M. Galanter (ed.), *Recent Developments in Alcoholism.* Vol. 1. New York: Plenum, 1983, 25–48.

Musto, D. M. *The American Disease: Origins of Narcotic Control.* (Rev. ed.) New York: Oxford University Press, 1987.

Nathan, P. "Alcohol Dependency Prevention and Early Intervention." *Public Health Reports,* 1988, *103* (6), 683–689.

Nathan, P., and McCrady, B. "Bases for the Use of Abstinence as a Goal in the Behavioral Treatment of Alcohol Abuses." *Drugs and Society,* 1987, *1* (2/3).

National Alcohol Tax Coalition. *Impact of Alcohol Tax Increases on Federal Revenues, Alcohol Consumption, and Alcohol Problems.* Washington, D.C.: Center for Science in the Public Interest, Feb. 1989.

National Cancer Institute. *COMMIT Protocol Summary: Community Intervention Trial for Smoking Cessation.* Washington, D.C.: U.S. Government Printing Office, 1988.

National Institute on Alcohol Abuse and Alcoholism. *Sixth Special Report to the U.S. Congress on Alcohol and Health.* Washington, D.C.: U.S. Government Printing Office, 1987.

National Institute on Alcohol Abuse and Alcoholism. *Seventh Special Report to the U.S. Congress on Alcohol and Health.* Washington, D.C.: U.S. Government Printing Office, 1990.

National Institute on Drug Abuse and National Institute on Alcohol Abuse and Alcoholism. *National Drug and Alcoholism Treatment Unit Survey (NDATUS).* U.S. Department of Health and Human Services, publication no. (ADM) 89-1626. Washington, D.C.: Government Printing Office, 1989.

National Institute on Drug Abuse. "Overview of the 1988 National Household Survey on Drug Abuse." *NIDA Capsules.* Washington, D.C.: U.S. Government Printing Office, 1989.

Neerhof, M. G., MacGregor, B. N., Retzky, S. S., and Sullivan, T. P. "Cocaine Abuse During Pregnancy: Peripartum Prevalence and Perinatal Outcome." *American Journal of Obstetrics and Gynecology,* 1989, *161* (3), 633–638.

Novotny, T. E., Pierce, J. P., Fiore, M. C., and Davis, R. M. "Smokeless Tobacco Use in the United States: The Adult Use of Tobacco Surveys." *NCI Monographs,* no. 8. Washington, D.C.: U.S. Government Printing Office, 1989, 25–28.

O'Connell, T. "Gangs Bring Violence and Drugs to Schools." *U.S. Journal of Drug and Alcohol Dependence,* 1990, *14* (2), 6.

Office of the Assistant Secretary for Health, Office of Disease Prevention, Public Health Service. *Promoting Health/Preventing*

Disease: Year 2000 Objectives for the Nation. Washington, D.C.: U.S. Government Printing Office, 1990.

Office of Disease Prevention and Health Promotion and Office on Smoking and Health. *A Decision Maker's Guide to Reducing Smoking at the Worksite.* Washington, D.C.: American Cancer Society, 1985.

Office of Justice Programs, U.S. Department of Justice. *Profile of State Prison Inmates, 1986.* Washington, D.C.: U.S. Government Printing Office, 1988.

Office of Justice Programs, U.S. Department of Justice. *Drugs and Crime Facts, 1989.* Washington, D.C.: U.S. Government Printing Office, 1990.

Office of National Drug Control Policy, Executive Office of the President. *National Drug Control Strategy.* Washington, D.C.: U.S. Government Printing Office, 1990.

Office on Smoking and Health. *The Health Consequences of Using Smokeless Tobacco.* Washington, D.C.: U.S. Government Printing Office, 1986.

Office on Smoking and Health. *Smoking, Tobacco, and Health: A Fact Book.* Washington, D.C.: U.S. Government Printing Office, 1989.

Office for Substance Abuse Prevention. *Prevention Plus II: Tools for Creating and Sustaining Drug-Free Communities.* Department of Health and Human Services publication no. (ADM) 89-1649. Washington, D.C.: U.S. Government Printing Office, 1989.

Office for Substance Abuse Prevention. "OSAP Responds to National Crisis." Fact sheet, Alcohol, Drug Abuse, and Mental Health Administration, Department of Health Administration, Department of Health and Human Services. Washington, D.C.: U.S. Government Printing Office, 1990a.

Office for Substance Abuse Prevention. *Breaking New Ground for Youth at Risk: Program Summaries.* Office for Substance Abuse Prevention Technical Report 1. Department of Health and Human Services publication no. (ADM) 89-1658. Washington, D.C.: U.S. Government Printing Office, 1990b.

Office for Substance Abuse Prevention. *Citizen's Alcohol and Other Drug Prevention Directory.* Department of Health and Human

Services publication no. (ADM) 90-1657. Washington, D.C.: U.S. Government Printing Office, 1990c.

Office of the Surgeon General, Public Health Service. *Surgeon General's Workshop on Drunk Driving [Dec. 14-16, 1983]: Proceedings.* Washington, D.C.: U.S. Government Printing Office, 1989.

O'Malley, P. M., and Wagenaar, A. C. "Effects of Minimum Drinking Age Laws on Alcohol Use, Related Behaviors, and Traffic Crash Involvement Among American Youth: 1976–1987." *Journal of Alcohol Studies,* forthcoming.

Pattison, E. "Rehabilitation of the Chronic Alcoholic." In B. Kissin and H. Begleiter (eds.), *The Biology of Alcoholism.* Vol. 3: *Clinical Pathology.* New York: Plenum, 1974.

Pearl, R. "Tobacco Smoking and Longevity." *Science,* 1938, *87,* 216–217.

Peele, S. "The Implications and Limitations of Genetic Models of Alcoholism and Other Addictions." *Journal of Studies on Alcohol,* 1986, *47* (1), 63–73.

Peele, S. "Why Do Controlled-Drinking Outcomes Vary by Investigator, by Country, and by Era? Cultural Conceptions of Release and Remission in Alcoholism." *Drug and Alcohol Dependence,* 1987, *20* (3), 173–201.

Peele, S. "Second Thoughts About a Gene for Alcoholism." *Atlantic Monthly,* Aug. 1990, pp. 52–58.

Pentz, M. A., and others. "A Multicommunity Trial for Primary Prevention of Adolescent Drug Abuse: Effects on Drug Use Prevalence." *Journal of the American Medical Association,* 1989, *261* (22), 3259–3266.

Perlman, D. "Gene Seems Linked to Alcoholism: Addiction Factor Discovered in 77% of Cases Studied." *San Francisco Chronicle,* Apr. 18, 1990, p. A1.

Perrine, M. W., and Sadler, D. D. "Alcohol Treatment Program Versus Licensed Suspension for Drunken Drivers: The Four-Year Traffic Safety Impact." In P. C. Noordzij and R. Roszbach (eds.), *Alcohol, Drugs, and Traffic Safety.* New York: Elsevier, 1987, 555–559.

Petronis, K. R., and Anthony, J. C. "An Epidemiologic Investigation of Marijuana- and Cocaine-Related Palpitations." *Drug and Alcohol Dependence,* 1989, *23* (3), 219–226.

Polich, J. M., Ellickson, P. L., Reuter, P., and Kahan, J. P. *Strategies for Controlling Adolescent Drug Use.* Santa Monica, Calif.: Rand Corporation, 1984.

Purvis, A. "DNA and the Desire to Drink." *Time,* Apr. 30, 1990, p. 88.

Rangel, C. "War on Drugs Must Begin on the Poverty Front." Letter to the editor, *New York Times,* Dec. 26, 1989, p. A18.

Ravenholt, R. "Addiction Mortality in the United States, 1980: Tobacco, Alcohol, and Other Substances." *Population and Development Review,* 1984, *10* (4), 697–724.

Reeves, R. "The French Do It Right When It Comes to Child Care." *San Francisco Chronicle,* Nov. 20, 1989a, p. A17.

Reeves, R. "U.S. Races into the '90's." *San Francisco Chronicle,* Dec. 21, 1989b, p. A25.

Reich, R. *The Next American Frontier.* New York: Penguin Books, 1984.

Reinarman, C., and Levine, H. G. "Crack in Context: Politics and Media in the Making of a Drug Scare." *Contemporary Drug Problems,* 1989, *16* (4), 535–577.

Reinhold, R. "Police, Hard Pressed in Drug War, Turning to Preventive Efforts." *New York Times,* reprinted in *San Francisco Chronicle,* Dec. 26, 1989, pp. A1, A13.

Reynolds, R. V., and others. "A Method for Studying Controlled Substance Use: A Preliminary Investigation." *Addictive Behaviors,* 1987, *12* (1), 53–62.

Rice, D. P., Kelman, S., Miller, L. S., and Dunmeyer, S. *The Economic Costs of Alcohol and Drug Abuse and Mental Illness: 1985.* Department of Health and Human Services publication no. (ADM) 90–1694. Rockville, Md.: Alcohol, Drug Abuse, and Mental Health Administration, 1990.

Rich, S. "The Hand of Hardship Falls Heavily on the Children." *Washington Post National Weekly Edition,* Dec. 25–31, 1989, p. 37.

Richardson J. L., and others. "Substance Use Among Eighth-Grade Students Who Take Care of Themselves After School." *Pediatrics,* 1989 *84* (3), 556–566.

Room, R. "Governing Images and the Prevention of Alcohol Problems." *Preventive Medicine,* 1974a, *3,* 1–23.

Room, R. "Minimizing Alcohol Problems." *Alcohol Health and Research World,* Fall 1974b, pp. 12–17.

Room, R. "Alcohol Control and the Field of Public Health." *Annual Review of Public Health,* 1984, *5,* 293–317.

Rootman, I. "Preventing Alcohol Problems: A Challenge for Health Promotion." *Health Education,* 1985, *24,* 2–7.

Rosenthal, A. "Many Promises, Few Specifics at Drug Summit." *San Francisco Chronicle,* Feb. 16, 1990, pp. 1, 22.

Ross, H. L. "Deterring Drunken Driving: An Analysis of Current Efforts." *Journal of Studies on Alcohol,* 1985, *S10,* 122–128.

Rouse, B. "Epidemiology of Smokeless Tobacco Use: A National Study." *NCI Monographs,* no. 8. Washington, D.C.: U.S. Government Printing Office, 1989, 29–33.

Rowland, W. D., Jr. *The Politics of TV Violence.* Newbury Park, Calif.: Sage, 1983.

Rundall, T. G., and Bruvold, W. H. "A Meta-Analysis of School-Based Smoking and Alcohol Use Prevention Programs." *Health Education Quarterly,* 1988, *15* (3), 317–334.

Saltz, R. F. "Research in Environmental and Community Strategies for the Prevention of Alcohol Problems." *Contemporary Drug Problems,* 1988, *15* (1), 67–81.

Savage, D. "Drug Czar Bennett Goes, But Not Quietly." *San Francisco Chronicle,* Nov. 9, 1990, p. A–18.

Schade, C. "The Drug War: The Wrong Efforts Aimed at Lesser Problems." *Nation's Health,* Mar. 1990, p. 20.

Schaffer, D., and others (eds.). *Prevention of Mental Disorders, Alcohol and Other Drug Use in Children and Adolescents.* Office for Substance Abuse Prevention Monograph 2. Washington, D.C.: U.S. Government Printing Office, 1989.

Schechter, D. *Alcohol Warning Signs: How to Get Legislation Passed in Your City.* Washington, D.C.: Center for Science in the Public Interest, Jan. 1986.

Schorr, L. B. *Within Our Reach: Breaking the Cycle of Disadvantage.* Garden City, N.Y.: Doubleday Anchor, 1989.

Schreibman, J. "Winemakers Response to Negative Image." *San Francisco Chronicle,* Jan. 18, 1990, p. C2.

Schuckit, M. A. "Alcoholism and Sociopathy—Diagnostic Confusion." *Quarterly Journal of Studies on Alcohol,* 1973, *34,* pp. 157–164.

Schuckit, M. A. "Why Don't We Diagnose Alcoholism in Our Patients?" *Journal of Family Practice,* 1987, *25* (3), 225–226.

Schuster, C. R. "The National Institute on Drug Abuse (NIDA)." *British Journal of Addiction,* 1989, *84,* 19–28.

Schwartz, J. L. *Review and Evaluation of Smoking Cessation Methods: The United States and Canada, 1978–1985.* Washington, D.C.: National Institutes of Health, National Cancer Institute, U.S. Department of Health and Human Services, National Institutes of Health Publication No. 87-2940, Apr. 1987.

Schwartz, R. H. "Marijuana: An Overview." *Pediatric Clinics of North America,* 1987, *34* (2), 305–317.

Searles, J. S. "The Role of Genetics in the Pathogenesis of Alcoholism." *Journal of Abnormal Psychology,* 1988, *97* (2), 153–167.

Secretary of Health and Human Services. *Sixth Special Report to the U.S. Congress on Alcohol and Health.* Washington, D.C.: U.S. Government Printing Office, 1987.

Segal, B. *Drugs and Behavior: Cause, Effects, and Treatment.* New York: Gardner Press, 1988.

Skog, O. J. "The Long Waves of Alcohol Consumption: A Social Network Perspective on Cultural Change." *Social Networks,* 1986, *8,* 1–31.

Skolnik, J. "A Critical Look at the National Drug Control Strategy." *Yale Law and Policy Review,* 1990, *8,* (1), 75–116.

Skrzycki, C. "Drugs in the Workplace." *Washington Post National Weekly Edition,* Jan. 1–7, 1990a, p. 38.

Skrzycki, C. "For Most Employers, Seeing Is Ignoring." *Washington Post National Weekly Edition,* Apr. 9–15, 1990b, p. 22.

Smart, R. G. "Does Alcohol Advertising Affect Overall Consumption? A Review of Empirical Studies." *Journal of Studies on Alcohol,* 1988, *49,* 314–323.

Smart, R. G. "Increased Exposure to Alcohol and Cannabis Education and Changes in Use Patterns." *Journal of Drug Education,* 1989, *19* (2), 183–194.

Smith, J. W., Schmeling, G., and Knowles, P. L. "A Marijuana Smoking Cessation Clinical Trial Utilizing THC-Free Marijuana, Aversion Therapy, and Self-Management Counseling." *Journal of Substance Abuse Treatment, 1988, 5* (2), 89–98.

"Smoking in Movies: License to Kill." *Wellness Letter,* University of California, Berkeley, Apr. 1990, p. 3.

Snyder, G. "Reports of Revolt and Defections Among MADD Volunteers." *San Francisco Chronicle,* Mar. 12, 1990, p. A7.

Solomon, N., amd Lipton, M. "Step-by-Step Plan to Stop Smoking." *San Francisco Chronicle,* Nov. 17, 1989, p. B3.

Squires, S. "Millions of Americans Still Go Hungry." *San Francisco Chronicle, This World* section, Nov. 26, 1989, p. 19.

State Alcohol Taxes: Case Studies of the Impact of Higher Excise Taxes in 14 States and the District of Columbia. Washington: Center for Science in the Public Interest, February 1990.

Stein, R. "Mimi Silbert Stays Tough for Delancey." *San Francisco Chronicle,* Mar. 1, 1990, pp. B3, B6.

Stroock, S. A. "Random Drug Test Challenge Upheld." *San Francisco Chronicle,* Feb. 23, 1990, p. A4.

Swisher, J. D., Crawford, J., Goldstein, R., and Yura, M. "Drug Education: Pushing or Preventing." *Peabody Journal of Education,* 1971, *49,* 68–75.

Taylor, P. "Legislating Under the Influence: The Booze Merchants, Money, and Congress." *Nutrition Action Newsletter.* Washington, D.C.: Center for Science in the Public Interest, Feb. 1989.

"Tobacco's Last Gasp." *Harper's Magazine,* Apr. 1990, p. 24.

Tobler, N. S. "Meta-Analysis of 143 Adolescent Drug Prevention Programs: Quantitative Outcome Results of Program Participants Compared to a Control or Comparison Group." *Journal of Drug Issues,* 1986, *16* (4), 537–567.

"Troubled Children." *San Francisco Chronicle, Sunday Punch* section, Apr. 1, 1990, p. 1.

"U.S. Agents Help Peru Repel Guerrillas." *San Francisco Chronicle,* Apr. 13, 1990, p. A22.

U.S. Department of Health and Human Services. *HHS News.* Washington, D.C.: November 6, 1990.

Uchitelle, L. "Everyone's Talking About a Tax Boost." *San Francisco Examiner,* Mar. 26, 1990, p. A11.

University of California at San Diego. "You Don't Have to Be a Man . . ." *Prevention File: Community Responses to Alcohol Problems,* Spring 1990a, pp. 6–7.

University of California at San Diego. "New Rules of the Road." *Prevention File: Community Responses to Alcohol Problems,* Spring 1990b, pp. 9–10.

University of California at San Diego. "Prevention Gains New Support from Foundations." *Prevention File: Community Responses to Alcohol Problems,* Spring 1990c, pp. 13–14.

University of California at San Diego. "Beverage Industry Gifts—A Conflict of Interest?" *Prevention File: Community Responses to Alcohol Problems,* Spring 1990d, p. 15.

University of California at San Diego. "Let's Get Organized." *Prevention File: Community Responses to Alcohol Problems,* Summer 1990e, pp. 10–11.

University of California at San Diego. "Tobacco Control: Where Do We Go from Here?" *Prevention File,* Winter 1991, 13–16.

Van Buren, A. "A Good Excuse to Quit Smoking." *San Francisco Chronicle,* Nov. 15, 1989, p. E12.

Wagenaar, A. C. "Preventing Highway Crashes by Raising the Legal Minimum Age for Drinking: The Michigan Experience 6 Years Later." *Journal of Safety Research,* 1986, *17* (3), 101–109.

Wagenaar, A. C., and Maybee, R. G. "The Legal Minimum Age in Texas: Effects of an Increase from 18 to 19." *Journal of Safety Research,* 1986, *17* (4), 165–178.

Wagenaar, A. C., and Streff, F. M. "Public Opinion on Alcohol Policies." *Journal of Public Health Policy,* 1990, *11,* 189–205.

Wallack, L. "The Problems of Preventing Problems: Barriers to Policy and Program." In I. M. Newman and W. E. Ford (eds.), *Opportunities for Prevention in Treatment Agencies and Settings: A Conference on Alcohol-Related Issues.* Lincoln: Nebraska Prevention Center for Alcohol and Drug Abuse, 1981.

Wallack, L. "Public Health and the Advertising of Alcoholic Beverages." In H. L. Holder and J. Hallan (eds.), *Control Issues in Alcohol Abuse Prevention: Local, State and National Designs for the '80s.* Chapel Hill, N.C.: Human Ecology Institute, 1984a, 95–107.

Wallack, L. "Television Programming, Advertising, and the Prevention of Alcohol-Related Problems." In D. Gerstein (ed.), *Toward the Prevention of Alcohol Problems: Government, Business, and Community Action.* Washington, D.C.: National Academy Press, 1984b.

Wallack, L. "Koop Calls for Increase in Alcohol Excise Taxes." *California Alcohol Forum,* a publication of the California Conference on Alcohol Problems, 1989, (11), 4–5.

Wallack, L. "Media Advocacy: Promoting Health Through Mass Communication." In K. Glanz, F.M. Lewis, B. K. Rimer, and Associates, *Health Behavior and Health Education: Theory, Research, and Practice.* San Francisco: Jossey-Bass, 1990a, 370–386.

Wallack, L. "Testimony Before the United States House of Representatives Energy and Commerce Committee Subcommittee on Transportation and Hazardous Materials, Regarding H.R. 4493, a Bill to Require Health Warnings to Be Included in Alcoholic Beverage Advertisements." Washington, D.C., July 18, 1990b.

Wallack, L., and Barrows, D. "Evaluating Primary Prevention: The California 'Winners' Alcohol Program." *International Quarterly of Community Health Education,* 1982–83, *3* (4), 307–336.

Wallack, L., Breed, W., and Cruz, J. "Alcohol on Prime Time Television." *Journal of Studies on Alcohol,* 1987, *48* (1), 33–38.

Warner, K. E., and Goldenhar, L. M. "The Cigarette Advertising Broadcast Ban and Magazine Coverage of Smoking and Health." *Journal of Public Health Policy,* 1989, *10* (1), 32–42.

Washton, A. M. "Preventing Relapse to Cocaine." *Journal of Clinical Psychiatry,* 1988, *49* (Suppl.), 34–38.

Weisner, C. M. "The Transformation of Alcohol Treatment: Access to Care and the Response to Drinking Driving." *Journal of Public Health Policy,* 1986, *7* (1), 78–92.

Weisner, C. M. "The Social Ecology of Alcohol Treatment in the U.S." In M. Galanter (ed.), *Recent Developments in Alcoholism.* Vol. 5. New York: Plenum, 1987.

Weisner, C. M. "Coercion in Alcohol Treatment." In L. Mazade (ed.), *Broadening the Base of Treatment for Alcohol Problems.* Washington, D.C.: Institute of Medicine, National Academy Press, 1990, 579–609.

"Where the Skies Are Not Smoky All Day." *Wellness Letter,* University of California, Berkeley, Feb. 1990, p. 5.

White, P. "Coca—An Ancient Herb Turns Deadly." *National Geographic,* Jan. 1989, *175* (1), 3–47.

Will, G. "Smoking, Custom, and the Law." *Washington Post National Weekly Edition,* Jan. 22–28, 1990, p. 28.

Williams, L. "The Cocaine Trail." *San Francisco Examiner,* Feb. 4, 1990, pp. A1, A14–A15.

Witkin, G., with Cuneo, A. "One Step Ahead of the Law." *San Francisco Examiner, This World* section, Jan. 14, 1990, p. 10.

Wojcik, J. V. "Social Learning Predictors of the Avoidance of Smoking Relapse." *Addictive Behaviors,* 1988, *13* (2), 177–180.

World Health Organization. *Mental Disorders: Glossary and Guide to Their Classification in Accordance with the Ninth Revision of the International Classification of Diseases.* Geneva: World Health Organization, 1978.

Yoffe, E. "How to Legalize." *Mother Jones,* Feb./Mar. 1990, pp. 18–19.

Zane, M. "A Drug-Free Pledge with Plenty of Class." *San Francisco Chronicle,* Mar. 22, 1990, p. A26.

Weigle, J. V., "[illegible]" [illegible] Science [illegible] 1: 180.

World Health Organization. [illegible] Geneva: World Health Organization, 1978.

Wolf, [illegible] Feb./Mar. 1990, p. [illegible]

Zane, A. F. "A [illegible] with [illegible] of Glass," [illegible] Mar. [illegible] 1990, p. [illegible]

Name Index

M

N

O

P

R

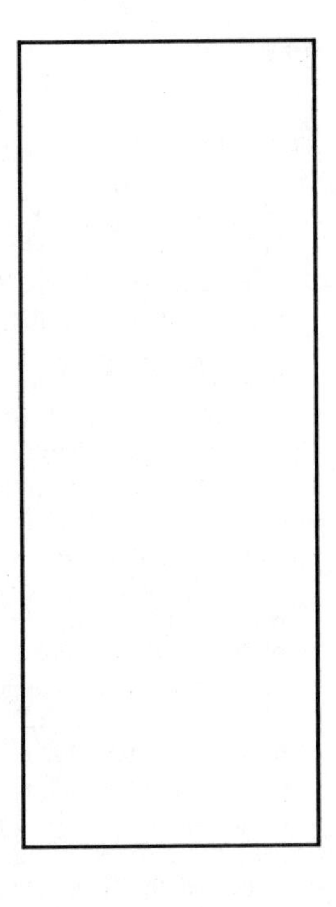

Subject Index

V

W

Y

DATE DUE

NO 09 '92			
JE 09 '93			
NOV 10 '94			
NOV 25 '94		WITHDRAWN	
12/2/94			
JUN 18 2001			